D0428650

# THE METHUSELAH FACTORS

# THE
# METHUSELAH
# FACTORS

## LEARNING FROM
## THE WORLD'S LONGEST
## LIVING PEOPLE

### COMPLETELY REVISED AND UPDATED

NATIONAL UNIVERSITY
LIBRARY     SAN DIEGO

# DAN GEORGAKAS

Academy
Chicago
Publishers

**1995**

Published in 1995 by
Academy Chicago Publishers
363 West Erie Street
Chicago, Illinois 60610

© Dan Georgakas 1995

Printed and bound in the U.S.A.

No part of this book may be reproduced in any form
without the express written permission of the publisher.

**Library of Congress Cataloging-in-Publication Data**

Georgakas, Dan.
      The Methuselah factors: learning from the world's longest
      living people/Dan Georgakas. —Rev. & updated.
           p.   cm.
      Includes bibliographical references and index.
      ISBN 0-89733-416-7
      1/ Longevity.  I. Title.
      QP85.G43  1995                    95-55
      612.6'8—dc20                 CIP

"Desirable Weight Tables for Men and Women," published 1959 by the
Metropolitan Life Insurance Company, are used herein by courtesy of
the Metropolitan Life Insurance Company.

*For Barbara Saltz*

# CONTENTS

Introduction . . . ix

## Part I: The Longevity Profile

1. Longevity Lore . . . 1
2. The Oldest of the Old . . . 11
3. The Long-Living People of Abkhasia . . . 37
4. Soviet Centenarianism . . . 67
5. Longevity in the Mountains . . . 81
6. The Hunzakuts . . . 95
7. Serendipitous Sheringham and Cambridgeshire . . . 117
8. Rethinking the First Ninety-Nine . . . 131

## Part II: The Longevity Agenda

9. The Longevous Personality . . . 153
10. Doctor Two Legs . . . 173
11. Food as Fuel . . . 191
12. Biochemical Individuality . . . 217
13. The Toxic Society . . . 233
14. Redefining the Biological Limits . . . 255
15. Longevity Now . . . 269

Glossary . . . 281
Notes and Further Reading . . . 285
Bibliography . . . 307
Index . . . 319
Photo section between pages 151-152

# Introduction

Tens of thousands of human beings who have already celebrated their 100th birthday are alive as I write these words. Hundreds of thousands more have already passed their 90th year. By the time this book reaches you, the ranks of nonagenarians and centenarians will have further increased. Nonetheless, most people now alive will not survive to celebrate their 70th birthday. How then is it that some people manage to live over 30 years longer than the majority of humanity? How good is the quality of these extended lives? And has anyone nearly doubled the average life span by living to 130 years? In this book I address these questions as a detective approaches any mystery, patiently separating longevity fact from longevity fiction.

My first challenge was to firmly separate those who had actually achieved longevity from the multitude making claims, most of which prove false. Having done that, I needed to determine if there was enough data concerning the genuinely longevous to yield common factors. What such persons said about themselves was not always reliable and many who told the truth might have forgotten crucial information or just didn't think to mention something which might be critical. The investigation was also haunted by the the possibility that prospects for long life might just be a matter of pure chance. Alternatively, longevity might be determined by factors programmed at birth, a matter of genetics,

ix

of biological destiny. In any case, from the start I was skeptical that the path to longevity could be reduced to a single cause, since human life is too complex and too long. Moreover, if disease and aging have many causes, then longevity must also involve many factors.

The more I delved into the mysteries of longevity, the more I saw both its complexity and its simplicity. Clearly the ultimate biological mechanisms within the human body had to be extraordinarily complex. Gerontologists are only now beginning to understand the fundamental hows and whys of aging. No gerontological Einstein has yet appeared to produce a general theory of aging which resolves all the separate credible, but often conflicting, theories now advanced. Nevertheless, many people with no scientific training whatsoever and no particular health agenda have managed to live comfortably for nine or more decades. These longevous birds may not be able to read geron-tological musical notes, but they have sung their longevous songs quite admirably.

My solution to the longevous puzzle is offered in two parts: the Longevous Profile and the Longevous Agenda. The Longevous Profile is drawn from what might be thought of as a cast of longevity characters, all the usual and some unusual. I deal in considerable detail with claims regarding specific individuals and regions in order to attempt to resolve the claim, and to examine the kind of unique wishful thinking that surrounds this topic. Many of the longevous tall tales are entertaining, but, more importantly, they occasionally yield unanticipated or serendipitous prizes. That is, the longevous claim is false, but the claimant's life style yields important data on some aspect of health in advanced age. A group of mountain people, for example, may not prove to be particularly long living, but because of the rugged terrain in which they live, both males and females have generally escaped osteoporosis, a major problem among people in the same age group who live in less challenging physical environments. The lives of these mountain people confirm the scientific thesis that osteoporosis is not inevitable, although some bone loss does occur with advancing years.

The genuine Longevity Profile that emerged was not much of a surprise. Much like Edgar Allan Poe's famous purloined letter, it had been in plain sight all along, once we understood how and where to look for it. It is a striking fact that although the essentials of the Longevity Agenda seem simple when they are outlined, they do not constitute the profile of the average human inhabitant of the planet earth, let alone the average American.

It is one thing to know what factors are necessary to achieve long life; it is quite a different thing to summon up the determination to put them into practice. I have learned from lecturing before live audiences and responding to questions on call-in talk shows that what most people want is a quick fix: a longevous pill or potion or a single longevous pattern to establish. However much I may emphasize that the data show that to succeed, all longevity factors need to be included, most people still tend to focus on those factors which they find most congenial and to ignore or downplay the others.

The Longevity Agenda in Part II of this book is a generalized "how to" based on the Longevity Profile supported on the best available health research. Readers who want to pursue the Agenda will have to adjust, adapt and refine it to meet their individual circumstances. To do that well, it is essential to understand how the Longevity Profile was formulated, the *why* of the factors and the usual misconceptions that must be avoided.

In the fifteen years since I did my original research on longevity, many of my conclusions have been born out. I have included considerable new data of this kind in the revised text and in the sections on additional readings in the notes. There has been an explosion of books on longevity and on health, like those discussing heart disease, significantly linked to longevity. Throughout this book I mention various popular works and evaluate them against the Longevity Agenda. To facilitate comparisons of different studies, I have used the following definitions: people aged 70-79 will be referred to as being in late maturity; those 80-89 will be called old; 90-109 longevous, and 110-114 superlongevous. Those claiming to be more than 115 years old will be called super-centenarians.

I have added a considerable amount of new material on my research in the former Soviet Georgia. Because of the collapse of the Soviet Union, I have been able to be far more candid than I was in 1980 when I feared putting at risk people who had helped me. This additional data further supports my original positions and implications.

Perhaps the most significant changes from the 1980 edition of this book constitute my response to what I believe to be the growing amount of disinformation disseminated by an irresponsible mass media on health issues in general and longevity issues in particular. I am not talking about supermarket tabloids and other sensationalist media, but about mainstream media, both print and electronic. They commonly treat these issues as entertainment, and usually with humor or cynicism. Each time a new study is issued which refines earlier observations or raises new issues, it is seized upon as if it contradicts an established body of knowledge. The result is that unwary consumers are left with the impression that there is no scientific consensus on the fundamentals of longevity, and that those who actively pursue a Longevity Agenda are gullible health junkies whose habits are more harmful than helpful.

Media treatment of information on body weight provides an excellent example of disinformation. Wide coverage has been given to the Baltimore Longitudinal Study which found that slightly overweight people in the study lived longer than those who were slightly or seriously underweight. This coverage gives the impression that one has to learn to live with one's weight and that it is foolish to diet in order to be fashionably thin. The point then often made is that fat can be beautiful: a point sometimes illustrated with a reproduction of a painting by Rubens.

This sort of "analysis" ignores the finding that a lean body mass is a longevity factor so well established that life insurance companies use it as a criterion for issuing policies. The statistic that slightly overweight people in a study group live longer than slightly or seriously underweight people, results from the fact that very ill people lose a great deal of weight, particularly when they are dying. Taking that into consideration and considering also that chronically unhealthy persons—like most alcoholics and drug addicts—are thin, there is no doubt that greater body weight over a lifetime is a prime risk factor for premature death. The media mishandling of this data is all the more troubling because for most people, adult body weight is one of the longevity factors that can be controlled through diet and exercise, however difficult that may be for some. *How* one achieves and maintains a desirable weight is always far more significant than the weight itself. Wherever relevant, I will point out distortions of this nature to clear up as much mass media static as possible.

No prospective longevity project would be complete without consideration of the various artificial means for extending life now being researched and experimented with throughout the world. Eventually, a series of such anti-aging interventions might carry life spans past supercentenarianism to the 969-years of Methuselah and even to the threshold of physical immortality. Anti-aging scientists usually discourage speculations of this sort by saying that their work is only the next logical step in the process that has given us blood transfusions, pacemakers, bionic limbs, wonder drugs, and other weapons in the life-sustaining arsenal. In any case, we appear on the brink of a longevity breakthrough in which a hundredth birthday will cease to be of note. Someone already alive is likely to become the first fully documented super-centenarian.

Whatever dazzling longevity prospects lie ahead, this book holds a fully researched longevous agenda for today. Its goal is to help the reader achieve vigorous longevity, and to live a healthy life that will automatically transcend the present average life span, which may one day seem as limited as the 23-year average life span of the citizen of the Roman Empire now seems to us.

# PART ONE  *The Longevity Profile*

# 1. LONGEVITY LORE

*She found the essence in which to bathe is to outlive*
*Generations, Faiths, and Empires. —She, H. Rider Haggard*

BEFORE WRITING HAD BEEN INVENTED, the Babylonian story-tellers sang of the hero Gilgamesh who, when he discovered that only the gods are permitted immortality, sought to be as healthy as a youth all the days of his life. After many tests of his valor, the secret of long life was revealed to him by the Old Man of the Mountain, who spoke of a fragrant plant that looked like a buckthorn and pricked like a rose. The Old Man confided that the plant grew at the bottom of the world's deepest sea, and "If anyone comes into possession of this plant, he can, by tasting it, regain his youth." [1]   In time, Gilgamesh was able to locate the fragrant buckthorn rose, but before he could benefit from its rejuvenating powers, it was stolen from him by a serpent seeking a new skin.

This fantastic adventure involving the physical courage and spiritual testing of a heroic figure is typical of ancient legends. Although simplistic in their longevity prescriptions, these ancient tales launched ideas still considered to have some validity. Building on categories found in Gerald J. Gruman's *History of Ideas About the Prolongation of Life*, it is possible to see that longevity has usually been associated with one or more of the following: magical substances, sacred places, golden ages, com-

1

plex regimens, and immutable fates. [2]

By far the most prevalent ideas focus on magical substances. Among the most ancient of these are Gilgamesh's undersea plant, Hebraic *manna*, Iranian *haoma*, Chinese peaches of immortality, and Indian *soma*. Other Indian tales dating to at least 700 B.C. describe a Pool of Youth—an idea repeated in sun-drenched Arabia in the form of a Well of Life said to exist in the oasis of El Hidr. Ssu-ma Ch'ien (156-87 B.C.), a Chinese precursor of European alchemists, theorized that mercury compounds might prolong life. That led to stories about a long line of magical substances with a base in precious metals or minerals. Throughout the European Middle Ages there were searches for ambrosia, and in the New World "discovered" by Columbus, the Native Americans spoke of a Fountain of Youth hidden in the Florida peninsula and a life-extending octli plant growing in the Andes.

The earliest magical substances tended to be immersed in religious lore, either as temptations by evil supernatural forces or as gifts from the most kindly gods. In time, the magical substances acquired a more scientific nomenclature, becoming, among other things, vitamins, enzymes, hormones, and trace elements. More recently, the magical substance has been a synthetic laboratory product or, at the other extreme, a rediscovered folk remedy involving a rare root or herb. What distinguishes all of these substances—aside from the fact that none of them has been proved to promote longevity unaided—is that they are relatively easy to use. As with Alice in her Wonderland who drank a potion or nibbled a cake to become instantly short or instantly tall, long life is thought to be a simple matter of sipping, chewing, bathing in, injecting, or swallowing the right magical substance.

Closely associated with the idea of a magical substance is the belief that there is a specially favored earthly habitat where longevity is the norm. This place may be where the magical substance abounds, or it may be the "perfect" human environment. Rather than being at the center of civilization, the terrestrial paradise is usually located beyond the farthest boundaries of the known world, a place only the boldest would dare seek. Indian myths spoke of the far-off land of Uttarakuru where the magic tree of life grew. Blessed isles figured in the mythology of Japan, Iran, and the Teutonic tribes. Some cultures had a variety of sacred places. The ever-inventive ancient Greeks had three: one high in the mountains of Asia Minor, another in the interior of Ethiopia, and a third on the island or continent beyond the Strait of Gibraltar. The more domesticated the surface of the earth has become, the deeper into jungles and the higher into mountains the sacred places have receded.

A variation of the theme of the sacred place is the legend of a sacred time when the human race enjoyed incredible lifespans. One Roman writer described a lost epoch in which childhood alone lasted a hundred years. Polynesian cultures believed in similar golden ages. And the legendary Methuselah was simply the longest-living of a whole line of longevous antediluvian Hebrews. Bypassing the unanswerable question of how "years" of the long-living epochs were calculated, most golden ages occurred in a period when the human race was thought to be in high favor with the divine forces that guide existence. Since that time, the race supposedly strayed from prescribed moral, dietary, sexual, and social teachings. The consequence of this disobedience was a shorter and more painful time on earth. The only way to restore spiritual harmony and possibly earn divine forgiveness was through a total reformation of self and society, to be achieved through a complex regimen that rigidly controlled all facets of behavior.

The reverse of the lost-age coin is the hope that a complex

regimen is the means for attaining an unprecedented utopia. An ancient if extreme example of this idea is found in a specific school of Taoists. Its monks combined breathing techniques, dietary principles, specific medicines, regular gymnastics, and spiritual exercises with a sexual discipline in which monks learned to retain their semen even after ejaculation had begun. This system, requiring a lifetime to master, was thought to lead to various planes of enlightenment, culminating in an immortal physical body which the spirit could inhabit or abandon at will. Although most complex regimens do not, like that of these Taoists, consciously exclude half the species or promise corporeal immortality, the regimens demand a total commitment in which life increasingly becomes devoted to the prolongation, enrichment, or surpassing of itself.

The worst aspect of these complex regimens is that individuals must relinquish a large amount of actual present time in the effort to gain an undeterminable amount of added future time. Any regimen that so mortgages and monopolizes the present is further suspect because most longevous people have not lived like that. More often than not, they have lived within the norms of their culture, and quite a few of them have been perceived by contemporaries to be exemplary citizens. In contrast, the complex regimens often remove people from society or involve them in cultish behavior. While some of the specific techniques can be incorporated into a more rational approach to life extension, none of the regimens has ever demonstrated that it can produce unusual health or longevity. Utopia never materializes. But like the concept of a lost golden age, the notion of a complex regimen is valid in its insistence that there is not a single longevity secret, but rather many factors. Unless each is represented in a conscious longevity agenda, the prospects of unusually long life are greatly diminished.

Lastly, there is the view that longevity is a matter largely beyond human manipulation. Those who favor an immutable-fate approach range from gamblers who believe long life is primarily a matter of luck to determinists who ascribe it to unalterable biological inheritance. The gamblers often speak of the futility of planning for longevity because one might die from an accident. This overlooks the fact that in a nation like the United States less than 5% of the entire adult population will die through accidents, while more than 70% will die from diseases greatly influenced by lifestyle.[3] Gamblers delight in speaking of some 95-year-old obese drunkard who chain-smokes cigarettes and has never exercised. Such characters may exist, but they are only slightly less rare than unicorns. Like the roulette addict, the gambler is banking on luck in a game in which the long-run odds of winning are nil.

The biological argument is another matter. The question is not whether biological inheritance is a longevity factor, but to what extent, and whether that inheritance is as immutable as was once believed. The studies of identical twins discussed later in this book are extremely useful in weighing the longevity impact of the genetic code. One important finding is that although inherited diseases and physiological weaknesses can have a definite adverse effect on longevity prospects, to date no genetic factor that positively promotes long life has been discovered. However, since longevous women far outnumber longevous men in every society, the possibility of a linkage between longevity and the genes that determine sex cannot be ruled out.[4] Other more observable, but less important, genetically influenced characteristics that affect longevity would include overall body size, the basal metabolic rate, and various chemical idosyncrasies.

Theoretically, the genetic code determines the outer limit for any given individual's development, while the quality of the environment determines how much of the potential capacity is actually realized. Present medical knowledge indicates that the body is programmed to endure, if it is not abused, for more than a century. If genetic manipulation becomes feasible, as now seems quite likely, current genetic limits will surely evaporate. Until that time, attaining the hundred-year mark in good health remains a reasonable objective, and substantially moving past one hundred a realistic challenge.

In order to examine the question of where the upper genetic limits are, we must return to the search for the oldest of the old. Ideally, verifying age should be done over a prescribed period in which a number of separate, independent proofs are observed, cases which employ established statistical and scientific principles. My search for the oldest of the old begins with an examination of the evidence offered for one of the oldest documentable centenarians, Delina Filkins (1815-1928), and moves on to consider historical and contemporary claims that others have lived much longer. The historical review concentrates most heavily on the period for which at least some documentation is available, and culminates in the investigation of centenarian claims for specific national groups and geographical locations. The most celebrated of these originate in the Caucasus, where, during the 1970s, hundreds of persons claimed to be over 120. Of equal interest are similar supercentenarian claims for the Vilcabamba Valley of the Ecuadorian Andes and for the Hunza Valley of the western Himalayas. Also investigated are the more modest but still extraordinary age claims for the Tarahumara Indians of the Sierra Madre range in Mexico, the village of Upper Sheringham in Great Britain, and mountain peoples of Eastern Europe and Turkey.

Just as important as age claims for indiviuals or regions are claims made for unusual physical vigor among the very old.

The wisdom of the oft-quoted epigram that we must add life to our years as well as years to our life should be self-evident. Few would want to accumulate calendar years filled with prolonged infirmity and discomfort. As will be seen, many of the investigations debunk extraordinary age claims, but confirm the reality of extremely vigorous septuagenarians and octogenarians and relatively active nonagenarians. These findings correlate with work done by physical fitness experts in the United States which demonstrates that the vitality commonly associated with a healthy 40-year-old can be enjoyed in one's 70s and 80s.[5] Whether or not the total life span exceeds one hundred years, this means that most people can add from two to three decades to what is now considered a prime time of life.

Studies devoted to every aspect of aging are legion, yet there is a serious communication gap between historians, anthropologists, physicians, chemists, and other specialists. It often seems that all the separate items needed for an effective longevity agenda were identified long ago but remain scattered in disconnected segments, much like the loose pieces of a jigsaw puzzle. A case in point is Hunza. Although it is usually depicted as an area nearly inaccessible to visitors and about which there is a paucity of information, there are, in fact, literally scores of books, journals, chapter entries, and diary notes by visitors going back over a century and commenting upon every facet of Hunzakut society. The pieces can be fitted together to provide a most coherent and credible portrait of Hunzakut longevity. Likewise, piecing together the longevity knowledge scattered through various disciplines produces a most lucid account of how the oldest of the old have lived and the best ways to emulate them.

For Christians, Moslems, and Jews, the scientific hubbub about life span may seem a colossal waste of energy. The limit most gerontologists currently put on human life can be found stated in Genesis 3: "And the Lord said, My Spirit shall not always strive with man, for that he also is flesh, yet his days shall be one hundred and twenty years." And the 90th Psalm provides a statement about average life span that describes longevity norms in the technologically advanced countries of the late twentieth century: "The days of our years are threescore and ten; and if by reason of strength they be fourscore years." Ecclesiassticus 18:9 follows suit by noting, "The number of man's days is great if he reaches a hundred years."

These Biblical pronouncements have not discouraged scientific inquiry into aging. As the Middle Ages drew to a close, Roger Bacon, the friar-scientist, opined that as the Almighty had set a maximum life span, it was the moral duty of humans to attempt to attain it. In the seventeenth century, René Descartes, the champion of logic, posited that in the new Age of Reason the aging process should be examined with the same rationalism with which other challenges were approached. In the following century the more secular Benjamin Franklin concluded that one day the causes of all diseases, including the disease of aging, would be discovered, making death strictly a matter of chance and accident. In our time Alex Comfort has observed that if humans could learn how to retain the same resistance to stress, injury, and death we enjoy at age ten, nearly half the species could expect a life span of seven hundred years.

The ages-long concern for longevity never abates. Ancient tales are forever rediscovered or recycled into a new form. What used to be pure fantasy is now presented in a science fiction genre which routinely features suspended animation, time travel, bionically enriched life, and extra-terrestrial forms that make our essence as well as our chronology appear primitive. In much the same spirit that aristocrats employed necromancers to formulate longevity brews, our governments fund gerontological research of every kind. Yoga masters who have learned to control complex biological processes through mental power are tested for their secrets with the most sophisticated medical equipment ever devised. Chemists walk in rain forests looking for life-saving plant life that might be on the brink of extinction, while biospheres are fabricated to test for a perfect human habitat. What underscores this storytelling, experimentation, and speculation is that the quest for longevity speaks to the how and why of life as much as its duration. How we spend the days of our lives ultimately determines their number, and why we behave as we do reveals who we think we are and what our place in the universe might be.

# 2. THE OLDEST OF THE OLD

*No single subject is more obscured by vanity, deceit, falsehood, and deliberate fraud than the extremes of human longevity.—Guinness Book of World Records*

AT THE TIME I BEGAN MY SEARCH for the oldest of the old, the best documented superlongevous centenarian was Delina Filkins of Herkimer County, New York (May 4, 1815–December 4, 1928) and the longest supercentenarian life span offered by officials of a major government was that for Shirali Mislimov of Barzavu, Azerbaijan, USSR, who died in 1973 at the reputed age of 170. Numerous other individuals have claimed life spans greater than the 113+ of Filkins but less than Mislimov's seventeen decades. Someone in that group has experienced the outer boundaries of achieved human longevity.

Looking at various claims I soon discovered that one kind of data configuration emerged from the authentic claims while other configurations characterized the less credible ones, particularly those for the longest life spans. Extremely useful in defining these data was the methodology of nineteenth century English researchers. Their standards and the patterns of fraud they established proved extremely useful in weighing all longevity claims.

The proofs and other circumstances surrounding the age claim for Delina "Grandma" Filkins proved to be models of valid data. Her life could be traced from 1850 to 1925 in every national and

11

state census record. This material established that the age of Mrs. Filkins (*nee* Ecker), the ages of her children, and the age of her husband remained constant. The ages consistently proceeded one year at a time. Interviews with her descendants established that for all her life she had lived within a ten-mile radius of the family's dairy farm and had been active in its extensive cheese business. Her father had been longevous (97), and her mother had reached late maturity (73). To the end of her life, despite some deafness, Filkins retained a keen interest in world affairs and enjoyed reading. She was said to be fond of bragging that the only medicines she had ever taken were "sleeping herbs."[1]

Confidence in Filkins's age is bolstered by the fact that in her own day, while her age was duly noted in the local papers and she enjoyed limited regional fame, she never sought to profit from her years. She was relatively obscure at the time of her death. Her major obituary appeared in the *Herkimer Evening Telegram*, and the only known portraits of her hang in the Van Hornesville Central School and in the Canajoharie Library and Art Gallery. Until A. Ross Eckler presented her documentation to the *Guinness Book of World Records*, Grandma Filkins was just another frontier character, and to this day there is no national or regional celebration of her.

Nor has A. Ross Eckler, the "discoverer" of Grandma Filkins, sought any personal limelight. A Ph.D. in mathematics from Princeton University, Eckler worked for more than a quarter of a century as a statistician for New Jersey Bell. After tracing the genealogy of his own family, he became involved in longevity studies as a hobby. By scrutinizing census data, Eckler discovered that many Americans seeking notoriety advanced their ages fifteen to twenty years for every ten years of the census, with the inflation usually commencing around age 70. He concluded that all of the unresolved American claims for longevity greater than that of Grandma Filkins were invalid, a good many being outright deceptions. Since there is an array of tax, legal, and census documentation on three levels of government, he found it difficult to believe that any American, particularly anyone living more than one hundred years, could have escaped repeated official documentation. The Filkins data also was satisfactory from a mathematical standpoint. Her life exceeded that of the previously recognized oldest person by only eighty-six days, a development quite in line with statistical probability. The only providential element in the claim was that Eckler's family happened to have a farm in Herkimer, and he had been intrigued by stories about the local centenarian told by his own longevous relatives.

The precedent for using mathematical probabilities and governmental records was set by the Englishman William J. Thoms, who wrote about centenarians in the latter half of the nineteenth century, publishing his landmark *The Longevity of Man* in 1873.[2] Thoms, who was a deputy librarian in the House of Lords, was intrigued by three British subjects who had been claimed as supercentenarians: the Countess of Desmond (140), Thomas Parr (152), and Henry Jenkins (169).

Thoms based his research on the fact that since 1538, every parson, vicar, and curate had been required by law to keep a record of all christenings, weddings, and funerals in his parish. To mandatory parish records could be added tax rolls, land contracts, court proceedings, military lists, and other documents. During times closer to Thoms's own era, there were records kept by life-insurance firms that were especially concerned about the correct age and identity of their clients. Thoms began the test of a claim by trying to find a parish record and continued it by looking for other materials that described the same person.

Certain bases for fraud were found to recur. Entries in the family

Bible often did not jibe with baptismal and marriage records. Frequently, this happened because related persons had identical names or because many parents, anticipating that one or more of their offspring would die during childhood, gave exactly the same name to two or more siblings. Another finding was that the claimed birth date and the written baptismal date could be separated by a gap of many years. The explanation for this was that the parents had put off the ritual until the child understood its significance or for financial or social reasons. The highest age claims were often found in conjunction with these delayed baptisms. Claimants also offered news clippings as verification when the story only repeated verbatim what they had told an obliging correspondent. The "proof" was their own word. The internal details of most stories fell apart under the mildest scrutiny, since the deceptions were primarily good-natured boasting rather than swindles.

At a certain point in his labors, Thoms began to doubt if anyone had ever turned 100; but gradually, from various sources, authentic case histories began to accumulate. The major breakthrough came from Canada, where Dr. Joseph Tache, Dominion Statistician at Ottawa, undertook a study of 421 centenarian claims made between 1609 and 1876. Finding that it was extremely difficult to get reliable data on those born outside Canada, Tache had narrowed his list to the 82 who were native-born. Of these 82, he determined that nine were valid centenarians.

Among those nine was Pierre Joubert, a French Canadian lumberjack who had lived from July 15, 1701, to November 16, 1814. His 113 years and 124 days was to stand as the longest documented life-span until the verification of Grandma Filkins's. Unlike so many others who proved to be liars, Joubert had shunned all publicity and had believed himself to be younger than his actual years. His age, however, was verified through church records found by parish priests working under the direction of Dr. Tache and Abbe Cyprien Tanguay, Canada's first genealogist.

Claims for the three fabled supercentenarians of the British Isles proved to be of much less substance. The case of the Countess of Desmond (1464-1604) was the weakest. A long-living Countess of Desmond had existed, but she had never claimed to be a super-centenarian and most likely was not aware of the myths surrounding her age. Testimony that purported to be firsthand fell under the weight of impossible internal contradictions. The final explanation for the supposed supercentenarianism was that the lives of two or three women who had borne the title had been grafted to create one fictitious superwoman.

On the surface, the tale of Thomas Parr (1483-1635) seemed to have more merit. Charles I had received him at court, and Sir William Harvey, the physician who discovered the circulation of blood, had performed an autopsy on him which was widely interpreted as having verified his great age. Parr's legend included the belief that he had been extraordinarily endowed sexually. In 1588, at the alleged age of 105, he had been ordered to do public penance for indecent sexual overtures to a woman, and seventeen years later, at the alleged age of 122, he had married for a second time.

Researching the story with his usual skepticism, Thoms became convinced that it was the invention of the Earl of Arundel, a courtier who wanted to regain lost favor with the sovereign, and that Harvey had obliged the Earl because of a personal debt. A reading of the actual autopsy report revealed that Harvey had made it clear that he was responsible only for the technical matter and that all else was "furnished by the person who accompanied Parr to London."[3] That person, of course, was the Earl of Arundel. Except for a whimsical comment that the stories of Parr's sexual powers had a physiological basis, the physician simply reported that Parr had indeed been a very old man.

Moving from Harvey's autopsy, Thoms delved into the matter of leases at the Parr cottage and discovered that on one occasion Parr had resorted to elaborate trickery to retain his right to the cottage and adjoining land. Subsequent research was to discover that three Thomas Parrs had lived consecutively at the Parr cottage: a father, his son, and his grandson. Old people who remembered Thomas Parr as being old when they were young were probably thinking of the father or grandfather. Several persons claiming to be Parr's children had substantiated his age with their own word, but according to Parr's own account, all the children of his first marriage had died and the second marriage had been childless.

The Parr legend held also that he continued to work in the fields until he was 130, that he enjoyed sexual relations until he was 140, and that he remained vigorous until he left Shropshire to go down to London, where he promptly expired as a result of frantic merrymaking. Investigation turned up a more credible portrait. Several sources agreed that Parr had been blind for at least twenty years, that he was quite frail, and that his memory was so greatly impaired that he could recall only recent events. Recognizing that Parr had probably been longevous, Thoms repeatedly requested surveys of all parish records in the region of Parr's birth. No documentation was ever forthcoming. The proof of having lived 152 years came to rest solely on the word of a frail, blind, poor old man and the ambitious courtier who had exploited him. Thomas Parr is still cited as a legitimate or probable supercentenarian in some books that are otherwise quite serious, and his myth is a standby of faddist literature.

The tale of Henry Jenkins (1511–1670) proved to be even weaker, with the strong possibility that Yorkshire officials had built it up in deliberate rivalry with Parr's earlier claim in Shropshire. Jenkins, who liked to call himself "the oldest man born upon the ruins of the postdiluvian world," was never able to keep his claim consistent. Depending on the occasion, his age went up and down like a yo-yo. One of the proofs his adherents thought strongest was that Jenkins had sworn that he was 157 years old in a court case involving Charles Anthony, a vicar. Yet twelve years later, after his burial, that same vicar discreetly listed Jenkins as "a very aged and poore man"[4] in the only parish record found for him. People who spoke up to confirm Jenkins's age were proved to be lying about their own and thus could not have witnessed the events they claimed to have seen.

As with so many undocumented individuals, Jenkins's notoriety began late in life—in this case after the asserted age of 130. This raises the question of why he was not famous at 110, or 120, particularly since Thoms had demonstrated that centenarianism was rare. The answer is self-evident. Like Parr's, Jenkins's claim was based entirely on his word, and like Parr, he was not telling the truth. An aspect of his legend illustrates how tales grow. Alternately, Jenkins was said to have been a soldier in the Battle of Flodden, to have brought arrows as a young man to soldiers in the battle, or to have brought arrows as a child to a young man who gave them to the soldiers. Most likely he had heard stories about the battle from his parents or grandparents.

The pattern of deception found in Parr and Jenkins was to be encountered by Thoms many times as he became the first to question why the most spectacular age claims were often made on behalf of illiterate people. His doubts were countered with the argument that the simple life of the peasant was more "natural" —a favorite theme of romantics influenced by Jean Jacques Rousseau. Yet throughout Europe, as soon as record-keeping with any degree of accuracy was established, the same peasant class that had boasted of longevity developed much shorter life spans and relatively poor health. In developed nations, education and longevity have had a consistently strong positive correlation.

Thoms concluded that centenarians were something of a biological fluke. He found that in Scotland the legal presumption of the limit of life was one hundred years. For him, this was folk wisdom at its best.

Writing twenty years after Thoms, T.E. Young pioneered another method of longevity verifications. The key to his approach is found in the dedication of his book to the Institute of Actuaries, an organization founded in 1848. Young believed the most reliable longevity data could be found in actuarial tables, since the solvency of powerful insurance companies depended on their accuracy. He noted that firms picked up their clients at a relatively young age, verified that age, and kept track of each person for life. While the clients of nineteenth-century firms were mainly the urban middle class, their statistics provided a guidepost for judging figures applicable to the general population. Confining himself to insurance records, Young established that of 30,000 persons covered by contracts from 1770 to 1890, there were only 22 indisputable centenarians, the oldest of them having lived to 105. Females had outnumbered males by two to one. Using this result and similar data, Young estimated that from 1821 to 1871, when the British population was increasing from 21 to 31 million, there had been 200 to 250 centenarians alive at any given moment.

Young fought against hearsay and flimsy evidence. He wrote that since tombstones usually used inflated sentiments and language, the dates carved on them were by no means dependable. He noted that one 78-year-old man had had his age recorded as 708 because the carver was told he was 70 and 8. Young's perusal of historical and medical records led him to conclude that from the thirteenth to the sixteenth century, 70 was usually considered a great age in Britain. He also attempted to deal with antediluvian biblical longevity by speculating as to what might have constituted a year on the basis of a variety of numerical theories. A more practical contribution was his inclusion of specific research used to reach his conclusions.[5] One of his consultants was Dr. G.M. Humphry, professor of surgery at Cambridge. Humphry had examined 900 patients thought to be at least 90 years of age. Of those 900, 52 were believed to be centenarians. The following data for the 36 women and 16 men were recorded:[6]

1. The majority were moderate or light eaters, consuming little meat.
3. The majority rose early and liked to do outdoor work.
4. Forty drank alcohol.
5. Few reported having had many illness.
6. Forty-four reported they were excellent sleepers, most averaging over eight hours a night for most of their lives.
7. A large percentage claimed to be from long-lived families, although "long-lived" was not carefully defined.
8. Twelve were first-born children.
9. Over two-thirds of the women had been married and had raised large families.
10. Ten of the 11 who were over 102 were female, the oldest person being 105.

In the 1930s, Maurice Ernest gave a larger European context to the tradition initiated by Thoms and Young.[7] Surveying historical records from Roman times onward, he was unable to locate a single credible case of a European who had lived as long as Pierre Joubert. What he did find was that monarchs were most enthusiastic about having the oldest specimens of humanity among their subjects, resulting in numerous hoaxes of the Desmond-Parr-Jenkins ilk. An example of this was Drakenberg the Dane, a Scandinavian sailor reputed to have reached 146 (1626-1772). Investigation showed the story to have no foundation whatsoever.

A more encouraging finding reported by Ernest originated in Scotland, where the Registrar General of Births had decided to examine every centenarian claim made from 1910 to 1932. 253 females and 48 males were involved. Ninety-nine claims were found inconclusive because of insufficient data. Of the remaining 202, the remarkably high number of 157 (137 females and 18 males) were found to be telling the truth. The oldest man was 103, and the oldest woman 106 years and 213 days.[8] These findings indicated either a sudden acceleration in longevity since the Thoms-Young period or a more accurate recognition of longevity that had existed all along.

Ernest located many other valid centenarians to go along with the Scottish group. Of greatest significance were the proofs found for Mrs. Ann Pouder (over 110), Mrs. Margaret Ann Neve (almost 111), and the Honorable Katherine Plunkett (almost 112). This trio, combined with Joubert, proved that a superlongevous club of 110 plus was indeed a human reality. The sample, it must be stressed, was limited to Anglo-American records (mainly from 1750 onward) and thus represented only a fraction of the human population; and even within this fraction, the number was confined to fully documented individuals.

Unlike his predecessors', Ernest's stated objective was to find the secret of longevity. He was knowledgeable about the medical opinions of his era and studied the biographies of longevous people, particularly those who had written about health. He speculated that if certain physical processes could be understood, the present maximal life spans could be doubled or even tripled. For practical purposes, however, he believed 120 was the realizable limit of human life. His prescription was:

— Eat frugally.

— Exercise and get plenty of fresh air.
— Choose a congenial occupation.
— Develop a placid and easygoing personality.
— Maintain a high level of personal hygiene.
— Drink wholesome liquids.
— Abstain from stimulants and sedatives.
— Get plenty of rest.
— Have a waste evacuation once a day.
— Live in a temperate climate.
— Enjoy a reasonable sex life.
— Get prompt medical attention in case of illness.

Ernest also reported on some of the hoaxes that had accumulated in the new century. Increasingly, the new sites of longevity were located beyond the Bosporus among non-Christian cultures. A typical case was that of Zaro Agha, an illiterate Turkish citizen from Kurdistan. Agha said he was 156 and claimed to have seen Napoleon when the General was residing in Egypt. While never able to convince researchers of his age, Agha had a brief moment of glory on theatrical stages before returning to Turkey, where he died in obscurity in 1933.[9]

Apparently that was a poor year for supercentenarians, for in May, Li Chung Yun, a Chinese herb seller, was reported by *The New York Times* to have perished at the incredible age of 197.[10] Written with obvious humor (a previous age claim would have made him 256), the story would not be worth citing if it did not involve yet another magical substance—the rare Oriental herb. In this case, the plant was called *fo-ti tien* (literal meaning: the elixir of life). Naturally, it could be found only in a difficult-to-reach region of China. Those who retold the story never explained why the herb was not used by the natives who brought it to Li Chung Yun or why he had withheld his secret from his reported

23 wives and their numerous offspring. Stranger still, the herbs Li Chung Yun sold to others were advertised as being able to extend life to a mere one hundred years. When tested under laboratory conditions, *fo-ti tien*, like ginseng and other miraculous roots and herbs, was found to have no prolongevous effects.[11]

A much more substantial Asian claim to long life belongs to Shigechiyo Izumi of Japan (1865-1986) who lived much of his life on a tiny fishing island located just south of Kyushu. Telephone communication with the registrar of the Isen town office on Tokonushima island, Kagoshima Perfecture, revealed that when the Family Registration Act of Emperor Meiji's government went into effect in 1871, a Shigechiyo Izumi was recorded as having been born on June 29, 1865.[12]

My reservations about the claim lie not with the credibility of the documents but whether they refer to only one person. The Japanese Ministry of Health and Welfare told me that Izumi lost his father when Izumi was only three months old and his mother three months later; he was raised by his uncle. Exactly what property or other wealth came with the Izumi identity has not been researched. I noticed that Izumi had not wed until age 39 and fathered his first child twelve years later. He had taken a porter's job at age 65 and had kept it until retiring at age 86. A Ministry report on his health at age 114 stated his blood pressure, eyesight, hearing, and internal organs were "normal," without giving the criteria for normality.

Newspaper accounts of his daily life described a kind of unique centenarian vigor. No mention was ever made of naps or fatigue. It was reported that Izumi went to sleep each evening at about nine after watching television and awoke at eight the next morning. He took a daily walk with his dog after breakfast. Reporters also noted that he was a moderate smoker and drank a pint of warm *shocku* (potato liquor) at his evening meal. Described as clearheaded and not much of a worrier, he had no dietary peculiarities but preferred fish and vegetables to meat.

Izumi's celebrity capped a more-than-decade-long longevity boom in the Japanese media. In addition to reports on the nearly 1,000 known Japanese centenarians, none of whom approached Izumi's age, there was extensive and somewhat uncritical coverage of various longevity claims around the world. Izumi may very well have attained the age the media so happily celebrated, but his summary biography begs for elaboration. Because he was an orphan born on a small island well before the Family Registration Act went into effect, greater scrutiny should certainly be given to determine that the documents all refer to him alone. The twelve-year gap between marriage and parenthood is somewhat unusual and the exact nature of the porter's job needs clarification. The "normal" health readings are the most suspicious, since loss of efficiency is observable in all humans as they age and should be especially apparent in anyone who has passed the age of 110. None of these questions about the data available on Izumi are insurmountable, but his age cannot be considered fully verified until professionals knowledgeable about Japanese culture have compiled family genealogies, cross-checked the records, assessed the health findings by more objective criteria, and otherwise filled in the details of his life.

Another intriguing claim for extraordinary age comes from Mali. In 1976 I interviewed Jean Rouch, the visual anthropologist famous for his pioneering films about traditional cultures in contemporary Africa. He told me that in 1969 while working on a film project, he was informed that Anai Dollo, the village elder of Bongo, had died. An unusual funeral was being prepared, for Anai Dollo was not only head of the Society of Masks, but he was believed to be over 122 years old.[13] Dollo belonged to the Auru subgroup of the Dogon people, and one of his tribe's most sacred rites is celebrated at sixty-year intervals. He had been present at three of these: once as a baby, once as a mature adult at 60, and finally two-and-a-half years before Rouch's visit.

Dollo's age claim was based on the testimony of an entire people, and not on the word of just one person. Genealogy in the tribe is kept by oral historians noted for their precision, and Dollo had become such a highly respected member of the Auru that unless there was progressive fraud throughout the tribe, any switch of identity would have to have occurred extremely early in his life. The possibility of a hoax was made even less likely by the fact that although his people considered him to be extraordinarily old, neither they, Rouch, nor the Mali government knew that if his story were true, he had lived a full eight years longer than the oldest documented person.

The dating for the rituals also appears to be authentic. The Dogon, who have long been the favorites of French anthropologists because of their sense of order, style, and precision, have a sophisticated astronomy. When questioned about the possibility that the sixty-year cycle might be inaccurate, Rouch thought it was extremely unlikely and noted that Europeans had been present at the ritual in 1907 and that the next cycle had taken place in 1967 right on schedule. There was no reason to doubt that the earlier one had occurred in 1847. Rouch thought it was also unlikely that there had been any falsification of Dollo's age. He emphasized the Dogon passion for exactness and the regularity with which the tribe's history was publicly recounted. Just as noteworthy in his opinion was the Dogons' respect for the old. If they became so feeble that they could not take care of themselves, they were placed on a platform in the vestibule of the family lodge. Everyone going in and coming out was required to speak with the oldster, maintaining his or her connection to daily life and preventing any sense of loneliness or abandonment. Dollo, blind for over two years and quite frail, had been treated in this manner.

Speculation on the longevity of Africans fed an interest in the United States during the 1950s and '60s when there was a rash of stories about black centenarians who had been slaves. Typical was an *Ebony* story about 114-year-old Henry Hudson who had spoken with Abraham Lincoln.[14] Popularizers advanced the notion that a black physical elite may have been created because the horrors of the slave trade had killed off the weaker men and women en route from Africa and the rigors of slavery had bred exceptional strength. It was further argued that slaves had eaten simple, wholesome food and had not been under the stress of economic worries. For whites, there was more than a little racism in the idea that people constantly in fear of being sold or physically abused could live without stress. Like that of the rich city-bred Europeans who idealized the peasantry, the American idea of longevous ex-slaves made it seem that slavery, like serfdom, had not been without its advantages. For African-Americans, there was some psychological pleasure in believing that the slaves had outlived their masters.

Investigation of plantation registers and post-emancipation census records soon proved most of these claims to be false. More difficult to prove were cases in which the claimant deliberately threw off the researchers with false information so that no documentation could be located. The most famous of these hoaxers was Charlie Smith, who told a Social Security official in 1955 that he had been born in Liberia in 1842. Sometimes he said he had been lured aboard a slave ship with false promises, and other times that he had been knocked from his bicycle and kidnapped. A man of considerable charm, Charlie told his stories well, aided, perhaps, by his background as a carnival worker. By 1979, claiming to be 137 years old, Smith had become a celebrity, his life extolled in a filmed docu-drama and his words reproduced in numerous newspaper and magazine articles. Most gerontologists, however, were not surprised when a researcher for the *Guinness Book of World Records* found a Florida marriage license which showed that Smith had added a whopping thirty-three years to his true age. He had become a genuine centenarian only in 1975. Smith died in October of 1979 without ever being told that his real age had been discovered.

The remaining unresolved ex-slave supercentenarian claims are quite doubtful. The researcher of Delina Filkins has found only two claimants with partial documentation. One is Mark Thrash, who died in 1943, and had said he was 123 years old. The 1900 federal census shows a Mark Thrash in the Crawfish Springs Militia District claiming to have been born on December 18, 1822. Whether this is indeed the same Mark Thrash has not been confirmed. No other Thrash records have been located. The second former slave is Martha Graham, who died in 1959 at the reputed age of 117 or 118. The 1900 census for Cumberland County, North Carolina, shows a Martha Graham married to a Henry Graham, and the same family unit appears in the 1880 count. The ages found in the two censuses would have made Graham 116 years old at her death if it is the same Martha. No other record for her has been found.[15]

Mark Thrash and Martha Graham notwithstanding, the known life spans of blacks in the United States do not augur well for the existence of superlongevity among them. African-Americans have consistently had poorer health and lower life expectancy than the general population. Only since the 1940s have they begun to approach its average life span. Despite rapid gains, life span equalization will probably not occur until the twenty-first century. The depressed living conditions and economic exploitation suffered by most blacks is more than sufficient explanation for this phenomenon. These factors are compounded by the fact that until the 1940s most blacks lived in the South, which traditionally has had the nation's poorest health. Of course, black centenarians do exist— Charlie Smith was one of them—but they do not seem to live any longer than other segments of the population or to appear in a different percentage from the national average.

Claims for black longevity based on the notion of a simple yet arduous life style have a parallel in Europe. When the Ottoman Empire began to contract in the late nineteenth century, there were hundreds of supercentenarian claims in the newly independent Balkan states and in regions of the Austro-Hungarian Empire. Like most patriotic tales, the longevity stories were told on national holidays accompanied by wine, music, and general festivity. With the establishment of even minimal record-keeping, it soon became evident that these areas had the poorest health, the lowest average life-spans, and the fewest centenarians in Europe. The scale of falsification was evident in a study of longevity in Bavaria. When the 1871 census turned up 37 centenarian claims, the government made an official inquiry. It was discovered that most of the claimants had not reached 90 and one person proved to be a mere 61. In the final count, there was only one genuine centenarian.[16]

In spite of many incidents of this kind, stories of longevity in Eastern and Southern Europe persisted, enhanced by scientists fascinated by what they believed was a link between cultured milk products and long life. Led by the brilliant Eli Metchnikoff, who had discovered the disease-fighting role of phagocytes, scientists believed that live yogurt bacillus penetrated into the intestinal tract, where it worked against toxins that might poison the body before being released as waste matter. Yogurt experts squabbled over which strain was best and whether a solid or semiliquid form was better. In addition to the obvious wishful thinking about magic potions, there was the mystique of the "golden age" and "sacred place" created by writers who wanted to idealize the "noble" Eastern European peasant.

Outstripping the reputation of all areas associated with longevous yogurt eaters is the region of the Caucasus. The problem of age verification in the region has been formidable. Under the Tsars, the region was poorly administrated; its people were left illiterate. When inhabitants were asked their ages, they might respond with reckonings in other than the Christian calendar. As in Central Asia, they might refer to twelve-year cycles, each named after an animal. Having been born in the Year of the Bear could mean in 1880, 1892 or 1904. Few of the minimal records kept by the Tsarist bureaucracy or religious authorities survived the fighting during the Revolution, the civil war, and World War II.

Confronted by this lack of documentation, contemporary researchers have had to rely heavily on detailed life histories obtained through personal interviews. Each centenarian is asked to recall his or her age at the time of important historical events. The responses are then compared with whatever records exist, the testimony of family members, and the histories of other persons living in the area. Clearly, such a method would be subject to error with even the most highly trained personnel. The problem was more severe in the former USSR because many of the old people did not understand Russian and it was not always possible to find a person skilled in the local language or dialect who was also professionally competent in taking oral histories. Untrained interpreters or interviewers often had to determine which war in the east and which Year of the Bear was being cited. Respect for the word of the old, ethnic chauvinism, and plain wishful thinking probably fostered more distortions than deliberate chicanery. Aware of this situation, the Soviet authorities issued a 272-page manual to interviewers. Its sheer size indicated the magnitude of the problem.

Particularly after 1970, when the announcement of some 500 supercentenarians' claims elicited worldwide awe at the same time that detente made travel much easier, many foreign reporters and scientists visited the longevous regions. Among the most important American researchers were Dr. Sula Benet, an anthropologist at the Institute for the Study of Man and Hunter College-City University of New York, and Dr. Alexander Leaf, a medical doctor on the staff of Boston General Hospital and the faculty of the Harvard Medical School. After several trips to the Caucasus, the Russian-speaking Benet enthusiastically endorsed the Soviet findings. A somewhat more skeptical Leaf, who studied longevity in the USSR, Ecuador, and Hunza for the National Geographic Society, was also impressed.

In 1976 a populist twist was given to the centenarian craze by an American advertising agency representing the Dannon Yogurt Company, which promoted yogurt sales in America by showing a centenarian parent sharing a cup of yogurt with a centenarian offspring. The agency people told me that they wanted to film in Bulgaria, which was already associated with yogurt consumption and longevity. But Bulgarian officials told them that no family of the age they required existed in Bulgaria and that they should try their luck in Soviet Georgia. Despite all the claims for superlongevity, the "best" they could do was a centenarian mother and her 89-year-old son. Nonetheless, that ad and other clever and entertaining ads featuring Soviet centenarians were fabulously successful in the American market.

The most vocal dissenter from the longevity euphoria was geneticist Zhores A. Medvedev. Although of Russian descent, Medvedev had been born in Tbilisi, Georgia, and had traveled throughout the Caucasus. He had been trained by the Soviet scientific establishment, had an insider's knowledge of Soviet methodology and a personal acquaintance with some of the longevity specialists. He also happened to come from a dissenter family. His father had been a purge victim, and he and his twin brother, Roy, also a renowned scientist, were among the most vocal critics of the Soviet system, arguing for a more humanistic form of socialism. Shortly after he was forced into exile in the early 1970s, Zhores Medvedev was asked to comment on Soviet longevity claims. His views were published in *The Gerontologist* in October of 1974. In that article and in subsequent writings and interviews, he detailed a number of scientific doubts about Soviet data and furnished political speculations on why they had been allowed to stand. His objections were manifold:[17]

— Internal passports and other Soviet documents go back no further than 1932, when information was obtained through oral interviews, with no verifying investigation. The census is taken the same way.

— No public official, church leader, or other person with a traceable career has been shown to be older than 108. Ages have been highest where illiteracy is highest and records most meager. Not one person among the 500 who claimed to be over 120 has pre-1932 documents.

— Soviet statistics have shown certain mathematical irregularities. For instance, in the 1959 census in the Altay region, there were more people (19) in the 114–116 group than in the younger 111-113 group (14).

— Another odd finding in the 1959 census is that after age 100 male survivors begin to overtake females, and all who claim to be over 150 are male. This is contrary to the established worldwide pattern that longevous women outnumber longevous men in all age categories.

— Yet another statistical oddity from 1959 deals with survival after age 80. In Estonia, the region with the least longevity, out of each 100,000 persons born, 1,600 will survive to 80. In Georgia, the region with the second-highest longevity, that number will be 1,500. However, during the next twenty years, only two of the 1,600 Estonian octogenarians will survive to 100, compared with about 85 Georgians.

— Almost all settlements of any size in Georgia claim at least one centenarian, an improbable distribution mathematically.

— Physical and biochemical tests show results for some of the 100-110-year-olds that would be normal for persons not much older than 60. Similar tests on documented centenarians in other countries do not yield this result.

— Older developed Christian cultures, like those in Armenia, have longevity rates similar to those in most European nations, even though Armenia is in the longevity belt of the Caucasus. Unlike many Moslem groups in the region who rebelled against Tsarist and Soviet policies, creating a need for some rebels to take new identities for safety, and generally distorting family genealogies, the Armenians sought Soviet protection following genocidal massacres in Turkey.

— In the Altay region, asserted longevity is higher among native people than among the Europeans who live with them, even though the Europeans have better standards of living and better access to medical care.

— The statistical odds against the supercentenarian marriages claimed are astronomical, even if a claim is for a second marriage contracted when both parties were already past 60. Any marriages in which both parties are centenarians should be extraordinarily rare.

To these objections Medvedev added a number of political interpretations, most of them involving Joseph Stalin. He believed that after the end of World War II, local Georgian officials seeking to flatter the Georgian-born dictator began to publicize stories about longevity in their area. One old chestnut that was revived dealt with a woman said to be 180 who had lived in the same Gori district where Stalin was born. Longevity was also advertised as another example of the superiority of the Soviet system. Whether he believed in the stories or not, the aging Stalin certainly did nothing to discourage them. Like many rulers before him, he seemed to enjoy the idea that among his subjects were the longest-living people in the world.

Whatever the original factual basis, tales of Soviet longevity soon got out of hand. Individuals, villages, and districts had always been zealous about making age claims. Now, with the sanction of the state, older and older centenarians were "discovered." The phenomenon began to take on nationalistic biases. Within the Caucasus, regions like Azerbaijan began to compete with Georgia, and within Georgia ethnic minorities like the Abkhasians began to compete with the Georgians. Soviet investigators exposed claims that were off by whole decades, with individuals, particularly men, doubling and even tripling their real ages. One hoax involved a man living in Siberia who announced he was 130. His photograph was published throughout the USSR and happened to be spotted by Ukrainian villagers who recognized him as a man who had used his father's papers to get out of military service in World War II. His real age was 78.

Another element in Medvedev's political critique touched on the reliability of Soviet statistics. At the end of World War II, a report was released which stated that the average life span in the USSR had jumped from the low twenties into the high fifties. Given the invasion of the Nazis and the difficult times before, this was indeed an amazing improvement. However, the Western press pointed out that the average life span in the capitalist bloc had already reached into the high sixties. A short time later, revised Soviet statistics showed that the USSR had caught up. The quick leap in the average life span was then followed by a flat line for nearly a decade. Medvedev thought that by the 1970s the average life spans in the developed world were about the same as those in the USSR and that the flat line was a correction needed to compensate for the false leap which had indicated parity before it had actually been achieved. Medvedev contended that other longevity data had been tampered with from similar political motives.

Medvedev's skepticism did not lead him to conclude that there was no unusual longevity in the Caucasus, only that the claims were inflated. None of the Soviet scientists he had spoken with confidentially before his exile had seen anyone they believed to be older than 112. In that connection, Medvedev noted that the fabled Shirali Mislimov had not been accessible to foreigners, ostensibly either because he was too frail or because he was living in a security zone. The lack of an autopsy report after his death was equally suspicious.

Critics of Medvedev noted that Soviet scientists had been reexamining and refining their work constantly, trying to resolve issues of the very type Medvedev had identified. Naturally, there had been mistakes. The Thomas Parr myth still took in the gullible. Why should the situation in the Soviet Union be any different? And although inexperienced investigators, charming braggarts and eager reporters had undoubtedly distorted Soviet surveys, the exposure of fraud had been the work mainly of Soviet researchers, not of outsiders. One also had to bear in mind that since supercentenarians did not exist elsewhere, established longevity patterns might not apply.

Dr. Jeffrey Bada, an organic chemist at the Scripps Institute of Oceanography in San Diego, also directly challenged Soviet experts. In 1976 he announced that his recently developed method for dating the age of fossils through changes in their amino acid molecules could be used to determine the age of humans. All that was required was a tooth fragment from a living or recently deceased centenarian. While the Soviets could perform the procedure on their own, using his published work as a guide, Bada volunteered to do the job personally in cooperation with whatever scientists the Soviets designated. As of this writing, there has been no acceptance of his offer.

The heat generated by Soviet findings came down to three essential issues: Were there really as many centenarians as claimed? Were they as vigorous as advertised? Were there hundreds of living supercentenarians? These questions could not be left in limbo as an isolated claim like Anai Dollo's might be, for they dealt on a massive scale with the fundamental question of the limits and nature of human longevity. But to assess all Soviet data, point by point and region by region, would require an effort approaching the scale of the original work. I concluded that a more reasonable and practical approach would be to single out a particular geographical area for intensive firsthand observation. The immediate objectives would be to examine Soviet research methods, to question officials on the doubts expressed about their data, to evaluate how longevity was presented to the Soviet public, and to meet with alleged centenarians. If the results of such an investigation were conclusive, a generalization based on printed materials might be possible for Soviet research as a whole.

My choice for an on-site study was not difficult. The 1970 census had established Abkhasia, an autonomous region within Georgia, as the longevity capital of the world. Here, where the old were referred to as the "long living," a population of half a million had produced no fewer than 294 centenarians, including 39 persons between 110 and 119, and 15 persons over 120. Among the supercentenarians was Shirali Mislimov's female counterpart, Khfaf Lazuria, "the oldest woman in the world," who had died in 1975 at the reputed age of 140. None of the centenarians lived more than 100 kilometers from the main highway, and the entire region, which is the size of Delaware, was open to foreign visitors. Over half-a-dozen Americans had made longevity studies of some kind in Abkhasia between 1966 and 1977, providing an American research base parallel with Soviet research. All these factors made one more visit from the outside far less threatening to the Soviets than a request to see people in the restricted zones of Azerbaijan might have been. My journey was approved for the autumn of 1978.

# 3. THE LONG-LIVING PEOPLE OF ABKHASIA

*A fat man on a horse is ridiculous.*
*—Abkhasian proverb*

THE CAUCASIAN MOUNTAIN RANGE STRADDLES the borders of the Soviet Union, Turkey, and Iran, linking the Black and Caspian seas. Its peaks, the highest in Europe, range over 18,000 feet above sea level. For centuries armies marching south from Moscow and Kiev battled forces coming northward from Teheran, Damascus, and Byzantium for control of strategic passes. Legendary world conquerors such as Tamerlane, Genghis Khan, and Alexander the Great spread the fingers of their empires into its rugged valleys. Still earlier, poets sang of the exploits of Amazon warriors and of Prometheus, who dared to bring fire to the human race, and was chained to a great rock in the same mountains where Noah's ark was said to have touched land, near the summit of Mt. Ararat. Here too came Jason in search of a real or proverbial golden fleece.

The strength and vigor of the people of the Caucasus are so striking that in the mid-eighteenth century Johann Blumenbach chose their name to represent all people of European origin, and some decades later romantic poets like Pushkin and Lermontov renewed the fame of the "cradle of myth" throughout the continent. Rebellious subjects of whatever political rule they fell under, by the turn of the twentieth century the inhabitants of the Russian Caucasus were extremely displeased with the Romanov Dynasty.

They were to furnish some of the top leadership of the October Revolution.

Before the breakup of the Soviet Union, Abkhasia was an autonomous region within the Georgian Republic. A two-lane highway hugged its 250 kilometers of Black Sea coastline, the southern end of the highway veering over the mountains to Tbilisi, capital of Georgia, and the northern extending to Sochi and other resort cities near the border. At midpoint was Sukhumi, the area's administrative center. Founded as Diascuria by Greeks in the fifth century B.C., Sukhumi housed a little over one hundred thousand of Abkhasia's half-million inhabitants. Abkhasians made up the largest of the region's thirty ethnic groups; Georgians composed the second largest; and there were significant numbers of Armenians, Russians, Ukrainians, and Greeks, all of whom had retained their ethnic identities. The region had three official languages: Abkhasian, Georgian, and Russian. Many signposts were in all three languages as were all government documents. In the early 1990s the area erupted into a bitter civil war which pitted the Abkhasians against the Georgians, with most of the other ethnic groups siding with the Abkhasians. Intense fighting took place along the entire coast, including Sukhumi. At the time of my visit, these ethnic rivalries were visible but had not yet become lethal as they were to do a decade later.

I arrived in Abkhasia with several disadvantages. I did not speak any of the official languages, I had a limited two-week time frame, and I had no academic affiliations. In short, I was highly dependent on the goodwill of the local authorities. I did however have some advantages over previous investigators. Precisely because others had gone before me, I had a list of some 30 centenarians and the ages they had given to different researchers at different times. I was eager to see if they were aging one year at a time or were accelerating the number of their years to achieve supercentenarian status. I had addresses for a number of them and hoped to visit them "unofficially," if possible. My other advantage was that as a journalist and professional historian, I had considerable experience in evaluating government documents and decoding the kind of officialese used by government officials of Soviet bloc nations.

What emerged as the semi-official government line on longevity was presented to me by Riso Katchelavo, head of Intourist Bureau at the Hotel Abkhasia in Sukhumi, who spoke an array of languages, including Georgian, Abkhasian, Russian, English, and two forms of Greek (Pontian and modern). He had traveled outside the USSR and had often accompanied foreign visitors when they did field work with centenarians. He immediately informed me that the government felt it was best not "to bother" the centenarians unless there was a scientific study in progress, of which fewer and fewer were being approved. The government felt there had been too much emphasis placed on longevity and that the centenarians had been exploited. The stress had gotten so great that supercentenarians had become an endangered species. From this, I understood that the government was retreating from its vigorous promotion of longevity claims. What was less clear was how far the Soviets were retreating and how candid they were going to be about past misrepresentations.

I asked Katchelavo if his words meant that the government would not permit me to visit centenarians. "Not at all," he replied, but the government would not arrange those visits. What he would do for me was to arrange a meeting with Dr. Shoto Gogoghian, the leading authority on Abkhasian longevity. Since 1976 Dr. Gogoghian had been Director of the Institute of Gerontology, a local unit of the Academy of Medical Science. Before this appointment, he had been Director of Public Health in Abkhasia for twenty-three years. He would answer any and all questions I wished to raise and would make his research available to me. Katchelavo assured me this would be a far more productive use of my time than chatting informally with a centenarian. Katchelavo had also arranged for me to meet with local authors and folklorists who were experts in Abkhasian culture. There were other institutions he thought I should visit, and if I were agreeable, he would be pleased to set them up after I met with Dr. Gogoghian.

At one level what Katchelavo had planned made sense and served many of my purposes, but I was also determined to have some firsthand experience of Abkhasian longevity. I asked if it would be possible for me to rent a car. He said, "Yes, of course." He further assured me that I was free to travel anywhere in Abkhasia, to take any kind of transportation available, and to speak with whomever I wished. Of course he knew that I did not speak Abkhasian, so even a chance meeting would need translators, and that without his direct assistance centenarians and their families might not be willing to meet with an American. Without formally restricting me in any way, he had every reason to believe he had effectively closed the door on any direct communication with centenarians. I was not surprised that a car was never available when I asked about renting one. Ironically, by throwing me entirely on my own devices but without formal restrictions, he created a situation in which I was eventually able to see centenarians under the "unofficial" circumstances I had hoped for.

Katchelavo was disingenuous in other ways as well. When I casually asked about the Greeks in Abkhasia, he said there were many and they were quite content. I asked if they had a coffeehouse or other community meeting place I might visit. He said no, they were just scattered about. Later, I was to discover that the Greek gathering place was in a cafe just across the street from the hotel. Although distressed by Katchelavo's lukewarm cooperation, I didn't take it personally. I understood he was obliged to carry out his government's policy. On the positive side, I was anxious to hear the "official story" they were prepared to offer. A major part of my agenda was to see just what the Soviet scientists with the most direct knowledge of Abkhasia had to say about longevity.

Katchelavo offered a "private opinion" that Abkhasian longevity had entered a new stage. With an increasingly higher standard of living available, the average life span would increase but the percentage of centenarians would decrease. This would occur because longevity appeared to be linked to arduous lifestyles and restricted diets which were now rare. No one was going to walk 20 kilometers from Atara to Sukhumi when one could ride in a car or bus, and increasingly, people were enjoying more meat, pastries, coffee, butter, tea, and other anti-longevous foods that had once been rare or totally unavailable. Inevitably, there would only be a handful of supercentenarians. This decline, however, was not health retrogression but the result of progress.

My major concern about the meeting with Dr. Gogoghian was how he would react to the challenges I had prepared to Soviet claims already in circulation. I did not want to appear hostile or confrontational, but I was not prepared to accept life spans at face value. I had a long list of Abkhasians who had given birth dates to different researchers that varied by as much as thirty years. (A few of these are recorded in the footnote section for those interested in specifics.[1])

Given the pattern of deception my list implied, I thought it would be more diplomatic to focus on just one individual and see where that inquiry led. The logical candidate for that purpose was Khfaf Lazuria, the most famous of all the Abkhasian supercentenarians. Renowned for her sense of humor, Lazuria loved to mug for the camera and had given countless interviews. A tiny wisp of a woman at only four feet two inches, she liked to say that because she had lived so long she was treated "like a man." At the time of her death in 1975, she was claiming to be 140 years old. That would have put her birth date in 1835, during the presidency of Andrew Jackson. Could that possibly be true?

Alexander Leaf hadn't thought so. When he visited in 1972, Lazuria was already claiming to be in her 141st year (b. 1832?). She told him she had been an inhabitant of her village all her life, marrying for the first time at 16. Her first-born son and her first husband were soon lost in a typhus epidemic. At 50 years of age, she married Lazuria and gave birth to another son, who was a grown man of 30 at the time of the Great Snow of 1910, when two meters of snow fell in one night. That same year she took up smoking for the first time, and she had continued the habit at the rate of a pack a day ever since. She said that both of her parents and one husband had passed the century mark. Judging one "big war in the North" to be the Crimean War of 1853-78, the cautious Leaf concluded, ". . . I have arrived at a degree of confidence that prompts me to place Mrs. Lazuria's age close to 130. In the absence of written records this is my best estimate, and it should be regarded as only that—an unverifiable estimate."[2]

Two years later, Sula Benet heard a different story.[3] Now, Lazuria was officially 139 by virtue of register number 439 of the village, which showed a birth date of October 18, 1835. To the longevous parents and spouse, Lazuria added one great grandfather who had lived to be 160 (one of whose grandsons lived to be 120) and a first cousin of 146. Instead of having been a lifelong resident of Kutol, she reported that she had been abducted by the Turks in 1853 while still a girl and not allowed to return home for ten years. There were four instead of two marriages. The one in which the husband and son were lost occurred when she was 40, not 16. The marriage to Lazuria, for which she converted from Islam to Christianity, took place around age 50 but no children were mentioned. Much more was said about her work in organizing collective farms and being a champion tea picker when already a centenarian. Tarkuk, the son in the 1910 story of the Great Snow, was now identified in the village record as a stepson. After getting to know the family, Benet concluded the old woman smoked only when photographers were present, because she thought it made her look modern and jaunty. Before actually meeting Lazuria, Benet had been given information and photographs in 1972 in which Lazuria was identified as being 131 (b. 1841?).[4] A brother and three sisters were said to have lived to be about 90.

Neither Leaf nor the Benet accounts match the one given to Peter Young of *Life* in 1966.[5] At that time, Lazuria claimed to be 124 (b. 1842?). She admitted not knowing her exact birth date but said her parents had told her when she was 15 and she had kept track ever since. In this variation she states she was married to Lazuria at 50 and that Tarkuk was already three at the time.

Yet another version of her life was told to journalist Henry Gris in 1973.[6] At first Lazuria tried to claim to be 160 (b. 1813?), but she was restrained by relatives, who said she was only teasing and that her real age was 139 (b. 1835?). The brother and three sisters were now said to have lived to be over a hundred; and she now said she had not been kidnapped by Turks; she had only heard stories about others who had been. The abductions took place during the Makhadzhir Raids dating to a period between the Crimean War and Turkish Wars identified by Leaf. Instead of the four marriages mentioned by Benet, she says there were only two, but the first was not at 16 (as told to Leaf) but at 25. Now Lazuria was married at age 48, and the birth of Tarkuk (the stepson of the Benet-Young accounts) took place when she was 53. She confided that she had been smoking cigarettes for a hundred years. When Gris asked how she could manage that in a culture where only widows and old women were allowed to smoke, Lazuria breezily assured him that she knew where to hide.

Before joining the staff of the sensationalist tabloid *National Enquirer*, Gris had spent thirty years as a reporter for United Press International. Thus he knew how to spot tall tales. While appreciative of Lazuria's charm, he notes how Tarkuk made a discreet exit, to return some time later mounted on a horse and wearing the traditional turban and *cherkesska* (Cossack uniform). He mentions too that the interpreter, a local poet, is "swollen with pride as though he were personally responsible for all centenarians encountered during the journey."[7] This same man informs him that visitors to the grand old lady are expected to leave a small gift. In Gris's case it is a pencil flashlight, which is much appreciated. Enjoying the drinks, stories, and equestrian show, Gris begins to think of Khfaf Lazuria as a kind of Abkhasian superstar. She and her family had been through this routine countless times, and they tried their best to tell guests whatever they thought guests most wanted to hear. His comment upon her death in 1975 sums it up well: "Her life was, indeed, a great performance."[8]

If the Abkhasian superstar of longevity, the fabulous "Coquette of the Caucasus," was a fraud, what about the other 293 centenarian claims? That was the question that obsessed me as I entered the Institute of Gerontology quartered on the ground floor of a newly built but modest housing development a few kilometers beyond central Sukhumi. On the wall of its foyer I found a series of easy-to-read charts summarizing the major longevity findings of the past decade. Directly opposite were photographs of the oldest Abkhasians. When Judy Janda, the photographer who had accompanied me to Abkhasia, asked if she could photograph the exhibit, permission was immediately granted.

This willingness to share charts valuable to both experts and lay people reflected Gogoghian's outgoing, unassuming manner which was similar to what one would expect of an American professional. Whenever possible, his statements were precise; and when exactitude was not possible, his phrasing tended to be cautious rather than rash. He was scrupulous about identifying some opinions as controversial or only a working hypothesis.[9] He was modest about his work and stated that he had a small staff of only three medical doctors and four technicians.

The need to press possibly embarrassing challenges to centenarian claims was averted, when Gogoghian volunteered the view that probably no one in the world had ever attained 120 years of age and that most definitely no one in Abkhasia had. This disclaimer was a stunning departure from many previously published Soviet opinions. It was even more startling in Abkhasia, which had been widely proclaimed the mecca of superlongevity. When I asked about the famous Khfaf Lazuria, a smiling Gogoghian replied that there was no doubt she had been an extremely old woman, perhaps the oldest in the history of the world, but she had not been 140! Although admitting that some officials disagreed with him, Gogoghian said he thought that Lazuria had not lived even 120 years. Questioned about the amino acid test developed by Bada, Gogoghian replied that it was known to him and other Soviet specialists. He immediately reaffirmed the conclusion that 120 was the outer boundary of achieved human longevity, based on numerous physiological examinations of centenarians, living and dead, and on familiarity with the longevity data available through frequent national conferences and consultations.

I didn't need to be an official diplomat to know that the point should not be pursued further. If a tooth had been found that could be proved to be more than 120 years old, it would have been displayed with the marvelous pomp and stagecraft the Soviets were noted for. Instead, Gogoghian stated that earlier age estimates had been exaggerated, often on hearsay or fragmentary evidence. There had been too many amateurs in the field, and his major task was to ensure a scientific basis for future longevity studies. For him the objectives of the institute were fourfold: 1) discover how long the oldest Abkhasian had really lived; 2) determine the number of genuine centenarians; 3) identify the factors contributing to their long life; and 4) attempt to replicate the prolongevous factors for the benefit of the general population.

To meet his objectives, Gogoghian had set his team the task of visiting each of the 294 centenarians identified in the 1970 census. He personally had visited 178 of them and his colleagues had seen another 50, for a total of 228 contacts. Most of those not seen had died before they could be interviewed. Gogoghian explained that although the geographical area of Abkhasia was not large, roads to the villages were difficult to use most of the year, communications were still inadequate, and centenarians moved about unexpectedly or were sometimes too ill to hold long conversations or undergo arduous physical examinations. Field work was primarily limited to the summer months.

Gogoghian produced a tin box filled with the small white index cards used by researchers throughout the world. There was a card for each centenarian, and in a nearby cabinet were corresponding files containing completed questionnaires and the results of various physical examinations. Gogoghian hoped that testing could be done annually to monitor the health of the long-living. One of his prime objectives was to make sure people aged only one year at a time. The institute also had begun tracking 200 nonagenarians in Sukhumi proper and the easier-to-reach hamlets. While he did not expect to see the final outcome of his work, Gogoghian expressed considerable pride that he had established a system which could resolve all future supercentenarian claims in Abkhasia.

The profile of Abkhasian longevity he outlined was compatible with findings elsewhere in the world. Longevous women out-numbered longevous men by two to one in all age groups. Most of the centenarians (189) died shortly after their hundredth birthdays, with another large group of 51 deaths occurring between 105 and 109. Putting another statistical nail into the supercentenarian coffin, Gogoghian reported that only a score or so of the 294 centenarians of 1970 were still alive. These included one supposed super-centenarian Biga Vouba (123), whose claim Gogoghian considered definitely untrue, and another person of 116 whose age Gogoghian also doubted. Most of the long-living were rural people, often slightly built, who had lived arduous lives, particularly in their youth. Generally, they moved higher into the mountains during the summer months, and frequently men climbed to even higher areas to herd sheep or to hunt. Centenarians were spread among all the national groups: 132 Abkhasians, 108 Georgians, 42 Armenians, three Greeks, two Russians, two Ukrainians, two Hebrews, two Turks, and one Azerbaijanian.

Half of the centenarians were able to function fairly well, taking care of major daily needs, while the other half required some degree of assistance. The most common disability was some hearing impairment. All lived with their families, and almost all had been married for the greater part of their lives, many having second or third spouses. In a study Gogoghian published in 1964,[10] 80 percent of all Abkhasians over 90 were described as mentally healthy and outgoing, a little over 45% had good hearing, and a little over a third had good vision. Only 10% were judged to have poor hearing, and fewer than 4% had poor eyesight. Evaluations of the health of men and women were comparable in all categories except the rather ominous "decrepit" ranking, which applied to 18.2% of the women and only 8.7% of the men. In contrast, the "healthy" category included 35% of both sexes. One could surmise that the proud Abkhasian males were likely to conceal their failing health, while the Abkhasian females, trained in modesty, spoke more truthfully. In any case, the physical well-being of the longevous was remarkable, and the finding of 1964 had not been significantly altered by subsequent observations.

One common thread mentioned by those interviewed was that few had ever stopped working. Instead, as they grew older, they had eased their schedules, working three to five hours rather than 8 to 10 or doing lighter physical tasks. Although no one was required to work after 60 because of the state pension system, Abkhasians enjoyed physical labor so much that they would have been as angry at being denied the right to work as they had been when landlords forced them to work when they wanted some time to hunt or race their beloved horses.

Commenting on age verification, Gogoghian observed that it was far more difficult for women to lie than for men. If a woman had a son of 40, she could not claim to be 100, for during Gogoghian's twenty-three years as head of public health in Abkhasia the oldest recorded childbearing was at age 47, and in the entire Soviet Union the oldest observed birth was by a woman of 55. The world record at the time was 57 years and 129 days.[11] Thus, any supercentenarian woman who claimed to have given birth beyond those limits would be a double wonder of the world: the longest-living human being and the oldest recorded mother. Men, on the other hand, could claim to have fathered children when between 60 and 100. I was reminded that storytelling is a fine Abkhasian art. Exaggerated accounts which added a few years at a time are not rare, especially in a society where immense honor accumulated with age. Being beneficiaries of a strict patriarchal society, men told most of the stories and liked to extol their sexual longevity. Adding to the verification difficulties was the fact that many persons did not really know exactly when they were born. About the only factor Gogoghian omitted was that many Abkhasians had never been enthusiastic about fighting for the central government and had done their best to avoid military duty by claiming to be too old. More specifically, throughout the nineteenth century the Abkhasians had periodically revolted against the Tsarist regime. Violent incidents connected to the unsuccessful attempts provided ample reason for men to assume the identities of relatives.

When the revolutionaries took control of Abkhasia in the 1920s, it was a backward region with an average life span in the 20s and an illiteracy rate of over 98 percent. Malaria was so rampant along the coast that no one lived in the Sukhumi lowlands. Soviet power began to deal decisively with the health situation. Mosquitoes were eradicated, swamps drained, and eucalyptus trees planted to make the area drier and more healthful. By the 1950s, public health measures had turned Sukhumi from a wasteland into a resort region. No less a personage than Joseph Stalin had a villa in the immediate vicinity, where he took advantage of the year-round warm weather. His example was followed by many dignitaries, including Lavrenti Beria, longtime head of the secret police. By the 1970s, Black Sea cruise ships accommodating Soviet and Eastern European tourists made regular dockings at Sukhumi, and Leonid Brezhnev had a retreat in nearby Pitsunda. In the lush hills overlooking the palm trees and subtropical vegetation of the coast were newly introduced crops grown on some of the nation's most successful collective farms. The average life span had risen to 86 for women and 76 for men. Although the weight of 294 centenarians may have artificially elevated the averages, there could be no doubt that Soviet rule had given the formerly impoverished peasants unprecedented prosperity.

Throughout the talks with Gogoghian, concern for public health was emphasized. Much of the institute's work involved teaching Soviet health professionals how to care for the old and how to put into general practice what had been learned about health from the study of centenarians. As elsewhere in the USSR and the developed world, the main killers in Sukhumi were heart disease and cancer. Trying to determine how centenarians had delayed the onset of these maladies was seen as a major practical as well as theoretical task.

Gogoghian pinpointed five factors contributing to Abkhasian longevity: respect for the aged, the nature of the life style, the diet, the climate, and genetics. Of these, the reverence enjoyed by the old throughout the region is remarkable. This is one of the few places in the world where people may genuinely look forward to old age. Traditional toasts include "May you live to be two hundred!" and "May you live to be as old as Moses (120)!" Even if an elder is ailing, his or her counsel is sought by all members of the family without a hint of any generational gap. Health permitting, the long-living preside over many official and informal social functions, enjoying numerous privileges. They are arbiters in family, village, and regional councils. For men, old age is the crown of a successful life; and for women, it is the only time when rough equality with men is finally possible. Many new freedoms accrue to women after menopause. The psychological climate for the old is so positive that the rest homes available through government auspices are rarely utilized, as even in the smallest of families there are many relatives who covet the honor of housing an elder.

The Soviet authorities incorporated this cultural phenomenon into their system by establishing a Soviet of Elders in each village to act as an advisory body to the formal government. When changes were being contemplated, the elders were among the first consulted. In the 1930s, some of them played leadership roles in the collectivization campaigns by relating the new system to Abkhasian traditions of cooperative labor. Later, the long-living helped introduce new crops such as tea. During the war years and after, centenarians who continued to work were accorded honors as a part of drives to raise agricultural productivity. Often, too, elders were called upon to tell of the infamies and hardships of the Tsarist era, and they were feted on a holiday called the Day of the Long-Living People.

Whatever their age, Abkhasians remain physically active. They follow regular and orderly daily patterns of hard work. Their routines have a tempo more linked to biological rhythms than the helter-skelter patterns that predominate in most developed nations. Abkhasians dislike being rushed, loathe deadlines, and never work to exhaustion. In the same vein, they consider it extremely impolite to eat quickly or to eat too much. Even after they pass the conventional age of retirement, they continue to work in the collectives and to walk many kilometers each day. Many chop wood, haul water, and bathe in mountain streams.

Cardiograms taken of Abkhasians show that, without feeling more than an upset stomach or experiencing a day of slight discomfort, some have suffered malfunctions or blockages of the type that would cause serious illness to sedentary people. Some studies of the cholesterol levels of centenarians have shown readings of 98 in a test in which the upper normal level for the middle-aged American would be 250. The cardiovascular benefits of their rigorous lives are enhanced during the summer when they move higher into the mountains. Although tobacco is grown in the area, few of the long living smoke.

The traditional diet followed by most of those who became centenarians contained between 1,500 and 2,000 calories a day. Seventy percent of that intake was from vegetables and dairy products. Fruits, nuts, grains, and a rare serving of meat made up the rest of the diet. (Many of the centenarians were nominal Moslems and had never eaten pork.) In addition, there was no coffee or sugar and little butter or salt. The major spice was red pepper, while honey was used as an occasional sweetener. A peculiarity of the diet not found anywhere else in Georgia, but that seems to have no longevity significance, was the absence of soups. A further unique aspect of the traditional diet was the insistence on freshness. Vegetables were picked just before cooking or serving, and if meat was to be part of the menu, guests were shown the animal before it was slaughtered. Whatever the food served, all leftovers were discarded, because they were considered harmful to good health. Such concern for freshness guaranteed that a minimal loss of nutrients took place between garden and table. Most food was consumed raw or boiled, with nothing fried.

The combination of light eating and heavy exercise led to the lean somatype prized for both sexes. The Abkhasians have been among the few people in the world so appreciative of the ill effects of fat that even their children and infants remain slim. The traditional Abkhasian body type was particularly easy to maintain in the past, when considerable time was spent raising and training horses. From the earliest possible ages, even at two and three, children were taught to ride. Horses provided the major sport, and the ability to do equestrian tricks was a mark of individual worth. The horses were never used as work animals, only for recreation and sports. For reasons not fully understood, Abkhasian women, despite their inferior social status, participated in the horse culture in a manner unknown elsewhere in the Caucasus. They became accomplished riders and were so skilled in the martial arts that they played a fighting role in armed combat with enemies. Love of horses remains an Abkhasian passion, and horse parades are a favorite part of the Day of the Long-Living People celebrations.

The genetic influence on Abkhasian longevity was not much elaborated on by Gogoghian, who said that there was some speculation that certain blood types might be prolongevous and that longevous people usually claimed to have had longevous parents. It had been noted, however, that when people left the villages to go to cities or to other parts of the Soviet Union, their average life spans tended to conform to those in the new territory, suggesting the primacy of environmental factors. There was less longevity in areas closer to industrialized coastal areas, where the terrain is flatter and where traditional customs had given way to many habits of the modern world.

Gogoghian's most controversial views involved climatic factors. Acknowledging that longevity had been observed in various climatic zones, he emphasized that Abkhasian centenarians lived the greater part of their lives at about 200 to 300 meters above sea level in a zone which experiences little snow or heavy winds. The mean temperature was 10 to 13 degrees Celsius, with minimal seasonal variations. Typically, homes were two-story dwellings in which only one room, the kitchen-dining area, was heated by a fireplace. To use Gogoghian's terminology, people in the villages are "slightly refrigerated." He believes this coolness served to slow down the metabolism and might be a key factor in prolonging each stage of life.

Throughout his presentations, Gogoghian stressed that Abkhasian longevity research was still moving from a folkloric to a scientific basis, and I needed to be careful about my sources of information. This was a valid warning. In the United States, one would never accept the average newspaper story at face value or equate it with an article appearing in a scholarly journal. Nor would the views of the local chamber of commerce, tourist office, booster club, and politicians be accepted as gospel.

I left my meetings with Dr. Gogoghian with great confidence in his scientific integrity. Without fanfare, he had brought research on Abkhasian longevity into line with longevity research elsewhere in the world. The man with the file cards on every Abkhasian centenarian had told me he had never personally seen anyone whom he believed to be older than 112, but that the rural Abkhasians did have unusual rates of longevity and reasonable health in old age.

I was to find the sharpest contrast to Dr. Gogoghian's assessments at the Abkhasian State Museum, an institution visited extensively by Soviet citizens and Sukhumi school children.[12] The neat, well-laid-out premises included a section devoted to a photographic exhibit of centenarians. The photos showed 11 centenarians of whom eight were identified as having lived more than 132 years. Most were ethnic Abkhasians, but there were also immigrants like Polish-born Yelif Kobachia (105). Quite a few of these photos had been reproduced in the Soviet press and had been made available to foreign publishers through Novosti News Agency. The distressing factor about the photos was that the alleged life spans varied tremendously from publication to publication.

The personnel of the museum who allowed photographs to be taken were genuinely convinced of the authenticity of the supercentenarians. They found Gogoghian's opinions surprising and said that while some exaggerations or doubts were possible, the essential facts had been checked many times. Some of the supercentenarians had been locally famous for their musical or handicraft skills and had verifiable histories. Like Gogoghian, the museum officials were open with their material and volunteered the names of centenarians, the villages where they lived, and how to reach them through public transportation.

The museum director was in close contact with the centenarian chorus, which was composed solely of men. Wearing national costume, the men sang traditional Abkhasian songs and performed traditional dances at major celebrations. Their dashing appearance—they had luxuriant mustaches and high spirits—had made them beloved throughout the region. A booklet chronicling their travels had been printed in Tbilisi, but as with so many Soviet publications, demand for it so far exceeded the supply that most officials did not even have a desk copy. At the Gerontological Institute, one of the inner corridors was decorated with photographs clipped from the booklet. Some were candid shots of major events, while others were posed shots in the villages to show typical scenes of bygone times.

To call the group a centenarian chorus, as is usually done, is to use a misnomer. The museum personnel told me that ever since the chorus was begun in the late 1930s, the minimum age had been 70, not 100 as calling it a centenarian chorus would indicate, or even 90 as many visitors were told. If the chorus really was limited to centenarians, that would provide an impressive secondary verification for age claims, for it would mean that since the late 1930s Abkhasia had always had at least 20 centenarian men vigorous enough to sing and dance in public performances. Even if the minimal age were 90, such a chorus would be of some importance. With a starting age of 70, however, the main significance of the group was that it provided another illustration that older people not only are capable of entertaining themselves, but can also entertain and instruct others.

Another local Sukhumi institution where the maximal ages on longevity were accepted was the local chess and stamp club. Its walls were covered with dozens of photographs of national and international celebrities visiting Abkhasia. Many were shown in the company of centenarians. A picture of Ho Chi Minh sharing a toast at the Duripsh Collective was quickly pointed out to me. The Soviet custom went back to the 1920s, when the French author Henri Barbusse was also toasted by Abkhasian supercentenarians. Other photographs showed centenarians with Leonid Brezhnev and Yuri Gagarin, the popular cosmonaut who made the first manned flight into space in 1961. Equally revealing were photographs of centenarians posing with young people, publicizing productivity campaigns, in which the young were implored to emulate their hardworking elders. Discussions at the club as well as other interviews with Sukhumi residents left no doubt that the general population was convinced of Abkhasian longevity. Everyone had heard of at least one supercentenarian, although few had met any personally. The local residents were very proud of the number of long-living people in the region; they seemed to attribute this to the uniqueness of the Caucasus and not to the socialist political system.

The legend of longevity in the Caucasus is long-standing. A typical nineteenth-century traveler whose major interest was the brigandage and feuding then associated with the area offhandedly wrote of meeting a 120-year-old Armenian monk.[13] The man was described as sleeping most of the time as well as being blind and lame. One doesn't have to accept the claim to appreciate that advanced age was not considered remarkable. While few writers took a specific interest in longevity, asides about old people and observations about the honors accorded to village elders are constantly encountered in writing about the Caucasus. One pre-Soviet traveler who was specifically interested in the long-living was Essed Bey, a man of Daghestani ancestry born in the city of Baku. In 1916, against the wishes of a father concerned for his safety, Bey took an extended horseback tour of the region. He concluded that once having reached adulthood, "The Caucasian, on the average, will attain the age of 80 to 90 years. Centenarians and even older persons are by no means uncommon."[14]

Evidence of similar nature is found in the literary traditions of the ethnic Abkhasians. When the Soviets took power, fewer than 2% of the Abkhasians were literate in any language, and they had no alphabet. Three attempts to form an alphabet, using mainly

Russian and Georgian characters, failed before the present system was adopted in 1954. Since that time, oral traditions going back to the ancient Nart epics have been written down, as have more recently composed songs and stories.[15] Longevity and the role of benevolent elders in society are frequent themes. It should be noted that jokes and tall tales are popular. One story repeated in many variations involves a centenarian being interviewed by an awed traveler (in the modern version: a gerontologist). The centenarian solemnly declares that the secret of long life is to avoid all alcohol and tobacco and to control one's temper. Suddenly, he is drowned out by shouting in the adjoining room. "Don't let that bother you," the poker-faced centenarian says. "That's just my older brother and my father. They've had too much to drink again and they're having their usual argument over cigarettes and women."

The Abkhasian scholars who gather these stories often serve as assistants to longevity researchers. Unfortunately, the proofs of old age they innocently accept include every error warned against by Thoms and Young. The repetition of hearsay and superficial evidence related by congenial old folks also has passed into the work of Sula Benet, the only American who has written extensively about Abkhasia. While providing excellent cultural and historical descriptions, her work, which draws heavily on Soviet sources, leaves much to be desired in the area of age verification and reflects the gossipy nature of so much that has been written about the Caucasus in the USSR and abroad. Benet has an appallingly cavalier attitude toward the supercentenarian claims, writing, "It seems to be mere quibbling to discredit reports of longevity by questions about precise age. If a person lives to 120 rather than 130 in health and vigor, the fact of old age is barely diminished."[16]

The mistakes that flow from such an outlook are evidenced in a story Benet tells about the 180-year-old woman from Gori referred to earlier. Giving no citations for her account, Benet reports that Metchnikoff interviewed the woman in 1904 and leaves the strong impression that he accepted the claim.[17] Metchnikoff's summation which appears in his *The Prolongation of Life* (1910) is quite different.[18] He refers to a newspaper clipping from the *Tiflissky Listok* of October 8, 1904, that had been sent to him by a kindly stranger, and that describes Thense Abalava, an Osete woman, living in the village Sva, Gori district. It is not clear whether the newspaper reporter had investigated the claim personally or was relaying the tale at second or third hand. Moreover, although Metchnikoff was justifiably honored as a great scientist, he was no expert on age verification, accepting already disproved claims such as those of Thomas Parr and Drakenberg the Dane.

A similar retelling of a story by Benet touches on an episode from a history written by O.B. Butkov.[19] In 1722 and again in 1796, the rebellious city of Derbent had to be subdued by the Russians. In each instance, a delegation of elders presented the victors with a plate upon which lay a silver key to the city. On the second occasion, when the chief elder was asked to identify himself, he responded that he had already given his name seventy-four years earlier when he surrendered the city to the army of Peter the Great. He was now 120! A nice story, to be sure, but no documentation is offered to show that it is not a fable. Nor is it explained why the elders of 1722 were led by a man then only 46 years of age. Many stories of this nature, especially those told by centenarians, are passed along without critical comment or examination.

Benet presents a linguistic proof that is far more persuasive of Abkhasian longevity. In her 1976 book *How to Live to Be 100*, she writes that the people in the Caucasus, ". . . have specific terms or expressions for great grandparents going back to six generations.

These expressions are used to refer to the living, not to those who have died. Very few languages contain expressions for so many generations of living relatives."[20] Her early study *The Abkhasians* (1974) was somewhat more conservative: ". . . the abundance of familiar names for such relatives as great-great grandfather is an indication that sufficient members of fifth-generational families exist to require their use."[21] In either case, the need for words to describe living relatives of fifth and sixth generations indicates a significant incidence of old age and probable longevity.

Benet also points out that Abkhasian language forms indicate the age relationship between speakers so that there is a constant re-affirmation of who is younger and who is older. This can be extremely useful in age verification. A solid identification for one person affects all other claims. For example, if Sheilach Butba acknowledges being approximately two years younger than Kama-chich Kvichenya, who says she is two years younger than Khfaf Lazuria, the total spread in their ages cannot be more than five years. If we accept Alexander Leaf's highest estimate for the age of Butba as 113, Kvichenya automatically drops to 115 and Lazuria to 117. All would be record breakers, but these constitute a con-siderable fall from the supercentenarian ages each claimed at one or another time.

Another argument put forth by Benet is that the privileges of old age are so great that the genuine longevous zealously guard their prerogatives against pretenders. This argument does not take into account the rivalry between villages, ethnic groups, and republics to have the oldest of the old. The view is further rebuffed by Benet's own observation that men will lie downward, claiming to be octogenarians when they are much older, because a man of 100 is thought to be in sexual decline. Sexuality in general is a whirlpool of longevity exaggerations, as can be seen in numerous claims of women who give birth after 55 and men who become fathers after

90.  A reasonable conclusion could be drawn that the astounding virility among the old and the longevous belongs to the same class of legend as the Thomas Parr stories. Then too, peasants traditionally have enjoyed pulling the legs of their city cousins, and as their literature illustrates, the Abkhasians' sense of humor is hardly underdeveloped. The difference between 92, 102, and 122 may not be taken quite as seriously by peasants as by gerontologists. Since everyone in the village knows the truth anyway, what's the harm in having some fun with the outsiders? By Benet's own admission, even she thinks the difference between 120 and 130 amounts to "mere quibbling." We can assume that some of her Soviet colleagues shared her view and were not as meticulous as Shoto Gogoghian.

Even though I was convinced that Dr. Gogoghian had indeed provided the best analysis of Abkhasian longevity available anywhere, I still thought it essential to meet some centenarians. I needed the assistance of native Sukhumians. To that end, I told Judy Janda that we should try to be as conspicuously American as possible as we made our way around the city, speaking to each other in English a little louder than necessary. This strategy bore fruit in the Sukhumi Public Park, but Janda's German camera rather than our English was the point of reference. The local park photographer, a blond man in his late twenties, told us in gestures that he wanted to buy our camera. When he understood that we were Americans and not Eastern Europeans, he pointed to his wristwatch to indicate we should meet him at the park entrance a little after dinner.

At this second meeting, the blond photographer brought another street photographer with him, a young man who spoke some English. But against very long odds, the man also happened to be a Pontian Greek with whom I could communicate in Greek as well as English. He told me the blond, whom I'll call John, was a Ukrainian who had a sister who spoke English fluently. If it were agreeable, we could visit her home the following day. The Greek seemed extremely uneasy. As I pressed him about the wisdom of Soviet citizens meeting this way with Americans, he explained that John was a religious dissident who had been in trouble with the police, but that his sister was a loyal member of the Communist party. The Greek quickly added that he was not himself a dissident and that the Greek minority was treated fairly. His only complaint was that he would like to be able to travel abroad, not to leave permanently but to be a tourist, perhaps to visit Greece. I tried to arrange for us to meet without John being present, but the Greek was evasive and I was not to see him again anyway. He probably felt he had taken enough risks. The meeting with John's sister was extraordinary. She was actually a cousin, but explained the term "sister" was used in Abkhasia for many close relationships. She had learned her English in college and was grateful that the Communist party had arranged her education through her union. All the males in her family had been killed in World War II and she was thankful for the care the Soviet system had provided for her, her mother, and her grandmother. She and John disagreed about almost all aspects of Soviet society, but she insisted that he had "a good heart." When I explained why I had come to Abkhasia, John said he would borrow a car from a friend and take us to the centenarians himself. His only request was that his name and that of his friends be sent to the Billy Graham Crusade once I returned to the United States. He was sure that Billy Graham would find a way to get him out of the USSR.[22]

During the many hours we spent together, we talked constantly about America, the USSR, and religion. John's "sister" was not surprised when I confirmed that the negative aspects of America projected in the Soviet media were indeed true, but John could not understand why a person who wanted to work could not find some job to do or that Christians could be racists. Both John and his sister were firm believers in Abkhasian longevity, but neither had ever met any long-lived people personally and thought the experience would be fun. On the day of the outing, we were quite a carload. There was John, his wife, his baby son, his cousin, Judy Janda and me.

The person I had selected to visit was Vanacha Temur of Lichny, a man frequently spoken of as among the healthiest and most vigorous of the centenarians. His claim of 110 was accepted as valid by Dr. Gogoghian and the same birth date had been cited by Benet and the Sukhumi State Museum. The first evidence of the centenarian's authority when we reached his farm was that his son would not open the garden gate to let us in until he secured his father's approval for the visit.

Wearing a snappy leather hat, the venerable, always referred to only by his first name, walked briskly across the garden and took up the responsibilities of a host. Spotting an infant among his guests, Vanacha insisted that a cow be milked so that the baby could have some wholesome country refreshment. For the other guests baskets of apples from his best tree and a round of drinks were brought out. Only when these necessities were seen to was he prepared to speak.

Familiar with international protocol, Vanacha, before proceeding to talk about himself, spoke about the need for world peace and increased understanding among nations. Unlike most of the other centenarians, he had a baptismal certificate. According to the dates of this document, he was 106, but he explained that his baptism had been delayed until he was four because his parents could not pay the priests. Although this was an echo of an excuse Thoms had frequently encountered, Vanacha's vigor was incredible. About five feet tall, with twinkling blue eyes and an elegant white mustache, he was the personification of a kindly and playful grandfather. He credited his slim, wiry body to light eating, horseback riding, farming, and walking in the mountains. These days he slept more than he had in the past, but he felt fine and was looking forward to the sixty-first anniversary of the Revolution, for the chorus was going to be filmed beside the ten-centuries-old Basletsky Bridge for a national television program.

The chorus was obviously one of Vanacha's great joys. He loved being with the other old men and being fussed over. In photographs of the group his impish antics were frequently the focus of attention. He said that he had helped form the group forty years earlier. At that time, he was 70 and one of the youngest members; now he was the oldest continuous member and probably the chorus elder. Again, the round numbers were somewhat suspicious, but it is unlikely that he had been less than 65 at the time of the chorus's establishment, which would bear out the age indicated by the baptismal record. Asked if the chorus would like to perform in the United States, Vanacha said he thought it would be a lot of fun, but that it wouldn't happen because a lot of them, himself included, did not like to fly. They wouldn't even take a plane to Moscow. So perhaps it would be better if the Americans came to Abkhasia. He obligingly pinned on an "I Love New York" button as a gesture of camaraderie.

After more than an hour's conversation, there was a round of toasting. Vanacha drank two full tumblers of strong applejack and confirmed that many of the long-living liked to take one shot every morning to get going. Otherwise, they drank only on festive occasions. He brought the interview to a close by embracing each of his visitors, lingering longest over the infant now sated with fresh milk. As he walked back to his house, he looked like a man who would be there to greet visitors for many years to come. The laurel of Abkhasian longevity clearly had passed into his hands, and Vanacha Temur was handling it with considerable dignity.

Vanacha suggested we visit Mikhail Kaslantzia, a centenarian in a neighboring village. We followed his instructions and found ourselves before a typical two-story Abkhasian home. The woman who answered our call could not speak Georgian or Russian, as Vanacha had. The very resourceful John dashed around the neighborhood until he found a man who could speak Abkhasian and translate to Russian for his sister. When Mr. Kaslantzia was informed of our purpose, she waved us through the iron gate. Mikhail was sitting at a table in the kitchen when we entered. He was not as vigorous as Vanacha, but he had extraordinarily clear eyes and responded quickly to every query.

Like Pierre Joubert , he was not much interested in age—"I'm pretty sure I'm over a hundred. I was fifty when I married my wife, who was then seventeen. Now she is seventy, so I must be about a hundred and three. It isn't important." The chorus did not interest him, and except for once when a Japanese television crew had filmed him with his neighbor Khfaf Lazuria, he had not participated in the centenarian boom. Speaking only in Abkhasian, he expressed interest in seeing photographs of other longevous people. Without using glasses, he studied the hand of an Ecuadorian peasant woman. "These are beautiful hands. They have done work," he said. Then, when he spotted a full-page color photo of Khfaf, his whole manner changed. He chortled and called his wife to his side for a good look. "She was a few years older than I," he said.

Khfaf's photograph prompted Mikhail to tell stories of how he, Khfaf, and others had begun the first tea collectives. They had all been champion tea pickers, he said, and striking a chord generally left untouched by others, he announced with considerable relish that he had joined the Communist party in 1919 before it took over in Abkhasia. He had been part of the local political bureau, and with energetic gestures he described the gun battles fought with local landlords. As far as he was concerned, the only good thing about life before the Revolution had been the trips he made into the mountains as a young man when he had the time to walk and hunt all summer. Up there he had been so free that he felt that if he wanted to fly all he had to do was spread out his arms. He spoke, too, of how he liked to eat the grasses of Abkhasia, by which he meant various leafy greens that grew wild and were the favorites of the older generation. "We didn't eat so much in the old days. Life was difficult."

An unusual feature of the small but immaculate Kaslantzia home was that even though it was the middle of a weekday afternoon, the center table was filled with snacks and drinks as if many guests were expected. Mikhail's wife quietly explained that their only child, an adopted son, had died four years before in an automobile accident. As a memorial, they had vowed to leave the table set just as it had been that night. A very large portrait of a handsome young man in his 30s was hanging on an outside wall of the house. The accident, which destroyed the continuity of generations, had obviously taken much out of their lives, but the Kaslantzias did not allow their grief and mourning to make them unduly somber. Like Vanacha, they scolded their guests for not having announced the visit beforehand. Next time, they wanted to prepare a proper Abkhasian feast, and the Americans were not allowed to leave before promising there would indeed be a next time.

I think about Mikhail and Vanacha whenever I read about the charming Abkhasian centenarians described by Benet, Leaf, Gris, and others. I think, too, of the longevous Abkhasian dressed in full traditional costume whom I saw dusting off the back seat of a white vintage Mercedes Benz convertible which had been hired to carry away a bride and groom from a wedding celebration, which the elder was stage managing with considerable glee. Contact with such individuals illuminates the special magic of old age in Abkhasia. These are not cardboard role models from a propaganda campaign, but very real, very winning people with a full range of individual idiosyncracies. With little prodding, they will talk about food, romance, work, horses, politics, family life, and all other topics of mutual interest. Their symbolic and actual leadership in community and family affairs highlights the foolishness of the notion that a life of advanced years needs to be bleak.

From a strictly statistical standpoint, the final evaluation of Abkhasian centenarianism may never be made. The ferocious civil war of the 1990s has disrupted the orderly research begun by Gogoghian and may have destroyed vital records as well. One can only guess at the mortality rate the conflict may have directly or indirectly increased among the aged. In ways Riso Katchelavo had not foreseen, his sense that Abkhasian longevity has already passed into history may prove prophetic. Governments committed to public health no longer exist. Benefits such as the traditional diet, a pollution-free atmosphere, rhythmic patterns of work in hilly terrain, and the unique psychological support of stable communities have decreased or vanished. But the legend of Abkhasian longevity contains considerable truth. Truly, the final images of this rugged land belong to the elders who were given so much attention in the 1970s. In Abkhasia these elders were never referred to as "old" but as "long-living."

# 4. SOVIET CENTENARIANISM

*We will be quite satisfied if we manage to reverse the*
*process of premature aging and sustain the biological age*
*commensurate with the calendar age; thus assuring man*
*a life span of well over a hundred years.*

—*Dimitri Chebotarev*

NO MODERN STATE INVESTED AS MUCH energy in longevity research for as long a period of time as did the former USSR. The spurs to that research were the longevity claims found in the three republics in the Caucasus: Azerbaijan, Georgia, and Armenia. Together they accounted for over 25% of the nation's 19,000 centenarians. Most gerontological interest focused on Georgia where the study of centenarians had gone on for the longest period and where the level of research was the most sophisticated. This was in contrast to the flamboyant claims made in Azerbaijan without data of any kind and the lower-keyed approach favored in Armenia. The 1970 census showed 1,844 centenarians (including the 294 Abkhasians) in the total Georgian population of some five million. This works out to 39.3 centenarians per 100,000 of population. The Azerbaijan figures work out to 48.2 centenarians per 100,000 and the Armenian to 24.3 per 100,000. In most developed nations with excellent birth records there are only from one to seven centenarians per 100,000 of population.[1]

Unfortunately, as demonstrated in the previous chapter, none of the Caucasus data can be accepted at face value. Any research that has come under scrutiny has resulted in drastically reduced age claims. Books in English by Soviet gerontologists in the field are not very useful either. A 1982 book on Georgian longevity written by the director of the Gerontology Center in Tbilisi is all too typical. Little if any attempt is made at age verification. Thus, even if the health data associated with these populations were rigorously collected, they could not be taken as having any validity on exceptionally long life spans. Most of the subjects were probably under 90. The competency of such work is further suspect because of its casual acceptance of noted fakers like Parr. Furthermore, all the extreme Abkhasian claims are accepted as confirmed, and more than a score of other individuals are said to have been over 160 years old. The author also states that a pair of twins were born in 1964 to a 95-year-old woman and her 127-year-old husband![2] Other works on Soviet longevity available in English demonstrate the same kind of gullibility.[3]

A much more scientific approach is found in the massive project undertaken in the 1960s by the Gerontological Institute of Kiev.[4] Working from the 1959 census, the project involved questioning 40,000 persons over 80 years of age, and giving a physical examination to 27,181 of them. The findings were similar to those of work done in other nations.

The Kiev project discovered that the overwhelming majority of those Soviet citizens over 80 had been employed as either farm workers or manual laborers. Fewer than 4% were teachers, office workers, medical workers, and the like. A high percentage had worked at the same occupation all their lives, including a resounding 90% of the manual workers. As in Abkhasia, most were found to have lean bodies and to be moderate eaters. Ninety-one percent reported they ate a mixed diet, 8.4% a vegetarian diet, and .6% a meat-oriented diet. The state of their health at the time of the survey was quite good. Seventy percent did all their own household chores, and 55.4% moved about unaided. Forty-four percent of the men and 31% of the women were judged to be practically healthy, which was defined to mean that they were no more affected by illness or disease than younger people. Ninety-seven percent of the women and 45% of the men had never smoked. Of possible sociopsychological importance, 99% of the men and 97% of the women had been married at least once.

The organizer of this study was Dr. Dimitri Fedorovich Chebotarev (sometimes spelled Chebotaryov), the director of the Institute, a member of the Academy of Medical Science and the leading Soviet authority on longevity. Drawing from his intimate knowledge of all Soviet gerontological research, by the 1970s Chebotarev had observed five prolongevous constants:[5]

1. The longevous tend to work continually throughout their lives. As they grow older, the volume of work diminishes but the longevous never totally retire. Their work and their lives follow rhythmical patterns so that energy is expended regularly over a period of time rather than in spasmodic, frantic bursts broken by rest periods or carried to exhaustion. The work of the longevous is physically demanding.

2. The longevous abstain from rich foods which can cause obesity and its associated health problems. Their diets are low in fat, sugar, and salt and high in vitamins. Their cholesterol levels are low. Their daily caloric intake is usually less than 2,000. While alcoholic drinks are usually part of the diet, consumption is moderate.

3. The longevous tend to do the same kind of work throughout life. The longest living often remain in the same village or region as their parents and relatives. Many live in mountain areas, and when older people move to cities or away from their immediate families, their death rate is high.

4. The longevous are most highly concentrated where "local tradition demands respect for elders."

5. The longevous report that they have long-living relatives, which suggests a genetic influence, although the specific role of heredity has not been clearly determined.

One notable divergence from the observations made by Gogoghian in Abkhasia is that Chebotarev had eliminated climatic conditions as a major factor. He also eliminated other locally based theories, such as the significance of cosmic radiation at the altitudes where most of the longevous people in the Caucasus live. Looking at the long-living phenomenon from a broad national perspective, Chebotarev had discounted such influences, considering them geographical idiosyncrasies rather than longevity universals.

Although Chebotarev included possible genetic factors in his five constants, he does not appear to consider them to be central. In the 1960s study there was a surprisingly low incidence of immediate blood relatives over 80 years of age.[6] The high of 40% was reached in the Ukraine, where longevity is not particularly pronounced, while in Abkhasia the rate was an unexpectedly low 31%. With so many longevous people living in the same region, even in the same village or household, as their parents, the similarity in environment and life styles could account for such a percentage quite as well as genetics.

That the de-emphasis on genetics was more than a holdover from the period when that subject was a Soviet taboo is supported by studies made in the United States. Contrary to the old aphorism that the best way to be longevous is to have longevous parents, various investigations indicate that having longevous parents adds only an average of three years to the life span.[7] While not a totally insignificant factor, this advantage can be compared to the five years that are gained by simply living in the country or the eight years that are lost smoking one pack of cigarettes a day. This consensus in American and Soviet research casts additional doubt on the frequent assertions by supercentenarians that both of their parents and many close relatives were longevous.

Soviet studies are usually most reliable when they deal with objective data and identify longevity factors found in mammoth samplings. In the area of age verification of specific individuals they are far weaker, with numerous indications of wishful thinking or sloppy methodology. Little commentary, for example, can be found on generational proofs of centenarianism. Simple arithmetic shows that if one starts with a newborn infant (one generation), one can derive a mother of 18 (two generations), a grandmother of 36 (three), a great grandmother of 54 (four), a great-great grandmother of 72 (five), and a great-great-great grandmother of 90 (six). Just such a family is documented in Dorothy Gallagher's *Hannah's Daughters—Six Generations of an American Family: 1876-1976.* Oral histories, genealogical charts, and photographs establish the identity of each member of the family. Included is a photograph showing Hannah (97), the family elder, holding Susan (two), the family baby.[8] The book, it should be noted, is not concerned with longevity but with changes in the lives of women over a hundred years.

Gallagher's family was not unique. In the 1890s, Alexander Graham Bell, the inventor of the telephone, became interested in families with a history of long life.[9] Lavinia McMurray was the mother of a remarkable clan. She had four generations of off-spring, 107 living descendants, by the time she was 85. Birth records were available for the family, and each member was clearly identifiable in four five-generation group photographs. McMurray's son Robert and her daughter Mrs. J.B. Gregory also parented four generations. If Lavinia had lived to be a centenarian, at age 105 she would have had five generations of offspring traceable through either her daughter or her son. Bell located another family of which the matriarch was Mrs. Karl Medlen, age 89. Her daughter was 61, her granddaughter 41, her great-granddaughter 21, and her great-great-granddaughter 7 months. If this pattern of motherhood at about age 20 had continued, a sixth generation would have been produced when Mrs. Medlen was 109.

Bell's four five-generational families in which the eldest was not even longevous does not mean that other four-or five-generational families might not include centenarians—simply that they cannot be thought of as proving it. The Gallagher example—of a six-generation family with the eldest being less than 100—demonstrates that only a seven-generation family would be a strong indication of supercentenarianism. If, as was claimed in the Soviet Union, there were many thousands of centenarians, there should have been a considerable number of six-generational families and perhaps some seven-generational. But this was not the case.

The explanation most often given, that the centenarians married late in life, is contradicted by individual histories. A typical one is Shirali Mislimov's, who first married in his 20s. A broad analysis of the marriage age in the Caucasus was made by Sula Benet, who determined that the usual age of marriage for Abkhasian women in modern times was an unremarkable 20-23[10] and that marriages in Azerbaijan occur at earlier ages.[11] There is no evidence that these patterns represent any drastic change from the recent past.

Some Azerbaijan doctors advanced the theory that longevity may be related to the occurrence of small family units within patterns of a slowed life cycle, marked by delayed menarche and delayed menopause. Benet produced a list of eight multi-generational Azerbaijan families as possible proof of this idea.[12] Though this is described as a list of people having "many offspring," there is only one five-generational example: a woman reputed to be 120 and to have 236 descendants. The other seven cases cite individuals aged 101 to 130, having four generations of offspring ranging in age from 38 to 53! The two men included are said to have fathered children at 93 and 104 respectively, and some of the women are said to have given birth after age 60.

These claims were at odds with official Soviet health records. Births after the mid-40s were rare, and none had been verified for a woman older than 55. As for family size, the 1959 census established the average Azerbaijan family as 4.5 persons, with 161 families out of every thousand having seven or more members. The figures are similar in Georgia (4.0 and 84) and Armenia (4.8 and 194). These were much higher, not lower than findings for the Baltic republics, the Soviet areas with the lowest longevity. There, the average family size ranged from a low of 3.1 in Estonia, with 14 households per thousand having seven or more members, to a high of 3.6 in Lithuania, with 43 households per thousand having seven or more members.[13] The claims were further undercut by the observation that Kiev women in the age group 80-104 had borne twice as many children as had those in the age group 60-79.[14] Like so much of the Azerbaijan-derived theories, the linkage of longevity to late marriages, small families, and delayed biological cycles was a back formation argument necessitated by the very oral histories it hoped to substantiate. This argument demanded exceptionalism from centenarian data available in the USSR and abroad.

A far more plausible explanation was that many of the long living had falsified their ages by from ten to thirty years. Correcting this would dissolve the generation gap for all but the most extravagant age claims and would mean that just as elsewhere in the world, great- and great-great grandparents would be in their late 80s, 90s, and early 100s. The total number of offspring would also make more statistical sense.

Mathematical irregularities pose another difficulty with the supercentenarian data that Soviet gerontologists never addressed adequately. If, for instance, Shirali Mislimov was actually 168 at his death, and Makhum Ayvazov, the previously recognized oldest person, died at 156, there is a gerontological chasm of a dozen years between them.[15] This compares with the mere ninety days separating Pierre Joubert from Delina Filkins. As soon as anyone over 120 is accepted as verified, comparable gaps appear for age categories going back to at least the late 90s, where Medvedev had already identified significant irregularities of a different nature.

Further evidence that falsification, particularly of the higher age claims, was at the root of the dilemma can be discerned in Georgian statistics. Of the 1,844 centenarians of 1970, 1,230 were women and 614 men. Proceeding at five-year intervals, the two-to-one ratio of women to men remains constant through age 115. From that point through age 119, there is a three-to-two ratio of 34 women to 20 men. In the ages above 120, however, there is cataclysmic reversal, with 42 surviving men and only 20 women.[16] This statistical improbability is best explained as a result of the patriarchs' boasting about their ages and their exaggerations being recorded as fact. Official unease with these figures is indicated by the lumping of all supercentenarians into one category rather than continuation of the five-year-interval method used to chart the other 1,782 centenarians.

Still more signs of sexist fraud are found when the longest-living women are compared with the longest-living men. Allowing Khfaf Lazuria the luxury of 140 years, there remain hundreds of men claiming to have outlived her and an incredible twenty-eight years separating her from Mislimov. Since everywhere in the world centenarian women outnumber men by at least 2 to 1 and since there is commingling of the sexes in that ratio in every age group through 115 even in Georgia, the sudden sex gap is unacceptable.

The flimsy nature of the supercentenarian claims reflects poorly on the oral-history verifications which, owing to the lack of primary sources, were the heart of Soviet field work. The staggering diversity of languages and cultures in the Soviet Union, the massive illiteracy of most of those born before the Revolution, and the difficulty of year-round access to mountain regions have already been cited as formidable obstacles to verification. Professionals doing oral histories in simpler contexts know that a considerable amount of time is required to do the job correctly. One cannot just walk in and take notes or run a tape recorder for half an hour and then go on to another centenarian. Second and third visits are essential to clear up ambiguities and other problems that will not be evident until the original material has been studied. The whole account, in turn, needs to be judged for accuracy against other available materials. There were roughly 20,000 centenarians to be interviewed. If only eight hours were spent on each person, a quarter-million hours, or six thousand forty-hour weeks, would be needed to complete the task. Finding field workers with the proper historical knowledge, language skills, and interviewing techniques to do such investigations would have been a major undertaking even if computers were available to tabulate data. As it was, local physicians not necessarily trained in social sciences did most of the verifications personally or through subordinates with a wide range of backgrounds.

Virtually all the proofs found in the oral histories made available to Westerners can be reduced to a matter of trust in the word of the particular respondent. When a venerable points to a mark on the wall of his home and insists his father made it one hundred and thirty years ago to record his birth, one can believe or disbelieve.

How many interviewers will have the intellectual courage to challenge such an assertion, especially in cultures where respect for elders is so high? Likewise an inscription in a Koran or a Bible may indicate the birth of one Makhtil Targil, but living in the same compound are Makhtil Targil I, II, and III. There were Makhtil Targils in earlier generations and cousins of the same or similar name. Given that there was no Abkhasian alphabet before the Revolution and illiteracy ran to 98 percent, the room for error is considerable. The rarely-available church record may be authentic, but to whom does it refer? Assessing the truth in oral histories is further complicated by rigid customs regulating male-female exchanges and by ethnic pride.

A major assumption in the oral-history approach is that the questions are so chronologically mixed that one could not lie consistently. But this mistakes illiteracy for lack of acumen. Peasants have always done complicated sums in their heads, and they can juggle dates as nimbly as university graduates. Nor must it be assumed they do not know that the Great Snow fell in 1910 or that the emancipation of the serfs in Abkhasia took place in 1870 (nine years later than in Russia proper, another opportunity for error). Khfaf Lazuria's accounts were all consistent and were supported by her family and neighbors. Discrepancies appeared only when stories told at different times were compared.

Vagueness is another shortcoming. Kamachich Kvichenya, an Abkhasian claiming to be a supercentenarian, asserted she had been kidnapped during the Turkish raids. This could be any time between 1858 and 1878, with the question of exactly how young she was a matter to be settled solely at her discretion. When pressed to explain how the incident demonstrated she was 137 and not 117, she explained that she was in pigtails when taken in one of the first raids. Assuming she was not lying, what does "first" mean? First for her village? For her region? For the whole era? How could she even know? Ten to twenty years could accrue to someone's age by misdating of such episodes. Often too, the personal details of life are related to famous historical events. But it is just these events which are most vividly recounted in the area's strong oral traditions. Many of the oldest of the long-living are consistently referred to as raconteurs, musicians, and story-tellers. Their ability to fashion credible fictitious histories should be self-evident. There also can be no doubt that at least some of the long-living are no longer sure whether they heard about the great war in the North at the time it happened or whether it was a story handed down by parents and grandparents. Locating the historical truth in this maze of confusion, legend, deceit, and vanity depends in great measure on the attitudes of the investigators. Are they, like Sula Benet, eager to believe? Or are they a doubting Thoms?

Soviet researchers acknowledged the inherent difficulties of the oral-history verifications and made constant revisions. After the original 1959 census identified 29,000 centenarians, 8,000 were totally eliminated by follow-up investigations, for a correction of 25%. Checks of the 1970 census results in Georgia dealt with 2,681 longevity claims and showed that 836 individuals had inflated their ages by from three to ten years and another 77 had inflated them by more than ten years, for a total downward correction of 35%. There were also 120 persons (a little over 4%) who had understated their ages.[17] Investigations of specific cases indicate that the incidence and magnitude of error increased as the age advanced beyond 109 into superlongevous territory. If highly trained persons redid the interviews, the number of centenarians per 100,000 of population would likely be substantially reduced. In view of the percentage of distortion, the vagueness of the oral histories, and the statistical abnormalities, none of the supercentenarian claims can be accepted as proven.

Detailed oral histories, physical-test results, genealogical charts, generational photographs, autopsy reports (when available), and other proofs of the 10 or 20 best cases have never been presented for international study.

The most monumental of all Soviet longevity programs was Project 2000, begun by Chebotarev and his associates in 1970.[18] It involved 2,000 urban dwellers who ranged in age from the early 20s to the 90s. All agreed to follow regimens set up for them by the gerontologists and to take periodic physical examinations, which were more frequent for the oldest participants. The specifics of the program were kept secret, but its components included psychological counseling, diet control, exercise programs, and chemical intervention. The last involved vitamins, hormones, and antioxidants. The volunteers were divided so that each combination of therapies was used by a portion of each age group. The *de facto* control group for Project 2000 was the general Soviet public as measured by the average life span, but among the volunteers there were those whose pills and injections were placebos. Any longevity gain on their part would have to be attributed to psychosomatic factors or the regular medical checkups. The institutional chaos which accompanied the collapse of the Soviet Union effectively put an end to Project 2000. Whether any valid findings can be salvaged from the first decade-and-a half of its existence remains to be seen.

Taking a different experimental direction from Chebotarev's were scientists organized in the late 1970s into the National Committee for the Artificial Prolongation of Human Life.[19] One of the key figures in the group was Dr. L.V. Komarov, a biologist at the Institute of General Genetics. He believed that artificial means would be found to extend life spans to more than three hundred years. He hoped to slow down the aging process through drug combinations. His personal research centered on adenosine triphosphate (ATP), an enzyme found in greater quantities in the bodies of the young than in the old. Earlier studies had determined that used alone, ATP could not retard aging, but Komarov thought ATP would become an anti-aging weapon when combined with other substances. Using magnetized sugar and other macroenergetic substances, he had doubled the life span of houseflies. His anti-aging work with human volunteers began in the 1980s. Other research on the artificial prolongation of life done in the USSR was coordinated through the National Committee. In Odessa, for example, the Filatov Institute conducted experiments using extracts from human placentas preserved after childbirth. As of the 1990s, none of this kind of research ever produced results worthy of publication in international journals.

Experiments on prolonging life were not without precedent in the Soviet Union. At the outbreak of World War II, Dr. Alexander A. Bogomoletz, the founder of the Kiev Institute and a pioneer in the investigation of centenarian claims, announced that he had developed a vaccine (antireticular cytotoxic serum) which seemed to prolong life. The work was interrupted by the war, and when it resumed in the late 1940s, the claim was withdrawn. In the mid-'50s a new combination called Gerovital which had been devised by Dr. Ana Aslan of Rumania was thought capable of revitalizing the body, but although Dr. Aslan reported that older people brought to her clinic treatment were rejuvenated, tests undertaken in other nations have failed to reproduce her results.

The basis of Aslan's formula is procaine hydrochloride—or as it is more commonly known in the United States, novocaine. To novocaine, Aslan added benzoic acid, a preservative, and potassium metabisulfate, an antioxidant. Her injections were given in conjunction with megavitamin treatments and close monitoring of the patients' vital signs. Zhores Medvedev deduced that the disparities between her results and those obtained by others was due to the source of her patients.[20] Rumania had one of Europe's lowest average life spans and one of its lowest standards of living. Aslan's patients were mainly sickly pensioners taken from old-age homes where treatment was not up to the standards of developed nations. The attention given to the pensioners, the vitamins, the good food, the proper exercise, and the comfortable surroundings, Medvedev argued, accounted for their improved health. He noted that testing in Kiev proved that Gerovital is worthless and led to its abandonment by the USSR. Aslan always claimed that incorrect combinations were used in the tests done outside Rumania, but it is inconceivable that the Soviets would not have been able to obtain and use her exact procedures and formulas. In spite of the failure to reproduce her results anywhere else, a health cult has emerged around Aslan's work. In major American cities, Gerovital is still sold clandestinely as a "forbidden" youth drug. Before the collapse of the Soviet system, Rumanian advertisements designed to attract American tourists shamelessly suggested that three points of interest in the country were the Carpathian Mountains, Dracula's castle, and "the youth clinics of Dr. Ana Aslan."[21]

What is most striking about the massive longevity research done in the USSR in the 1960s and 1970s is the conclusion that artificial means would be required to achieve new highs in life spans and even to get large numbers of people into the centenarian ranks. Komarov stated unequivocally that without the discovery of appropriate chemical combinations, the limits of life would remain less than 120. This figure is in line with the research of Soviet gerontologists such as Chebotarev and Gogoghian. Thus, Caucasian theatrics notwithstanding, the ultimate Soviet findings were the same as those elsewhere in the developed world. The highest documentable life spans were between 110 and 115 and the probable natural biological limit of human life was thought to be approximately 120.

# 5. LONGEVITY IN THE MOUNTAINS

*Vilcabamba is in a hollow in the mountains where
five valleys converge and, seen from above, looks
like the arms of a star, Vilcabamba being in the
center... —David Davies*

MOUNTAIN REGIONS HAVE ALWAYS BRED legends of long-
living people. The explanation most commonly advanced in
national literatures is that the harsh weather conditions and the
physical exertion required for simple survival have produced men
and women sure-footed, ornery, and sturdy as the hoofed and
horned animals with which they share the heights. As postwar
interest in the Soviet Caucasus grew, gerontologists wondered if
areas with similar topography might not also contain longevous
populations. In widely scattered regions of the world, the connection between mountain terrain and long life was promising. The
most exciting prospects involved the Vilcabamba Valley of
southeastern Ecuador, where supercentenarian claims were
backed by religious and civil records.

Vilcabamba enjoys an association with good health dating
back to the Incas, but its most recent fame began in the 1950s
when heart specialists wrote about the impressive cardiovascular vigor of its inhabitants. Popular interest was fanned by a
spirited 1956 press conference in New York City featuring Javier
Pereira, reputed to be 167, who had been brought to the United

States by the owners of *Believe It or Not,* a syndicated newspaper feature.[1] Fifteen years later came the sensational news that a census had found nine centenarians in a village of 819 persons. If accurate, this number would give Vilcabamba a centenarian population nearly 400 times that of the United States and nearly 30 times that of Soviet Georgia. This was all the more remarkable as Vilcabamba was in one of the poorest areas of South America, where health facilities were inadequate, hygiene poorly understood, and social relations strained by a brutal feudalistic economy.

Dr. David Davies of the Gerontological Unit, University College, London, was among the most enthusiastic boosters of the Vilcabamba claims. Aided by a number of Ecuadorian scientists and with some technical help from various levels of the Ecuadorian government, Davies made four visits to the valley between 1971 and 1973. The main evidence he found for longevity was a series of records kept by the Roman Catholic church.[2] They stretched back to the eighteenth century, and their authenticity was beyond dispute. The records were far more substantial than any documentation available in the Caucasus, and there were civil records going back to 1900 which could be used as a cross-reference.

Davies questioned many of the reputed superlongevous. A person who particularly impressed him was the oldest of the Vilcabamba centenarians, Miguel Carpio, who claimed to be 123. Satisfied with the documentation presented, Davies thought Carpio "very lucid" and took down a description of the Peruvian War of 1894 in which Carpio claimed to have fought. Three old women in the village, one of them a centenarian herself, remembered Carpio as already grown when they were still children. A number of men who attested to Carpio's age also claimed to be superlongevous.[3] The cluster of interrelated verifications and remembered historical events was similar to those encountered in the Caucasus.

Observations in Vilcabamba and the immediate area were to turn up a number of discordant elements, which Davies recorded but did not consider critical. For example, many of the men smoked from one to forty cigarettes a day, and on Saturday nights it was common for men to drink steadily until they passed out. Nonetheless, there were numerous male centenarians, and after age 105 they far outnumbered the women. Another element not found in other observations of long-living people was the social distance between generations. Speaking of specific centenarian families, Davies wrote, "They did not seem particularly close to their children or vice versa. They would meet each other regularly after church on Sunday morning but other meetings were not frequent."[4]

Rather than pursue these matters, Davies concentrated his study on the physical environment. He determined that the critical feature of Vilcabamba was that the soil was unusually rich in minerals, particularly selenium. This fitted his already formed hypothesis that trace elements might be critical to longevity. However, the accuracy of his tests cannot be accepted at face value, because his writing demonstrated a marked penchant for exaggeration and inaccuracy. He suggested, for instance, that "any heart patient, from any part of the world, improves after a visit to the village."[5] Trying to compare Vilcabamba to Abkhasia, he reported erroneously that there were 150,000 Abkhasians instead of the 500,000 of the 1970 census and 2,000 reputed centenarians instead of the actual 294. He thought Shirali Mislimov was an Abkhasian and seemed oblivious to the distinctions between Georgia, Azerbaijan, and Abkhasia.[6]

Equally excited about Vilcabamba was Grace Halsell, an author who lived in Ecuador for most of 1974 and spent considerable time in Vilcabamba. Halsell had made a career of changing identities in order to write books about specific cultures. She dyed her skin black and lived as a black woman in Harlem and Mississippi for one book and lived as an illegal Mexican alien for another project. She could not age for Vilcabamba, but she thought the length of time she spent living in the area as an ordinary inhabitant would give her work a poignancy and authenticity that brief visits could not provide. Her experiences were recorded in *Los Viejos*, published in 1976 by Rodale Press, a major publisher of health books in the United States.

Like Davies, Halsell made a point of searching out the records and described herself as "a little awed" by the age of the documents.[7] Her only other attempts at verification were the usual ones in which individuals in at least their 70s remembered that the centenarians had already been "old" when they were "young." Her explanation for Vilcabamba longevity did not stray far beyond the organic-food, pollution-free, natural life style approach advocated in the pages of *Prevention* and *Organic Gardening*, the best known publications issued by Rodale Press.

Halsell also made a stab at social analysis that is typical of the illusions often spread about underdeveloped areas with reputedly longevous inhabitants. Not finding the kind of tension and stress common in developed nations, she believed that the people Frantz Fanon characterized as the wretched of the earth—the social base that has fed one contemporary revolutionary movement after another—achieved longevity because of the serene nature of their life style. Like a nineteenth-century liberal commentator on American slavery, she wrote, "I could see the evils of the *hacienda* system and would, under no circumstances, exchange my life for the role of a *peon*. Yet, I also noted the *viejos* had used their harsh circumstances to build strong, good characters . . . It seemed ironic that the *viejos*, among the poorest people of the world, would worry less about money and possessions than the richest people in the world."[8] Brushing aside her own anecdotes of sexual passion, jealousies, violence, and anger, Halsell canonized the old with observations that "A *viejo* does not hate, he is not bitter"[8] and "I have never heard them quarrel or fight or dispute with each other."[9]

Such romanticization does not stand up when compared with detailed Vilcabamba biographies of longevous people, who invariably display all the normal human reactions to pain and adversity. The notion that poverty somehow produces strong character, physical fitness, and mental health is a delusion. The massive migration of young people from underdeveloped mountain areas clearly demonstrates their feelings, and it has been amply documented that the effects of poverty on the old can be as devastating in the Andean hut as in the North American rooming house.[10]

The somber realities of Andean poverty made a deep impression on Alexander Leaf, who visited Vilcabamba in 1970 and 1974. Even though he accepted the authenticity of the church records, his studies of the centenarians left him puzzled. The terrain, the low cholesterol level in the blood, and the meager 1,200-calorie daily intake might explain the low incidence of heart disease, but such factors were found throughout the mountains. There were also the numerous negative factors already cited. Leaf came to favor the thesis that whatever longevity existed was a product of genetics. The Vilcabambans were of a slightly different ethnic line than most of the neighboring people, and many of the longevous were blood relatives.[11]

Leaf was aware, too, of specific exaggerations of age. A brother of Miguel Carpio who claimed to be 122 on the 1970 visit had zoomed to 134 four years later.[12] José David Toledo, who told Leaf in 1970 that he was 107, claimed to *The New York Times* to be 141 in 1973.[13] Leaf thought a detailed examination of church and civil records might be profitable.

The challenge was taken up by Dr. Sylvia H. Forman, a specialist in quantitative anthropology, and Dr. Richard B. Mazess, who wanted to determine the rate of calcium loss in the bones of the longevous. In 1974 they conducted a survey of the skeletal status of the long-living and did a household census which involved 80% of the population. The church records and civil registry were examined after family genealogies had been worked out. In 1976 and 1978, Mazess returned for further work. A familiar longevity hoax emerged: the records of older relatives had been appropriated by younger people, sons taking the records of fathers and nieces the records of aunts.[14] Some false claims were the result of honest confusion and semi-literacy, but many, particularly the supercentenarian claims of the men, were conscious deceptions. Of the nine centenarians of the 1971 census, none were genuine. The oldest in the group was 96, and some were only septuagenarians.

Miguel Carpio's falsifications were typical. Because of the similarity of family names, various records had become confused, and the local officials came to believe he was born in 1864, which led to the official age of 112 recorded at the time of his death in 1976. This already cut some fifteen years off his highest age claim, but methodical work by Mazess and Forman was to eliminate another nineteen. It was established that Carpio's mother had been born in 1855 and that he had been born in 1883. Seven other entries between 1905 and 1915 made the identifications conclusive. For Carpio to have been 127 in 1976, he would have had to be born six years before his mother, and for him to be 112, his mother would have had to have given birth at age nine. Still more entries established that he began to lie about his age in 1944, when he claimed to be 70 while he was actually only 61. Five years later his age had jumped to 80.

With the linchpin of Carpio pulled, all the claims connected with his fell through as well. However, Mazess and Forman went beyond such circumstantial evidence. They were able to locate records for nearly all of the longevous claimants. Their conclusions stunned the gerontologists and faddists who had wanted to accept Vilcabamban stories: "None of the 23 'centenarians' investigated had, in fact, survived to 100 years. Similarly, none of the 15 'nonagenarians' investigated had, in fact, survived 90 years."[15] The very records that had once been the bulwark of the claims now disproved them. An important element in the de-verifications was the genealogies worked out by Forman which made it possible to sort out family relationships.

A significant ancillary discovery was that exaggerations of age had been a tradition since at least the turn of the century, so that the postwar tourist and scientific interest only fed an established custom. The apparently high concentration of older people was another illusion. Its cause was the mass exodus of young people to the cities, leaving depopulated villages with deceptively high numbers of abandoned old people. Without a massive demographic study, no absolute judgments could be made, but Mazess and Forman were confident about the conclusions to be drawn from their efforts: "Individual longevity in Vilcabamba is little, if any, different from that found throughout the rest of the world."[16]

Fortunately, as is so often the case in longevity hoaxes involving studies of large populations, the research in Vilcabamba had not been entirely fruitless in establishing useful data about the nature of aging. At a conference held in 1978, Japanese, French, Canadian, Ecuadorian, and American scientists correlated the Vilcabamba research they had done independently. The conferees agreed that the over–70 population of Vilcabamba had unusual cardiovascular health. Some indications of this were their low blood pressure, their low heart rates after exertion, and the finding that they had only one-third of the cardiac abnormalities usually found in the same age categories in developed nations.

Their cardiovascular health appeared to be linked to their leanness, their diet, their low cholesterol levels, and their high level of physical activity. It was found also that the older Vilcabambans were relatively free of the symptoms of aging (spinal curvature, pain, fractures) associated with osteoporosis.[17]

The scope of the Vilcabamba hoax is sobering for anyone wishing to give the benefit of the doubt to undocumented claims supported only by oral histories and local traditions. In this case, the longevity myth was rooted in the low rate of cancer and heart diseases in the area. Upon this factual base, some Ecuadorian officials had hoped that Vilcabamba might be transformed into a health resort. Writers, publishers, and scientists eager to find their pet theories proved added their own distortions. In response to this attention, the inhabitants made the most of their possibilities, gaining relief from the tedium of their existence and perhaps hoping for some financial benefit or a trip to the United States. As elsewhere, men lied more brazenly than women, and there was a tendency for baffled observers to believe the population might possess unique genetic inheritance.

Another area in the Western Hemisphere frequently thought to be prolongevous is the hot and arid Sierra Madre range of northern Mexico. The region's most celebrated inhabitants are the Tarahumara Indians, a people who have the distinction of being the world's only jogging nation. Their name can be roughly translated as "foot runners," and foot running is their basic means of travel and the basis of their sports. "Run, don't walk," would be an apt national motto for them.

Tarahumara hunters can chase deer for two and three days on end until the animal either drops from exhaustion or is run over the edge of a ravine. The stalking involves considerable tracking and walking, but long stretches of jogging are an essential ingredient of the kill. Even more common among the Tarahumara are foot-races, the national pastime. In 1928 two Tarahumara men, José Torres and Aurelio Terrazas, took part in the Olympic marathon in Amsterdam. They lost first place by several minutes, but claimed they had thought the race was going to be much longer or they would have run faster. Another Tarahumara sport is a kickball game which is played over a range of two to a dozen miles and can last from noon to sunset. Occasionally some games are said to go on for days.

Physical endurance of this kind would be impressive in any terrain, but it is doubly so in the Sierra Madre, one of the least hospitable environments in North America. Its demanding climate and poor soil make the continuing existence of Tarahumara culture a kind of ecological marvel. Even though the major crops of corn, pumpkins, and beans were often in short supply and most Tarahumara still did not speak Spanish, in the 1970s the group numbered 40,000.

Owing to the enthusiasm for jogging in the adjacent United States, legends about Tarahumara longevity have multiplied. The verification problem, however, is even more difficult than in Azerbaijan. In the 1930s, long before the American jogging craze, Wendell Bennett and Robert Zingg made an anthropological survey of Tarahumara culture. They discovered that while the tribal language had words for "day" and "week", the word for "month" was the same as that for "moon," and the year was only crudely reckoned by the position of the sun in the sky in relation to certain fixed points. The Tarahumara did not know how many days were in a month or how many months were in a year. They did not have names for individual months, and they did not bother to keep track of years.[18] Thus, any statement that a Tarahumara has lived a hundred years must be speculative.

Noticeable by its absence in the Bennett-and-Zingg work is any reference to large numbers of old people or the hint of longevity.

What was striking to the anthropologists was the low level of medical knowledge and basic hygiene. They were told many plants could cure bruises and abrasions, but the injuries they saw were usually neglected, and the most minor skin breaks could lead to severe infections.

Some forty years after the investigation of Bennett and Zingg, a *National Geographic* team reported on another anti-longevous aspect of the culture: the musical and drinking feasts known as the *tuturi*. One of these affairs was described as ". . . a cacophony of chanting, fiddles, rattles, guitars, stomping dances, shouts, raucous laughter, and howling dogs. Both men and women dropped out to drink corn beer (they rarely drink anything stronger) and soon were staggering about in a stupor."[19] The commentator, James Norman, goes on to call the massive drunkenness a "strange and sad phenomenon."[19] He judged that each Tarahumara spent about one hundred days a year preparing, drinking, and recovering from drinking corn beer, with some individuals taking part in as many as ninety parties. A minimum of two hundred pounds of corn per family was estimated to be needed for the preparation of corn beer annually, even though the usage cut into the already minimal food supply. This alcohol abuse would likely neutralize the health benefits of jogging even without the other negative factors of poor medical treatment and a diet inadequate to the point of malnutrition.

Even more disappointing than the Vilcabamba and Sierra Madre studies have been investigations dealing with the Carpathian Mountains. In the Soviet sector of the range no significant longevity was found,[20] and in the Rumanian sector the rates were lower than those found among Western European city dwellers.[21] The Rumanian study, done in the 1960s, is still important, however, because it identified longevity factors similar to those in the Caucasus. Patterning its work on Soviet models, the Rumanian government sponsored a study of 5,123 persons over 85 years old. Not mountaineers, but agricultural workers made up 54% of the group, housewives another 24%, and manual workers 22%. Most of these people had done the same kind of work for most of their lives, and few had ever formally retired. Thirty-five percent were lacto-vegetarians and 5% were primarily fish eaters, with the rest consuming a mixed diet. Thirty-eight percent reported that neither parent was longevous, and 16% did not know. One unusual finding was that in the group over 95, 20% were primarily fish eaters. This 20% also had the lowest number of bedridden persons. The researchers did not determine how much this phenomenon was due to diet and how much was related to the arduous life of the sea. The study further determined that 77% of those over 85 and 95% of those over 95 had never smoked.

Yet another study which produced results similar to the longevity profile found in the Caucasus was done in the 1970s.[22] This time the target was a mountain region of Turkey, and the investigators, Suha Beller and Erdman Palmore, were less concerned with the percentages of longevous people and verifying their ages than with making detailed biographical sketches. They located 50 individuals claiming to be over 90 and 13 claiming to be over 100. Although documentation was lacking, the investigators were confident that all the participants were at least octogenarians. Again, the longevity factors resembled those in the USSR. The long-living diets were very simple, including little meat or animal fat. Their body types were described as normal to lean, but definitely much leaner than that of the general population. The long-living also had a vigorous life style, exemplified by one man who insisted on walking at least five miles a day for his health. Eighty-six percent of the group had never smoked, and only 4% had ever smoked more than a pack of cigarettes a day.

Social relationships also were similar to those in the Caucasus.

All had been married at least once, and belonged to extended family networks in which they held honored and secure positions. While the social prestige was not as formalized as in the Caucasus, it was considerable. Most likely as a result of this psychological support, the group was found to have a positive mental outlook and a high rate of sociability.

A number of biochemical tests constituted another aspect of the survey. Eighty-six percent of those tested were judged to be in good health, with only 14% housebound. Vision and hearing were generally good. The only unusual results were some common blood factors. Since the sampling was so small, the investigators did not think it wise to form any generalization, and subsequent blood work remains inconclusive.

Tracking down the tales of longevity in the mountains sometimes appears to be little more than an exercise in debunking, but this isn't so. The studies of mountain people have revealed that significant benefits to the cardiovascular, respiratory, and skeletal systems can be derived from living on a rugged terrain. The advantages to the heart and lungs are linked to the physical challenge of walking on inclines. The process is comparable to the way a biceps is built up through the repeated strain of lifting an iron bar. The cardiovascular and respiratory health of mountain people of every age also indicates that those in the 50-90 age bracket are not doomed to heart disease. As the majority of people in that age range in the developed world suffer from degenerative diseases, it is possible to hypothesize that sedentary populations presently suffer from an epidemic of premature and preventable deaths not unlike the premature deaths once caused by infectious diseases.

This view is supported by numerous studies of occupations and activity patterns. Among the best known is a survey involving 31,000 London transport workers. Heart diseases were much more frequent among the drivers of double-decker buses than among ticket takers on the same buses, who walked back and forth and up and down the bus stairs all day.[23] A Finnish study discovered that woodcutters live seven to eight years longer than office workers.[24] An American study that compared a group of male Irish immigrants in Boston with their brothers still in Ireland found the Irish siblings to be longer living. The primary difference was that in Ireland the men had to walk or cycle several miles a day to agricultural jobs, while those in the United States used motorized transportation to reach their city jobs.[25] Other studies of 17,000 college graduates,[26] 6,551 stevedores,[27] 16,882 office workers,[28] and 119,000 postal carriers[23] have shown similar positive correlations between longer life and strenuous physical activity.

Exercise also confers great benefits on the skeletal system. In the mountains, a tougher system less subject to fracture seems to be due to the stimulation of the bone marrow caused by walking and climbing. Just moving about mountainous terrain performing daily survival tasks is equivalent to hours of formal exercise. Like heart disease, fragile bones, the curse of so many aging Americans, result more from lack of conditioning than from the passage of time.

The mountain studies thus provide useful evidence that calendar age is less significant than biological or physiological age, which in turn is highly dependent upon the kinds of physical demands made on the body. At the same time, the studies demonstrate that terrain, altitude, and exercise in and of themselves are not a sufficient combination to produce unusual longevity. To them must be added the dietary and psychological factors found in the Caucasus, and there must be no horrendously negative habits like alcoholism or cigarette smoking.

Authentic centenarians may yet be found in the Sierra Madre, the Andes, and the Carpathians. Certainly there is evidence that healthy octogenarian and nonagenarian individuals may be found in higher percentages there than in less demanding geographic zones. It is predictable that the belief in the wholesale longevity of mountain people and the existence of supercentenarians among them will persist until the respective governments become interested enough in vital statistics to devise systems for gathering accurate data. Someone will suggest that if Vilcabamba doesn't have centenarians, then other Andean villages do. Or if the Tarahumara visited by the *National Geographic* are drunkards, the more traditional groups deeper in the mountains are not. The supercentenarian haven will always be in that neglected valley over the far horizon.

# 6. THE HUNZAKUTS

*The point of Gilgit, now as always, is strategic. High above the snowline, somewhere midst the peaks and glaciers that wall in the Gilgit valley, the long and jealously guarded frontiers of India, China, Russia, Afghanistan and Pakistan meet. It is the hub, the crow's nest, the fulcrum of Asia.—John Keay*

THE MOST EXOTIC MOUNTAIN VALLEY ever associated with longevity is the one cut by the Hunza River amid the peaks of the Karakoram Range. Unlike the Caucasus or Vilcabamba, where tales of long-living people have historic roots, the Hunza claims are of recent vintage, their source traceable to the writings of a single individual: Sir Robert McCarrison. The background to his work was laid in the closing decades of the nineteenth century when the British extended the frontiers of their Indian empire into the western Himalayas. In a sustained effort that Rudyard Kipling called the Great Game, British agents, explorers, and adventurers sought to find passes leading into central Asia and to forge local military alliances for back-door challenges to the Russian and Chinese empires. As the decade of the 1890s opened, the last outpost in what is now Pakistan and was then the North-west Frontier was the village of Gilgit. From that group of buildings, a narrow trail led into some of the most magnificent mountain grandeur to be seen anywhere on earth. Mount Rakaposhi, the goddess of the snows, dominated the immediate vista, a peak of over 25,000 feet; and to the east was K-2, inferior in elevation only to Everest. Nestled among this splendor were minuscule robber states governed by autocratic despots called Mirs. No state was of more strategic importance than Hunza, a realm extending 50 miles east to west and 40 miles north to south.[1]

Given the British origins of the claims for Hunzakut longevity, I thought the logical starting point for any scholarly evaluation of those claims would be the library of the British Museum. In addition to the military reports and memoirs I had expected, I found that despite the fact that Hunza was inaccessible for most of each year, numerous outsiders had spent considerable time there and had written extensively about their experiences.

Among the first commentators on Hunza was Robert McCarrison who arrived in India in 1901 at the age of 23 after completing his medical studies at Oxford University. Serving as a regimental officer in the Foreign Service, he quickly distinguished himself by correctly identifying a sand fly as the carrier of the Three Day Fever of Chitral. In 1904, McCarrison was appointed army surgeon to the nine villages of the Gilgit Agency, a post in which he was to serve until 1911. Shortly after his promotion, the young scientist began to do research on the goiter disease endemic throughout the agency. Finding eight villages afflicted with goiter and one free of it, McCarrison was able to discover the link to iodine deficiency. While traveling about in the area and making various health studies, McCarrison also came to certain conclusions about the health and longevity of the neighboring Hunzakuts.

McCarrison's claims for Hunza were threefold. The most important for him was that Hunzakuts were relatively free of many common diseases, especially diseases of the gastroenteritis tract. Ailments like goiter and cretinism, scourges of Hunza's neighbors, were also said to be rare or nonexistent. McCarrison further stated that the Hunzakuts were long-living and that their incredible vigor persisted even at advanced ages. He credited this splendid health profile to the quality of their diet. His summary view of Hunza appeared in *Studies in Deficiency Diseases*, written in 1921:

> My own experience provides an example of a race unsurpassed in perfection of physique and in freedom from disease in general, whose sole food consists to this day of grains, vegetables and fruit with a certain amount of milk and butter, and goat's meat only on feast days. I refer to the people of the state of Hunza, situated in the extreme northernmost point of India . . . .When the severe nature of the winter in that part of the Himalayas is considered, and the fact that their housing accommodations and conservancy arrangements are of the most primitive, it becomes obvious that the enforced restriction to the unsophisticated foodstuffs of nature is compatible with long life, continued vigor, and perfect physique.[2]

In 1938, McCarrison's views were given a more popular treatment in G.T. Wrench's well-written *The Wheel of Health*.[3] Never having been to India himself, Wrench quoted McCarrison extensively to establish the uniqueness of the Hunzakuts and then augmented McCarrison's claims with corroborating material from the writings of explorers and soldiers. For Wrench, as for McCarrison, Hunza was a land where the dietary habits and life style he thought ideal had been tested successfully in nature's own laboratory. This view was buttressed by medical studies and presented in a manner that studiously avoided sensationalism. Over the years, Wrench's book became a standard reference on Hunza, referred to by other authors more frequently than McCarrison's own comments, which were scattered in various essays written for a professional audience.

The mythologizing of Hunza was also stimulated by the 1930s

best seller *Lost Horizon*, which spawned successful film, stage, radio, and television adaptations. In this popular romance, James Hilton wrote of Shangri-La, a valley found high in the Himalayas. Access was along a treacherous ice-laden path open only for limited times of the year, but within Shangri-La itself the climate was perfect. People entering from the outside world found that the aging process was slowed so that it took many decades to register the slightest signs of wear. Led by a European priest, the outsiders eventually formed a lamahood whose mission was to preserve human knowledge through the holocaust of wars the twentieth century was doomed to endure. While not quite pacifists in the Gandhian sense, the men and women of the lamahood prized wisdom and virtue above all else. As the high lama explained, "We govern with moderate authority and we are pleased with moderate obedience."[4] This attitude and other characteristics of the fictional Shangri-La slowly became identified with Hunza.

American exposure to Hunza got into high gear after 1949 with the publication of *The Healthy Hunzas* by J.I. Rodale, founder of the press that was to publish Grace Halsell's Vilcabamba book in 1976.[5] Like Wrench, Rodale had never been to India, and his views were based almost exclusively on the claims of McCarrison, again fleshed out with a few supportive quotations from other sources. His language was much less moderate than Wrench's and his views were later to be restated in flamboyantly exaggerated terms by writers on health.

After some well-publicized trips by Lowell Thomas into the Himalayas in the 1950s, a new thread began to be woven into the Hunza cloth by people like Nebraska optometrist George Banik, who visited Hunza under the sponsorship of the *People Are Funny* television show, and Jay Hoffman, a health lecturer seeking confirmation of his favorite theories. The quality of the observations of such travelers ran from amateurish to foolish. Jay Hoffman was to call Hunza a "Fountain of Youth" where people frequently lived to be well over 100.[6] His enthusiasm was exceeded by an author in *The American Mercury*, who wrote, "No Hunzakut has ever suffered from indigestion, constipation, ulcers, cancer, or any venereal disease."[7] When told that some Hunzakuts had lived to be 120 and even 140, Hoffman and Banik cheerfully passed along the claims without asking for any proof.[8] The champion of the faddist commentators was Renee Taylor, who wrote or coauthored five books dealing with life in Hunza.

The Hunza depicted as virtually untouched since the march of Alexander was actually a hub of international communications and espionage. During the latter part of the nineteenth century, the British had discovered that many travelers from Central Asia were accustomed to using Hunza as one of the passageways to India. The writings of British agents active in the region provide a fund of information about the society any centenarian surviving into the 1960s and '70s would have been born into. There are also accounts by various mountaineers, who, although usually more intrigued by glaciers than by human beings, sometimes dropped interesting asides on culture in their diaries. In 1934, Col. David Lorimer, who had served as the British agent in Gilgit from 1920 to 1924, commenced a fifteen-month stay in Hunza to study the native language. His wife wrote a detailed memoir of their experiences: the first year-round observation and substantial account of Hunzakut society.[9]

The decade of the '40s was to bring a flurry of visitors. Among the most unusual were a quartet of Norwegians who made a spectacular trip from Sweden through the Soviet Union into Hunza in an ostensible effort to join British forces in India for transport to an air school in Canada. The journal published by one of them appears somewhat naive, but the communication links cited are extremely sophisticated, and many native leaders thought the Great Game had entered a new phase.[10] In 1944 John Clark became active in Chinese Turkestan as a reconnaissance engineer for General Joseph Stilwell, and from 1948 to 1951 he was in Hunza on various occasions. Clark was to write the most comprehensive and perceptive account of Hunza.[11] At about the same period as Clark's activities, the American journalists Jean and Frank Shor sought to retrace Marco Polo's journey. Their adventures included a stay in Hunza. They made a second journey to Hunza in 1952.[12] A few years later, Barbara Mons, a British woman inspired by reading Wrench and Lorimer, made a pilgrimage to Hunza, and in 1973 came Alexander Leaf on the final leg of his longevity pilgrimage.[13] In addition to these major commentators there were mountaineers, health teams, food faddists, hunters, and curiosity seekers of every description. Thus, there is a century-long continuum of information on Hunza against which to evaluate McCarrison's thesis on Hunzakuts' health.

In view of subsequent attempts to explain Hunzakut longevity partly as a function of a serene life style amid idyllic surroundings, it is instructive to know something of the Hunzakut socio-economic system prior to 1900. Politically, the state was ruled by the Mir and his retinue of village chiefs. Their authority was absolute but unstable: the Mir's immediate relatives, backed by alternative village leaders, constantly plotted for power. Fratricide and patricide were frequent. Mir Mohammed Safdar Ali Khan, the ruler with whom the British negotiated in 1891, had gained his throne by murdering his father and at least one brother. Each successful revolt of this kind reshaped the pecking order in every village, unless the local headman had betrayed the former Mir by shifting allegiances beforehand. Any losers in the power struggle who managed to escape with their lives retreated through the passes to neighboring states, where they spent most of their time trying to regain power.

Economically, Hunza's barely adequate agricultural output was dependent upon an excellent terrace and irrigation system engineered with a finesse that was the envy of surrounding peoples. Like their neighbors, the Hunzakuts also collected tribute from or raided passing caravans. Independently or in alliance with others, the Hunzakuts would sweep out of their strongholds in periodic assaults on wealthy travelers. They could strike out at will and return to their valley, where various traps and fortifications made their villages impregnable. At times the road was just a series of rocks hammered into the side of the mountain. In an emergency, the rocks could be pulled loose, leaving a bare cliff face as Hunzakut warriors waited to start rockslides or use their weapons against any who dared venture farther. The value system was that of a typical warrior society in which, matters of politics aside, there was almost no crime within the society, but pillage, rape, murder, and enslavement of outsiders were taken for granted.

The Hunzakuts claimed to be descended from stragglers in the army of Alexander the Great, namely three Greek soldiers and their Persian wives. Although nominally Moslem, they drank a grape wine flavored with the oil of bitter apricots, their major crop; and it was customary until the 1930s for them to share their wives with respected visitors—a courtesy Europeans usually declined. Hunzakut women went about unveiled and had more freedom than their sisters in other Islamic mirdoms. But the role of women was far from enviable. Permitted to do all the work men did except fighting, women were still considered congenitally stupid, and they were not allowed to travel alone, to be educated, or to own property. Males did not speak to females who were not in their families, and in Hunzakut homes there was only minimal communication between the sexes. The general contempt for women was so pronounced that as late as the 1950s outside observers noted that despondent women committed suicide by leaping from high ledges or by eating large quantities of apricot pits, which contain a substantial amount of cyanide. There was no possibility that an ebullient female like Khfaf Lazuria would emerge from this society.

Sexism governed the treatment of domesticated animals as well. When winter approached, instead of reducing sheep herds by cutting them down to a majority of the sturdiest ewes and a few of the best rams, as is done in most cultures, the Hunzakuts maintained their herds at nearly full strength, with an equal number of ewes and rams. This method placed an unnecessary strain on the limited vegetation and prevented a rapid spring buildup in the number of lambs. Likewise, the Hunzakuts preferred stallions to mares even if the mares were hardier, on the assumption that the male of the species is always stronger. Rarely has male chauvinism taken such an awesome toll on the available food supply and immediate well-being of a people.

Old age was not honored either. McCarrison himself was shocked when the Mirs throughout the Gilgit region could not understand why he wanted to "waste" medicine and other medical treatment on their aged.[14] One Mir suggested that it would be a better idea to create a lethal chamber to do away with the old quickly. As it was, many tribes required, upon pain of death, that the eldest son use a conical basket to carry his old and decrepit parent to a summit, where he was to drop them to their deaths. Similarly, after the major battles of the winter of 1891, old men were sent to deal with the British victors because it was feared envoys might be shot on sight and the old were deemed expendable. Except for a Council of Elders, whose members were appointed by the Mir and could be dismissed at his pleasure, in traditional Hunza there were no social structures supportive of old age.

Until the war of 1891, the Mir of Hunza was contemptuous of all outsiders. The British were considered just one more warlike tribe of the kind that periodically rode up from Kashmir. When British demands became overbearing, the Mir would shout that his Chinese allies would send troops, or he would refer to his conversation with Captain Grombtchevski, the Russian explorer who had brought a Cossack troop through the northern passes with an offer of an alliance with the Tsar. In all these intrigues, the Mir sought to trade temporary concessions to any given foreign power for weapons and money. Eventually he overplayed his hand, was defeated by Pathan troops under British command, and fled to exile in Sinkiang.

Mohammed Nazim Khan, a brother of the deposed Mir, agreed to accept British policy and became the new ruler of Hunza.[15] He was to prove a shrewd leader, and except for an end to the caravan raids, Hunzakut life under his reign and that of his successors, Ghazan Khan (1938–45) and Jamal Khan (1945–74), remained virtually unchanged. Of importance to the longevity tale about to unfold is the fact that the British military post remained at Gilgit, 60 miles from a semi-autonomous Hunza.

At the core of McCarrison's assertions had been the absence of certain common ailments among the Hunzakuts he treated. In his Mellon Lecture of 1921, McCarrison reported, "During my association with these people, I never saw a case of asthenic dyspepsia, of gastro or duodenal ulcer, or appendicitis . . . . While I cannot aver that all the maladies were quite unknown, I have the strongest reasons for the assertion that they were remarkably infrequent."[16] In *Studies in Deficiency Diseases*, published that same year, he put his point more boldly: "Such service as I was able to render them during the seven years I spent in their midst was confined chiefly to the treatments of accidental lesions, the removal of senile cataracts, plastic operations for granular lids, or the treatment of maladies wholly unconnected with the food supply. Appendicitis, so common in Europe, was unknown."[17] Later writings were to claim that Hunzakuts were free of cancer, heart disease, goiter, and cretinism.[18] What most intrigued McCarrison was the Hunzakut diet.

On the issue of the Hunzakuts' overall health and the superiority of their natural diet, McCarrison was spectacularly off base. The most persistent thread in the Hunza commentary, from the first notes by Dr. G.W. Leitner[19] and Major Bidulph[20] in the 1860s and '80s to the most recent governmental reports, is the insufficiency of the food supply. In spite of the marvelous terraces carved on slopes as steep as 60 degrees, the amount of land available for cultivation is so meager and the arid soil so poor that not enough food can be grown to sustain the population. By the late spring of each year the food reserves run out, bringing on what is called Starvation Springtime. A pattern of two or three meals a week is common during this time. The Hunzakuts become so undernourished that vitamin-deficiency diseases cause ugly sores to appear on their bodies. Subclinical rickets and scurvy occur. If the winter is unusually long or the first harvest poor, the effect is calamitous. Only massive emigration has kept the valley from periodic famines. It is ironic that McCarrison, a pioneer in understanding the central importance of vitamins and minerals to good health, should have chosen Hunza as an example of a place where people had good dietary habits. Rather it is an example of a place where people suffer from bad diet, from vitamin and mineral deficiencies. It would have served better as a warning of what happens when there are vitamin and mineral deficiencies. Indeed, if the Hunzakuts were as healthy as McCarrison believed, then the whole relationship of quality diet to good health would be called into question. But the Hunzakuts are far from healthy.

The most devastating evidence about diseases in Hunza is found in the work of John Clark. As we have said, Clark spent long periods of time in Hunza during every season, and he was one of the few Westerners to live independently of the Mir's largess. His interest in Hunza was based partly on his conviction that a modestly funded self-help program could create viable mountain economies that would be hostile to the central planning of the Communist regimes in China and the Soviet Union. To pursue his idea, Clark, a vertebrate paleontologist who was on the staff of the Chicago Museum of Natural History for many years, arrived in Hunza in 1950 with over a ton and a half of equipment and medicine. He had secured the cooperation of the Pakistan government by agreeing to make a free geological survey beyond that government's technical means, and he had obtained the Mir's lukewarm acceptance by pledging to open a dispensary. Nevertheless, regional officials in Gilgit accused him of being an American spy and plotted against him. In addition to the geological survey and dispensary, Clark opened a handicraft school for boys, planted three experimental gardens, and taught all who would listen about new seeds he was prepared to give away. His plans were so thorough that he even brought along butterfly nets to collect specimens for the Carnegie Collection of High Altitude Butterflies. The work was to be done by Hunzakut boys who would be paid for their efforts.

The Hunza that Clark came to know bore little resemblance to the Shangri-La depicted by Wrench and Rodale. From the first day, his dispensary was mobbed by the ailing. Although the facility kept irregular hours, Clark eventually treated 5,685 patients, or roughly one-fourth of the entire population. A great many of those he saw suffered from vitamin deficiencies or had stomach problems. Among the most common diseases were chronic dysentery, cataracts, malaria, impetigo, ringworm, trachoma, pneumonia, and some cases of tuberculosis.[21] Clark found that many Hunzakuts suffered from gastrointestinal pains, which he believed were due to the bitter apricot nut they used to flavor their wine. Malaria and dysentery reached epidemic proportions at various periods while he was in Hunza, and diseases were not confined to any one class. The royal family commandeered nearly a quarter of all medical supplies, particularly stomach remedies, and they would have taken more if he had not resisted their demands. Whenever Clark undertook local trips, he discovered that the Mir would spread word of his coming by telephone so that people from some of the outer villages could consult him for medical treatment.

Wrench had written that Hunza's vegetables were "much like ours,"[22] yet among the new crops introduced by Clark in 1950 were beets, lettuce, endive, radishes, turnips, spinach, yellow pear tomatoes, Brussels sprouts, and parsley: the heart of the Anglo-American garden. Clark also noted that the apricot trees had reddish leaves at the growing tips, a sign of soil deficiency. He found that manure was not plentiful and except for human waste had to be laboriously brought down from the heights where there were goats and sheep. There was so little vitamin D in the diet that calcium was difficult to assimilate. This caused the teeth of the Hunzakuts to be extremely soft and loose. Clark developed beriberi during his first winter there and thought the whole population had a deficiency of vitamin A, vitamin D, and vitamin B complex.

Support for Clark's observations was provided later in the decade by Barbara Mons, whose agenda included an inquiry into Hunzakut diseases. To that end she questioned Dr. Safdar Mahmood of the Pakistan Medical Corps, who had established a clinic in Hunza. Dr. Mahmood showed her how the light in his operating room was adjusted for the numerous appendectomies he performed. In 1958, he said, he had treated 348 cases of dysentery, one case of typhoid, 734 cases of intestinal disease, 290 malaria cases, 113 cases of rheumatic fever, and 426 goiters for a total of more than 1,900 cases in a population of from 26,000 to 30,000 persons.[23] Mons reported that spring was still a most difficult time of the year, but that the potatoes introduced by the British had helped stave off starvation.

Fifteen years after the Mons visit, the trail from Gilgit was being transformed into a military road to enable China to reinforce Pakistan in case of war with India. Using the new artery in the making was Alexander Leaf, who found health conditions in Hunza not much better than those observed by Mons and Clark. Dr. Sahoor Ahmed, who had volunteered to serve as a medical doctor in Hunza to fulfill his required two years of military duty, had been at his post for eight months when Leaf arrived. Dr. Ahmed reported that there were now eight dispensaries and one hospital in Hunza, with the dispensaries staffed by nonphysicians. Infant mortality was higher than in Punjab, and diarrheal disorders were the major cause. Leaf summarized Ahmed's views as follows:

[Ahmed] found malnutrition, anemia, worms, goiter with many cretins, and pneumonia to be common. There was a smallpox outbreak with three or four deaths in the past year . . . . Tuberculosis is found among the young males who go "down country" for military service and employment in Pakistan, but women also have tuberculosis. There is much bronchial asthma . . . . Everyone, he claimed, had worms—round worms, tape worms, and thread worms.[24]

How is it possible to square the observations of Clark, Mons, Mahmood, and Ahmed with that of McCarrison and the food faddists? One answer is that most visitors came to Hunza when the weather had cleared and the valley was in full bloom. By this time, many symptoms of malnutrition had been cured or ameliorated by the first harvest. In addition, visitors were usually guests of the Mir and had little familiarity with the local language or with Asian culture in general. Understandably, the Mir, seeking good publicity for his realm, was not about to show his sick and lame or to talk about the perennial threat of famine. One might argue that pre-1940 Hunza was more prosperous, but this is contradicted by repeated observations from the earliest visitors about the inadequate food supply and the fact that new crops and medicines introduced by the Europeans had been helpful. But McCarrison had spent seven full years at the Gilgit Agency. Surely he knew Hunza better than those who stayed even as long as two years.

Perhaps not. It is possible that McCarrison's visits were limited to the summer season or that he never actually set foot in Hunza proper at all! McCarrison's station was Gilgit; he would not have gone to Hunza at the end of the summer for fear of getting snowed in, and he would not have gone immediately at the end of winter because of the dangerous trail. His writings give no indication that he ever saw the cycle of seasons as Clark and the Lorimers did. It is noticeable, too, that while McCarrison comments on the precarious nature of the food supply, he does not mention the diseases of malnutrition that his physician's eye would have spotted at once. It is also extremely suspicious that in his writings about the Hunzakuts he is coy about naming them, usually referring to "peoples of the Himalayan foothills." In one essay, McCarrison stated that his Hunzakut patients came 60 miles to be treated: the exact distance between Gilgit and Hunza.[25] There is every likelihood that the majority of Hunzakuts he treated, perhaps the only ones, were soldiers of the Hunza Rifles, the finest specimens of Hunzakut manhood. This interpretation is strengthened by his admission that he never treated a female. Other sources indicate that the Hunzakuts did not shield their women from outsiders, and even though it was forty years later, Clark, Mahmood, and Ahmed all treated female patients. With the exception of the royal entourage, women were not allowed to travel and could not venture as far as Gilgit. The Mirs, in fact, restricted all travel unless it was for a permanent move or in their service. Only the most unusual circumstances would have brought the seriously ill, the old, and children to Gilgit.

McCarrison's terminology is not very satisfactory either. References to Indian peoples habitually mix caste, religious, and ethnic classifications. His often-used phrase "the fighting races of India" includes Pathans, Sikhs, Punjabis, Dogras, Rajputs, Brahmins, and Jats. He wrote, "Among these, the Sikhs, the Pathans, and certain Himalayan tribes, one cannot find whether in the East or West, finer physical development, hardihood, and powers of energy."[26] He credits these to diet. The Sikhs favored food with a root base and the Pathans cereal, while the Hunzakuts had a combination of both. Other McCarrison essays compare Hunzakuts to tribes of the Nile and the west coast of Africa. None of these African or Asian groups has ever been cited for long life or immunity to disease. The impression is strong that McCarrison imbued the Hunzakuts with the benefits of his perfect diet without closely examining their lives or their general health. He was to be in India many times after his 1904-11 tour of duty, but he never again visited Hunza, and in his collected writings, published in 1972, no work dealing with Hunza is included. Nor did McCarrison ever write an essay in which the Hunzakuts were the major topic. All this seems odd treatment for a people he had identified early in his distinguished career as the living confirmation of his basic theories.

Except for McCarrison, none of the on-site writers before the 1950s mentions extraordinary longevity in Hunza, or large numbers of older inhabitants, much less supercentenarians. Rudyard Kipling, who used every legend he could when writing about India, did not mention longevity when he used Hunza as a setting for episodes in *Kim* and *The Man Who Would Be King*. At best, the historical record contains an occasional reference to an individual's being old, without a specific age cited. The Lorimers, when told one man was a centenarian, thought him to be in his 90s, and they described a woman of 50 as "a beautiful old woman."[27] At the handicraft school, Clark found that his boys and their parents had only an approximate sense of their age. One boy jumped in age from 13 to 17 in less than two full years. Clark concluded, "There is no evidence that anyone ever reached one hundred years of age in Hunza."[28] Mons supplemented this view by commenting, "That they are abnormally long-lived is impossible to prove for the simple reason that no record is kept of a child's birth. They do not know how old they are."[29]

At the time McCarrison first went to Gilgit, the average life span in the Kashmir Valley was in the early twenties. People in their 50s were considered old, and a nonagenarian was thought a wonder.[30] By this standard, if Hunzakuts were reaching their 70s and 80s in any number, they might well be thought of as long-living. Likewise, while Hunzakut infant mortality rates were much higher than those in the developed world, they always compared well with those of Kashmir. By taking McCarrison's comments out of their historical context, popularizers may have seriously distorted his original intent. In any case, his claims were never expressed in numbers but only in generalities.

Among the few visitors to give specific ages of Hunzakuts were the Shors. They wrote that the 12-man Council of Elders had one 97-year-old representative, while the rest were in their 70s and 80s. At social events, the Shors found other men who claimed to be nonagenarians even though they were not members of the Council. They did not report on any centenarians. At about the time of their first visit, the Mir had received an inquiry from J. Rodale concerning Hunzakut life spans. The Mir responded in a letter dated August 24, 1947 that, barring accidents, most of his people lived at least into their mid-80s.[31] A few years later, after the Mir had visited the West, he was telling visitors like Banik and Hoffman that some of his subjects had lived to 120 and an isolated few to 140—a rather spectacular revision. By the time Leaf came on the scene, the maximum age cited by the Mir was under 110. Only a few centenarians were available for actual examination at that time, but Leaf was assured that previous generations had been healthier, happier, and longer-lived. The only attempt at a proof of old age was the statement of one man that when he was in his 20s he had served in the War of 1891 as one of the Mir's bodyguards.

Women are noticeably absent from Hunzakut longevity claims. Apparently, like the Hunzakut ewes and mares, they are not as strong as the male of the species, an exception to the worldwide rule. Also absent are multi-generational families. Since Hunzakuts often marry while in their teens, if many people were living into their 90s, five-generation families should be available. This would certainly be true if, as later claimed by the Mir, there were scores of centenarians alive in the 1940s and 50s. Yet Leaf saw only four-generational families, and Clark, while told of five-generational families, saw only four generations among Hunzakuts he knew well. Clark made the further point that since the poor mineral content of the food produced extremely soft and loose teeth, a genuine Hunzakut centenarian would likely have all of his or her teeth ground to the gums. He had never seen such a Hunzakut. His own evaluation was that because of the terrible hardships of mountain life, those who succeeded in living past 60 were good septuagenarian and octogenarian bets, but that only a few survived much of their tenth decade.

All that remains of McCarrison's vision is the strong physique of the Hunzakuts. Here he is on unassailable ground. The strength, agility, and hardiness of the Hunzakuts has been remarked on by every visitor. One veteran mountaineer considered them "the world's best slab climbers."[32] Another saw a man dive into an ice-filled river.[33] Several observed that Hunzakuts could travel over Himalayan terrain at the rate of more than 40 miles a day.[34] Other examples of endurance lace every Hunza diary or book. The over-all strength of the Hunzakuts has been confirmed in repeated medical tests as well.

The toughness of the Hunzakuts can be misunderstood if it is taken out of the context of Himalayan culture. Many explorers who extolled the virtues of the Hunzakuts made equally flattering comments about Pathans and Sherpas. Faddist writers who quote them overlook this, giving the impression that the Hunzakuts were considered a unique biological elite. Racist overtones also creep into much Hunza commentary. The Hunzakuts are described as being lighter-skinned and taller than their neighbors, as if these were attributes of health. Some of the most balanced judgments came from the British military. The legendary Colonel Young-husband wrote:

> they [the Hunzakuts] were capable of marching 40 miles in the day armed and equipped across the mountains. And they had an extraordinary élan and capacity for working rapidly under their own leaders. In Chital, Yesin, and other little states on the frontier, *I subsequently found the same thing.* [Emphasis added].[35]

Generally when there is a sustained comparison of Hunzakuts with other Himalayans, it is with their nearest neighbors, the Na-girs, who live on the opposite side of the Hunza River. In 1893 the British staged sports contests, and the Hunzakuts emerged victori-ous every time. Most subsequent writing refers to their continuing physical superiority to the Nagirs. The Hunzakuts are said to be neat, friendly, and hygienic, while the Nagirs are described as slovenly, surly, and dirty. The Hunzakuts also are praised for being better agriculturalists, engineers, hunters, and soldiers. While there may be an element of truth in these dichotomies, the qualities mentioned often focus on just those areas most favorable to the Hunzakuts and prove much less than the authors believe. Much too much has certainly been made of the belief that the two groups had a common ancestor and that they are separated only by a single river. The shorter and darker cast of the Nagir physical type comes from frequent intermarriage with the people of the Kashmir Valley, who have influenced Nagir in numerous ways. And the Hunza River is no quaint mountain stream. For centuries it was traversed by a narrow rope bridge which collapsed several times every summer. As a cultural barrier it was every bit as formidable as the Great Wall of China.

Of possible health significance is the extraordinary personal hygiene of the Hunzakuts which is in marked contrast to all the surrounding peoples. This could have had a positive effect, particularly during the time when infectious diseases, unchecked by modern drugs, were the most common threat to health. Even this virtue, however, may have been overstressed or confused by subjective value judgments. Too often, references to slovenly dress simply mean that clothing styles are unlike those seen in Europe.

Another factor not fully appreciated by naive travelers was the rivalry between Hunza and Nagir. If one journeyed to Hunza first and became friendly with its Mir, the reception across the river was not likely to be cordial. The British officers who happened to befriend the Nagirs first usually preferred them to the Hunzakuts, believing them to be quicker learners and to possess a more democratic temperament. The military certainly was not impressed by the bravery or skills of the Hunzakut fighters. After losing the major battles of 1891, the Hunzakuts had not waged a guerrilla war but had meekly accepted the new Mir's authority.

The only reason they had ever been the senior partners in the Nagir-Hunza alliance was their geographic situation. Nagir was in a cul-de-sac, which made it more vulnerable than Hunza to a prolonged siege or to a frontal assault. Military diarists noted other significant terrain factors. Hunza faced south and got far more sunlight than Nagir. During two months of the year, some villages in Nagir could count the daily sunlight in minutes if they got any sun at all. The effects on the growing season, crop quality, and individual dispositions are obvious.

The Hunza Council of Elders too has been described in various ways. The faddists have tried to liken it to a democratic or people's court of venerables. Such a view sadly underestimates the absolute authority of the Mir. Early in the British contact, Younghusband showed a new rifle to a Mir, who told him to fire at a man across the valley. When Younghusband objected, the Mir became incensed, stating that the target was his man and had no more rights than his goats or sheep.[36] The shrewdest evaluation of the council was made by Clark. He saw that the council members did not hold office by virtue of age or as representatives of their local villages, but were appointees of the Mir. Clark witnessed overnight changes in the council when the Mir became displeased. This sort of arrangement has little relation to Western concepts of parliament or even a jury of peers. The daily convening of the council was more akin to the practice in Saudi Arabia, where even the humblest subject may come to court to present a direct appeal to the ruling aristocracy. The justice obtained may be swift, fair, and humane, but it is linked to the notion of the divine right of sovereigns.

The policy of the Mirs from 1892 to 1974 was consistent. They hoped to hold on to their power by keeping the population as insulated from outside influence as possible. The Hunza Rifles were disbanded at the first opportunity and with varying success.

The Mirs discouraged the idea of their young men being eligible for military duty "down country." Travel that did not result in permanent migration was discouraged, foreign visitors were carefully monitored with shortwave radios, and the telephones installed by the British were handled in a way that strengthened the Mirs' control rather than opening Hunza to wider cross-cultural contacts.

For more than eighty years, the Mirs maneuvered adroitly between contending foreign and regional powers. When the Hindu leadership in Kashmir decided to align that state with India even though the population was predominantly Moslem, the Mir withdrew Hunza from Kashmir to become part of Islamic Pakistan. In 1971, he explained to Leaf that he had been successful in combating corrosive outside influences, especially among "the students" who were restless.[37] Early in 1974, when informed that the Pakistan government intended to terminate Hunza's autonomy, the Mir said the people supported him overwhelmingly and would revolt if he were displaced. But that September, nine hundred years of autonomous and sometimes benevolent feudalism came to an end with the support of most of the Hunzakuts. Although the Mir was stripped of his secular power, he was allowed to continue to serve as a representative of the Aga Khan and was given a princely pension and a lowland palace. To the end, the man who had done so much to promote the myth of Hunzakut longevity continued to play the Shangri-La game. He told reporters of the international press that there were only five or six centenarians presently alive, but that before the work on the military road had begun in 1958 there had been 50 to 60.[38] He did not explain why Mons, the Shors, Clark, the Lorimers, and so many others had never seen them. By 1979, when the Karakoram Highway was formally opened, the Mir had died, but his 36-year-old son and successor, Ghazanfar Ali, was still fielding queries about supercentenarians. "No, no, not 120 and 130 years. But we do have a lot of people between 90 and 100 years old," he replied. The reasons given for such ages were "good, pure food, peace, freedom from stress, and no crime."[39]

It is amazing that the myth of Hunzakut longevity has persisted for such a long time on such flimsy evidence. Hunza was never significantly different from dozens of other tiny Himalayan mirdoms. Since the first British contacts in the nineteenth century, the specifics have altered, but not the patterns of internal life and foreign contacts. The Dowager Empress and the Tsar have been replaced by feuding commissars. The British influence has given way to that of the United States. Territorial and religious rivalries have created the states of Pakistan and India, still squabbling with each other and with Afghanistani and Kashmiri politicians about viable frontiers. Meanwhile, the old trade route coming down from Central Asia has become the Karakoram Highway, with the little huts once maintained by the Mir for travelers replaced by hotels and camping grounds capable of accommodating 12,000 annual visitors.

The Hunza myth demonstrates anew that however depressing the human record may be, the species wants to believe that somewhere on earth it has managed to produce a society where war, crime, poverty, injustice, and disease have been abolished. For almost a hundred years, the Anglo-American world has believed that the society existed in a tiny kingdom just beyond the last imperial outpost. But Hunza was never Shangri-La. The only Valley of the Blue Moon is in the fiction of James Hilton, and unless they are in the entourage of the Abominable Snowman, there are no supercentenarians in the Himalyas.

# 7. SERENDIPITOUS SHERINGHAM AND CAMBRIDGESHIRE

*I was born in a garden, and I have been in one ever since.—James Chapman, age 103*

GERONTOLOGISTS WHO HAD BEEN WARY of longevity stories emanating from isolated and distant regions of the world were startled in the early 1970s when a village only 125 miles from London was thrust into the longevity spotlight.[1] David Davies, one of the advocates of the Vilcabamba claims, had discovered that in Upper Sheringham the number of inhabitants over age 60 was more than triple the national British average. The population of approximately 300 contained a number of nonagenarians and a vigorous centenarian. Davies' analysis of the Sheringham soil had shown that it was unusually rich in minerals, particularly selenium, identified previously as a possible prolongevous substance. As almost every villager ate vegetables grown in the local gardens and greenhouses, the tentative linkage of mineral-rich soil and long life showed promise.

Proceeding on these few facts, journalists and television reporters from several nations descended on the quiet Norfolk village, which seemed to belong to another and better era. Its houses, built of gray sea stone in styles that blend into the natural landscape as if planned by a consummate architect, caught the attention of many of the photojournalists. Others took haunting shots of All

Saints Church, built in the 1300s, and made appropriate close-ups of the graveyard stones marking the long life spans of deceased villagers. Still others favored the Red Lion Pub, which still served a gigantic "Ploughman's Share" luncheon. If serenity and beauty were Methuselah factors, then Upper Sheringham was a Britannic Shangri-La.

My own visit to Upper Sheringham in 1978 went beyond these diverting aesthetic factors to consideration of more prosaic census figures. While it was quite true that 18 percent of the Upper Sheringham population was over 60, compared with the national average of 5% and regional average of 12%, it was also true that the entire region was in demographic imbalance due to economic factors.[2] At the same time that the lovely shoreline, sloping hills, and relatively low cost of living had attracted an influx of retirees, economic stagnation had been driving out many younger people. "Chick" Denis, an elected official of Sheringham proper, told me that from 65 to 85% of the population was not native-born and that many of those in the age range of 25 to 45 had left the area to find employment.[3]

The pattern Denis described was typical for the whole coast. Consulting the census figures for the 1970s, I determined that the population over 60 in areas surrounding Sheringham differed from it by only a few percentage points. The same results occurred when the percentage of longevous people was calculated, with some neighboring areas having a slightly higher and some a slightly lower number than Sheringham.[4]

The results for Upper Sheringham, a village separated from the main town by less than a mile, were further imbalanced by a retiree's home located at the edge of one of the approaches to the village. The Dales, a beautiful residence which once belonged to the vicar, generally housed about 30 persons over age 60. Its most famous occupant in the decade of the '70s was Frederick

Cornelius, who had been born on January 14, 1874, in Dover and died on December 24, 1979, three weeks short of 106.[5] At 104, Cornelius was still taking buses and taxicabs unaided and liked to stroll the quarter-mile to the local post office. He conversed lucidly, telling visitors of his fighting days in India, when he had been a color sergeant in the Scottish Rifles. Enjoying his notoriety as one of the oldest men in Great Britain, Cornelius talked about awards from his old regiment, payments from his insurance company, telegrams from Queen Elizabeth, and similar events. Most mornings he would be up before six, bathing, shaving, and dressing himself before going out for a walk in the lovely garden adjacent to The Dales. The final phase of his morning routine was to take up a position under a broad-branched tree where he fed birds with a tranquil dignity that conjured up images of St. Francis of Assisi.

I visited with Frederick Cornelius in The Dales' garden and found him charming, but his longevity had little significance for the selenium theorists, as he was already in his late 90s before coming to The Dales, and unlike most others in the home, he had not even lived much of his life in Norfolk. After his military service he had sold insurance and then had been a greengrocer in Kent. In one of those ironies which make longevity research so fascinating, Cornelius was advised at age 49 to retire because of a heart ailment. The worried doctor had long since died, while Cornelius, though frail and sleeping away a goodly part of the day, could still handle his own affairs with considerable humor. Pointing to his ears, Cornelius informed me that his deafness made "a proper conversation difficult," but he knew what I was interested in and began a discourse about his personal habits, diet, and views of the world. Mrs. Musgrove, the director of The Dales, who joked with him a great deal, commented, "I think he's at a point where he only hears what he wishes to hear." Although newspaper photographs showed him clutching a bottle of stout or a cigar, Cornelius did not drink alcohol in any form, had never smoked, and had been a light eater all his life. Until his final days he kept a watchful eye on his finances, flirted with the staff, and took pleasure in playing whist, checkers, and dominoes.

The Upper Sheringham longevity legend might be put to rest at this point except for the work of a remarkable local scholar, A. Campbell Erroll. After retiring from a banking firm in London, Erroll made a hobby of local history. His greatest service was the methodical tabulating of registers of local parishes. Gathering together every scrap of information available about the area, he published a history of Sheringham in 1970 and deposited research materials in the Norfolk Library in Norwich.[6]

Long before the longevity story became popular, Erroll had computed all the births, baptisms, and deaths recorded in Old Saints Church from 1789 through the mid-1860s. After 1868 the church records cease to be comprehensive, because of new churches in the area and dissent within the Church of England. Persons born in Upper Sheringham might be buried elsewhere, and vice versa, making the reconstruction of individual life spans difficult or impossible. During the early periods, however, one can follow most persons from the cradle to the grave with some knowledge of the kind of work they did and which part of Sheringham they lived in. Not the least of Erroll's contributions was to point out that the persons buried in Old Saints include not only the inhabitants of Upper Sheringham, but those of the town as well, people who generally obtained their vegetables from the same sources as the rest of Norfolk.

A study within the wider Sheringham project was Erroll's attempt to re-create the life of the village from 1791 to 1838. Out of a population of about 350 persons, Erroll found that most of the population were agricultural workers and fishermen, followed by craftspeople and mechanics. There were also a handful of merchants, one schoolmaster, one vicar, and one gentleman. Then Erroll made a fascinating discovery: "It may be significant to note that of the 206 persons whose age at death is known, seven attained the age of 90 or more, forty-four were 80 or over, and one hundred and six were over 70."[7] These figures work out to at least 30 percent of the population living to an age greater than 70. Making a further breakdown, Erroll was able to determine that there were no significant differences in life span between those residing in Upper Sheringham and those in the town.

Erroll had stumbled upon a two-tier longevity profile. Throughout most of the nineteenth century, those who did not die as infants or children had a very good probability of living past 60. Page after page of the registers, written in the neat script of various vicars, shows that deaths occurred mainly either under the age of 20 or after 60.[8] From 1813 to 1857, out of 800 burials there are 66 septuagenarians, 63 octogenarians, and nine nonagenarians. From 1858 to 1921, there are 1,600 burials, with 381 septuagenarians, 160 octogenarians, and 30 nonagenarians. Both time periods work out to about 18 percent of the total population living over seventy years. Even accounting for the fact that after the mid-1800s the records do not give a comprehensive picture of the area's population, there is the strongest suggestion that Sheringham, while not having phenomenal longevity, has been an area where life spans have constantly been at the upper levels of normal. The oldest recorded age at death before 1960 was 98.

In follow-up work covering the period 1960-78, Erroll consulted the burial records for the six major religious institutions in the district. While the significance of the number of persons dying at advanced ages cannot be determined because of the tremendous immigration of retirees, in a period of eighteen years, there had been 74 deaths of persons over age 90, nine of whom exceeded the longest life span recorded in the preceding two centuries. There were three centenarians, one person over 99, and three over 98. At the very least these findings indicate that the Sheringham environment was not hostile to long life.

Life in seaside Sheringham during the nineteenth century has been graphically reconstructed by Stanley Craske, another dedicated local historian. He has drawn extensively from stories told to him by grandparents, parents, and fisherfolk. Until mid-century, Upper Sheringham had been the undisputed center of social gravity, where the gentry, vicar, and schoolmaster lived and entertained. On the shoreline were fishing families operating some two hundred fifty boats. Constantly referred to as insolent rebels, the people of Lower Sheringham came to be called Shannocks, from the old English word "shanny" meaning "reckless" or "daredevil." The Shannocks asserted their independence by leaving the Church of England in great numbers to become Methodists or to enroll in the Salvation Army. One of the prides of the community was a lifeboat service established in 1838. When ships floundered in the North Sea, the Shannocks rowed out to save lives and to claim salvage rights.

The fisherfolk were extremely hardy, and like the Abkhasians, they never really retired. Men worked in the boats until their 70s and 80s and then mended nets and performed other shore work. Because the males went to sea during their early teens, the women had more formal education. As a consequence, in addition to traditional household duties, women managed the family finances and often instructed their husbands in reading and writing, thus enjoying a status unusual for most working-class women of that era.

Many of the octogenarians and nonagenarians found in the Sheringham registers belong to the strong-willed fishing clans. Anecdotes about them recorded by Craske confirm what Thoms had written about the same name running in a family. It is said that at one time in Sheringham there may have been as many as 16 men named John Henry Grice. They were differentiated by their nicknames. This same practice occurred in the West family, in which fishermen of the same name were known as Spider West, Never Sweat West, Sugar West, Teapot West, and other charming sobriquets.

Returning to contemporary Upper Sheringham, if people living at The Dales are excluded, in 1978 the oldest inhabitant was Rosie Runcieman, age 90, and the oldest native-born inhabitant was Reggie Chastney, age 83, whose family name is frequently found among the long lives recorded in Old Saints Church. Chastney informed me that his parents and relatives used to tell him that it was typical for workers to walk both ways to farms five and ten miles distant each day, an observation repeated by several persons knowledgeable about the area. Ivy Chastney, age 73, Reggie's wife, thought it might be important that the area had a tradition of homemade fruit wines and beer. It was the couple's opinion that people weren't living as long as they used to because life had gotten considerably softer.

A health advantage enjoyed by the people of the entire Norfolk coast is that they have been able to relish their pastoral cake without passing up the benefits of modern medicine. Easy access to medicines and treatment relating to minor diseases, which are thus kept from developing into something more serious, are probably more important to longevity than surgery or high-technology medicine. The people of Norfolk also share in the welfare state. The Dales belongs to a category of homes operated for seniors who need some assistance but can manage most of their daily tasks on their own. It provides only minimal medical assistance, being more like a government-run boardinghouse than a hospital. Meals and housekeeping are provided for residents, but if they wish, they may help with both. Half the residents at The Dales have private rooms, while the other half share their quarters. Roommates are chosen by the residents rather than being assigned by the director, and individuals volunteer to become residents rather than being assigned by an agency. The waiting lists are long, and health professionals feel that less than 10% of the population that would like to use the service are being accommodated. Frederick Cornelius stated bluntly that he would not have been able to enjoy as many birthdays as he had if he had not been able to live in a place like The Dales where he could be helped when the need arose, yet could preserve his independence.

A similar home is in Overstrand, less than an hour's drive from Sheringham. Called Sea Marge, it was once owned by a German industrialist. Later the mansion served as a hotel for British dignitaries, including Winston Churchill, George Bernard Shaw, and King George V. Gracing one of the rooms of Sea Marge in 1978 was a huge photograph taken seven years earlier showing eleven women with a combined age of 1,039 years. The occasion was the celebration by ten nonagenarians of the hundredth birthday of Mr. M. E. Cubitt. Robert Devenny, the director of Sea Marge, told me that the nonagenarian residents he had known through the years had lived rather ordinary lives before coming to Sea Marge and had no peculiar dietary or personal habits. Most had been agricultural workers, housewives, and domestics, but he thought this mainly reflected the need of the poor to take advantage of government services while the middle class and the rich made other provisions. Few of the nonagenarians he had known had ever consumed much alcohol or smoked at any time during their lives. Devenny emphasized that homes like The Dales and Sea Marge were unusual in that they had been converted from luxury housing. In most of the system, the homes were expressly constructed for older people, having such facilities as ramps and roomy elevators.

Orchard House, a low-slung modern edifice of the kind Devenny had in mind, is located in Sawston, a town just outside Cambridge. What drew me to this institution was that in 1978 it was the home of the oldest woman in Great Britain, 108-year-old Alice Empelton. The ambiance at Orchard was much more dynamic than at Sea Marge or The Dales. Although housing many permanent residents, it was also an active service center. Hot meals were prepared and taken to persons living at home, and many individuals used the facilities for daytime social functions. One service that Brenda Tarrant, the director, thought important in promoting longevity was allowing old people to live in the facility if the families they usually resided with wanted to take a vacation or were temporarily unable to care for them. At the time of my visit, there were three centenarians living at Orchard House. The youngest, Flo Evans, a little over a hundred, was too ill to be seen, but Alice Empelton was more than pleased to have a visitor.

Until the age of 106 Alice had lived by herself in a small bungalow, having an occasional meal brought in or getting assistance for heavier house chores. She expressed a strong desire to get back on her own if she could somehow regain her strength. In spite of poor hearing and frailty, Alice was alert and extremely congenial. After a whole morning's interview, instead of being tired, she said she felt invigorated. She enjoyed being with other people and didn't mind expressing her views. Far from harping on the "good old days," she felt there had been tremendous improvements in society since her birth in 1870, and she looked forward to more. Having been a victim of poverty, she had no love for the well-to-do:

> I'm Labor. Always was. I worked for them. I canvassed for
> them. Yes, I'm Labor. Staunch. So was my husband. He was

for them too. I'd work for them again. You know, I saw Queen
Victoria at her Diamond Jubilee in 1897. I was on my honey-
moon. I thought she looked rather shabby for a queen . . . .
When I was young, girls couldn't have a career. I wanted to be a
schoolteacher. I went through exams, but when it came to the
supplementary, I couldn't take it, because my mother could not
afford to support me for three more years. There was no factory
work then, so I had to get work as a domestic. To this day I
remember how I walked up the stairs for two hours at a time
every day hauling hot water for them. There were only jugs and
washstands in those days. You don't know what a miracle a
hot-water faucet is. You just can't imagine. Another thing to
remember is that we didn't have help then. There was no un-
employment benefits, no medical assistance. We just suffered.

Alice went on to say that until her marriage at age 27, she had
never ceased to feel tired. Although she had never had any children of her own, she had brought up eight, with some of whom
she was still in contact. "I didn't have time to darn my stockings,"
she says without a hint of regret. In later life, particularly after
she became widowed in 1939, she spent a lot of time in her
flower and vegetable gardens as well as remaining active in
social causes. Alice had never had much use for medicine and
was not a big eater. "I've always liked fruit. An orange a day is
good to keep you going."

As the interview with Alice drew to a close, her reminiscences
were interrupted by the entrance of a jaunty white-haired woman
using an aluminum walker. The newcomer was Rachel Rennie,
who could have been taken for 74 as easily as her actual 104. She
had come to report to Alice on newspaper and television coverage
of Alice's recent birthday party. Almost totally blind, Rachel had
a cheerful disposition and a blissful singsong cadence in her

voice. She quipped that she listened to rather than watched the television program. The two centenarians had met only recently, and Rachel was eager to know more about her new friend's life. A temporary resident at Orchard House, who would return to her daughter's home when her daughter came back from a vacation, Rachel spoke little about her own life except to say that she had walked a great deal and liked to exercise. Asked her reaction to Orchard House, she thought it was "a bit quiet" and was anxious to get home. "It's unsettling to be away from your things."

Brenda Tarrant and her husband knew of several other centenarians living in Cambridgeshire. One of their favorites was Mrs. Florence Jeaps, age 104, a lively conversationalist. Another was Mrs. Polly Wilson, also 104, who had had a sweet pea named in her honor by the W.J. Unwin Seed Company, where she had been employed for seventy years. Mrs. Wilson had been among the firm's first women employees, and she had held her position until age 100. Her special relationship to the company dated back many decades to a time when, as a midwife, she had saved the life of the firm's present chairman, grandson of its founder. She lived in Histon, some miles on the other side of Cambridgeshire, but she had attended Alice's 108th birthday party. The Tarrants mentioned still other lively centenarians and commented that most of them took an occasional drink. Without naming names, Norman Tarrant said that at least one of the ladies over 103 kept a bottle of brandy in her walker in case a nip was needed for a quick spurt of energy.

Having three centenarians under one roof and a cluster of even more in a small geographic area was a far cry from the time William Thoms had feared there might not be any genuine centenarians at all. The existence of the longevous ladies of Cambridgeshire also underscored the rapid rise in the number of British centenarians since the conclusion of World War II.

Additional information about what kind of people were becoming centenarians in a place like Cambridgeshire was available in local newspapers. From January, 1974, through September, 1978, the *Cambridge Evening News* published numerous stories, mainly obituaries and birthday coverage, concerning 37 centenarians. These included 33 local people, two visitors, and two individuals living elsewhere in Great Britain. Fourteen of the local centenarians could not be traced beyond a name and address, but backup material on the others was available through reporters, relatives, neighbors, medical personnel, and personal interviews.[9]

Thirty of the 33 local people were women—a percentage generally considered a consequence of the casualties suffered in the wars fought by Great Britain in the preceding hundred years. Of the 16 women for whom there were substantial data, 15 were from working-class or agricultural backgrounds. Most had worked as domestics at some time during their lives. The exception was Dame Harriet Chick, a professional nutritionist whose ideas about diet were similar to McCarrison's. Most of the women and all of the men had been residents of the many rural hamlets characteristic of the region. Nine of the women had led full lives that they or others considered vigorous. Sarah Fullard, for example, had taken many cycling trips around Great Britain with her father. More typical were the accounts of long walks to work. By 1978 the majority of the women were deceased, only a few of them having lived more than a short time past their 101st birthdays, but there were four still alive who were over 104: Florence Jeaps, Rachel Rennie, Polly Wilson, and Alice Empelton.

The three male centenarians, Horace Williams, James Sellers, and Horace Bull, had slightly different collective profiles in terms of professions, having been, respectively, a headmaster, an accountant, and a butcher, but they had all been extremely vigorous individuals. Williams and Sellers had been cycling enthusiasts,

Sellers stating that as a young Romeo he had frequently cycled from London to Cambridge to court the woman he eventually married. Horace Bull had devoted many of his later years to outdoor activities, presiding at sporting events and earning the title of Britain's eldest and most celebrated angler. At 99 he had climbed up on the roof of his cottage to make needed repairs, and he had celebrated his hundredth birthday with a day of deep-sea fishing. Bull died at 101, of a virus which had made his housekeeper and daughter seriously ill as well. Before then, his housekeeper stated that Mr. Bull had given no indication of physical decline and was planning hunting and fishing trips in various parts of Great Britain.

The two centenarian visitors described by the press were Walter Terry, age 100, an active horse owner, and James Chapman, age 103, who had had tea with Mrs. Empelton. Since his retirement, Chapman had taken his first rides in an airplane, a glider, and a balloon. He was hoping to arrange for his first rides in a submarine and a helicopter. Two other centenarians written about were the deceased Sarah Ellen Morgan, age 111, the most recent British member of the exclusive superlongevous club, and lively Elizabeth Archer, age 100, who had made a stir with her annual trip to a Norfolk seaside holiday camp. Mrs. Archer had worked as a home helper until into her 80s and still did her own housework, mowed her own lawn, and gardened. She continued to enjoy a glass of sherry and liked to play bingo.

The hamlets of Sheringham and Cambridgeshire are examples of communities where the residents have maintained the superior environment of the past while still enjoying the advantages of a highly developed modern society. As elsewhere, the major ingredients for unusual life spans appear to be a highly developed self-esteem, a lifelong history of physical activity, and a diet of common foods rich in natural nutrients. Sophisticated social and medical services and rapid communications also have played a role in the British longevity boom. Most importantly, the high spirits of the British centenarians and the long life spans recorded in Sheringham for more than two hundred years should be eye-openers for those who believe that lively long-living people can be found only in exotic locales.

# 8. Rethinking The First Ninety-Nine

*For when they [the worthy young men] saw their parents and kindred snatcht away in the midst of their days and me contrarwise, at the age of eightie and one, strong and lustie; they had a great desire to know the way of my life . . . —Luigi Cornaro*

RESEARCHERS ALL OVER THE GLOBE have carried on the age verification work begun by William Thoms in the 1870s. None of them has ever found verifiable documentation for a human whose life span extended to 123 years. A small cluster of individuals, mostly deceased, with claimed life spans of 116 to 122 years have been identified, but their verifications are faulty or incomplete. Thus supercentenarians, if they exist at all, are truly wonders of nature in whom chance has played a decisive role. Much the same can be said of the superlongevous group of 110- to 115-year-olds. Proofs for this age group are valid, but the total numbers of those living and dead are exceedingly small. They too compose a rare breed, the outer limits of fully verifiable longevity.

In contrast, centenarians aged 100 to 109 are not particularly difficult to locate or verify. Just within the United States the number of living centenarians at any given moment since the 1980s has always been at least 2,000 to 3,000. Most of this population dies shortly after passing its 100th year which links it more closely with nonagenarians than the biological elite of hypothetical supercentenarians or even the superlongevous. This is in line with the finding by gerontologists that the maximum life span for humans has remained constant for all of recorded history. Short of revolutionary medical breakthroughs, the maximum human life span is not likely to change even if the percentage and number of individuals who become centenarians rises dramatically.

This apparent anomaly stems from the fact that while the maximum life span has remained constant, the average life span has been increasing. Starting with records available from the Classical Age in Greece and proceeding to the eighteenth century, we can determine that the average life span in Europe has been between 20 and 40. Beginning in the 1800s that average began to rise and has now reached the mid-70s. But this gain in average life span has resulted from wiping out early death in infancy and childhood, not from more people living longer. Generally speaking, until recently, once Europeans reached adulthood, their remaining life span was relatively constant whatever epoch they were born in. Average life spans in the United States reflect this phenomenon. From the time of the signing of the Declaration of Independence in 1776 through the 1990s, the years remaining to anyone who reaches 60 have remained stable at 15 to 20 years.

The implications of this for those who seek to achieve a life span of 100 years and beyond is heartening. The average life expectancy for any American born in 1995 has risen to 75. Given that great numbers of Americans continue to have very unhealthy habits, live in unhealthy conditions, or work at dangerous occupations, simple logic leads to the conclusion that anyone who avoids the most obvious antilongevous habits and pays even minimal attention to prolongevous factors should do much better than average. Adding even a rudimentary longevity agenda makes the prospect of living a vigorous 80 to 100 years a reasonable goal.

The best guidelines to any longevity agenda are found in studies of people who actually achieved long life. The available data on such populations is overwhelming. Studies of particular interest to Americans include the Duke Longitudinal Study of Aging, the Baltimore Longitudinal Study of Aging, the National Institute of Mental Health Longitudinal Study, and the Duke-Chapel Hill Study of Aging. These projects have involved a total of 2,000 individuals at least 60 years of age at the time the particular study began. Of additional value is research directed at preventing heart disease, the major cause of death in the United States. The works of Nathan Pritikin and Dean Ornish are especially relevant. A broader context to the problem is provided by the classic Framingham Massachusetts Longitudinal Study. Numerous other projects deal exclusively with persons reasonably identifiable as centenarians. Using Social Security records, which are far from infallible but certainly identify the longevous, Osborn Segerberg has derived a longevity profile based on the lives of 1,200 reputed centenarians.[1] Belle Boone Beard based a similar agenda on 500 specific case studies drawn from her fabled longevity archives at Lynchburg College which include 12,000 named centenarians, 3,000 completed longevity trait observations, and several hundred personal interviews.[2] And Jim Heynen has provided one hundred short biographies with photographs of centenarians he personally interviewed from 1987-1989.[3]

One of the fundamental conclusions of these studies is that long life spans are highly dependent on individual decision-making. Major exceptions on the negative side are those individuals born with physical handicaps of some kind. On the positive side, being born female is a definite advantage. But even the gender advantage is secondary to life style and not all physical handicaps preclude long life. In any case, due to life patterns chosen or forced on individuals, as the decades of life begin to mount, chronological age reveals less and less about biological age. One septuagenarian will be able to row a lifeboat into a North Sea gale to help rescue shipwrecked sailors, while a retiree of the same age can barely muster the energy to rise from a rocking chair. Most observers of these two septuagenarians would assume the seaman has extended his youth beyond the usual limits. In actuality, the retiree has aged prematurely.

To keep biological age from racing ahead of chronological age is the essence of the Longevity Agenda. The major longevity factors involve psychological outlook, physical exercise, diet, and life style. The exact nature of each of these will be addressed in detail in succeeding chapters. Each factor must be examined separately and none neglected, any more than one would put high grade gasoline into a car but neglect to oil it. In the process of examining the longevity factors, many popular notions about health and long life need to be discarded. Some are not only useless but counterproductive.

A great irony that the study of the longevous has uncovered is that most, especially centenarians, say that long life was never a conscious goal. The factors that produced their unusual life spans were primarily fortuitous. Even so, since at least the time of the Italian Renaissance, a number of persons willing to experiment with their lives have lived by longevity agendas devised while they were relatively young. The perspectives of some of the more successful of these individuals conclude this chapter and serve as a bridge to Part II, which details the specific longevity factors those wishing to develop their own agendas must take into account. Before proceeding to discussion of those lives, however, we must ask if longevity is truly a worthwhile goal. What finally is the quality of life after age 85, much less 100? If pain, infirmity, and senility are synonymous with advanced years, why should anyone want them? If long life adds monumental burdens to families and society, would it not be immoral to consciously seek it?

The starting point for a rational response to such concerns is the biographies and interviews featured in volumes such as those produced by Segerberg, Beard, and Heynen. While infirmity among the very old is certainly more common than in younger persons, dependence on others usually occurs only in the last stages of life (characteristic throughout the population whatever the age of death) and the mood is usually one of satisfaction, if not joy. A sensational example of the vibrancy often present in the longest lives is available in yet another source: *Having Our Say*, a book about the lives and thoughts of Sarah Delaney (age 101) and Bessie Delaney (age 103), as recorded by Amy Hill Hearth. These centenarian sisters are members of a prominent African-American family. Their father was born a slave and their life experiences offer a thumbnail portrait of the history of African–Americans over the past century. But what propelled the book to the *New York Times* Best Seller list was the delightful wit and acerbic observations of the sisters, who live independently in Mt. Vernon, New York. Most endearing of all was the complex, humorous, and loving relationship between the feisty Bessie and the more serene Sadie. A second book, *The Delaney Sisters' Book of Wisdom*, appeared in 1994 when the sisters were 103 and 105 respectively.

Another powerful affirmation of long life and a persuasive in-dicator that mental abilities do not necessarily decline with age are the number of individuals over 70 who have made extraor-dinary contributions to their society. The percentages may very well be higher than those at most other age levels. Authors of advanced years have written many of the works that are acknowl-edged to be classics of European literature. Cervantes completed *Don Quixote* at age 69, Goethe finished *Faust* at 83, and Sophocles was in his late 80s when he wrote the final plays in the *Oedipus* cycle. Two of the best surveys of men and women who did outstanding work after age 70 are those done by Harvey Lehman and Ruth Hubbell.[4] They are unique, yet with their focus on the fine arts and theoretical science, many exceptional individuals are excluded. Neither list, for example, includes a political figure like Mother Jones, who was socially active throughout her 90s, wrote a spirited autobiography at age 95, and attended her last May Day rally on her hundredth birthday.

The life of Mother Jones also shows how fallacious it is to assume that humans become politically more conservative and generally more cautious as they grow older. Studies of the longevous reveal that just the opposite is often true. Many of the social pressures felt at other ages seem less important or are thought to be irrelevant. In Abkhasia, women grow bolder and more liberated the older they become. The old are often so direct and uncompromising in their views that they are accused of being gruff, garrulous, or crude. On a more sophisticated level, persons with strong social commitments usually pursue their visions to the end of their lives, often spurred by the notion that the time left to make changes is short. Two remarkable examples are Bertrand Russell and Welthy Honsinger Fisher.

World-famous as a philosopher and long forgiven his pacifism, in 1960, at the age of 88, Bertrand Russell formed the Committee of One Hundred to fight the threat of nuclear annihilation. His ban-the-bomb group was a breakaway from a more conservative organization, and its tactics of civil disobedience were to be adopted throughout the developed world by various political movements of the 1960s. In the last ten years of his life, Russell interceded in the Cuban missile crisis with appeals to the heads of the Soviet and American governments, and he launched a tribunal to investigate the charges of American war crimes in Vietnam. During the same time span he completed a three-volume autobiography; its sales helped finance his many interests.

The name of Welthy Fisher is not as recognizable as Russell's, yet she is typical of many people dedicated to religious or humanitarian causes. Having given up a promising career in opera to become a missionary, she spent eleven years in China teaching at a school that became a prototype for women's education. After her return to the West in 1917, Fisher continued to work on various programs of the Methodist Church, always known for her feminist and anti-racist point of view. She married at age 44. Although her husband was a highly placed church official, she did not curb her independent commitments. In 1947 she met Mahatma Gandhi, an old friend of her deceased husband, and she was persuaded to begin a school in India much like the one she had run in China. Following years of preparation, in 1956, at the age of 77, Welthy opened Literacy House on a 23-acre site in Lucknow. Twenty-two years later, suffering from a broken knee-cap and facing sub-zero temperatures, she accepted an invitation for a return visit to China. Now 99 years of age, she consulted with Madame Sun Yat-sen and others she had known from her missionary days about the progress Chinese women had been making toward a goal of full social equality. Interviewed on her return, Fisher made a statement that could be the credo of many longevous people who share her spirit even though their lives might be less spectacular: "I could never manage to feel as I was supposed to about my chronological age. Maybe I was too busy. The future always seemed limitless and I have never stopped expecting something to happen, some invitation for another adventure."[5] On September 18, 1979, at a birthday dinner for 250 friends at the St. Regis Hotel in New York, Welthy Honsinger Fisher became a centenarian.

Complementing accounts of those who reach the summit of their careers in old age are others about those who embark on new phases of their careers late in life. Artists and scholars provide many examples. Thomas Hardy, already considered a great

English novelist, began to concentrate on writing poetry from his mid-60s onward. Similarly, after reaching their 70s, Claude Monet began his famous water lily series, and Henrik Ibsen changed his literary style. Writers from Cato to Somerset Maugham have insisted that the 80s are a splendid time to start the study of a new language. Others have embarked late in life on entirely new forms of personal expression. When already well into her 70s, Anna Mary Moses found that her fingers were becoming too stiff to hold a needle to embroider on canvas as had been her custom. Although unschooled, she decided to concentrate on her oil painting. Before long, she had become world-famous as Grandma Moses, "the grand old lady of American art." She continued to be an active artist until several months before her death at age 101. Among her final works were illustrations done at age 100 for a new edition of *A Visit from St. Nicholas.*

About the only area of mental competence in which there appears to be a significant incidence of degeneration is near memory. This condition can be redressed through mental exercises if one is concerned about it, and experiments with choline indicate that some vitamins can foster better near and remote memory, even though most older people have little difficulty with the latter.[6] Older persons who keep their minds engaged in activities such as crossword puzzles, complex card games, chess, and personal finances have been observed to suffer far less from loss of memory than those who are intellectually more passive.[7] Moreover, memory and rote-learning abilities decline much less in persons with a formal education—indicating, perhaps, that many tests measure test-taking "savvy" as much as raw mental capacity.

The circumstances surrounding loss of memory can be extremely critical. When a busy executive forgets something, it is chalked up to overwork. The same memory lapse in the old may be considered a sign of approaching senility. It is common for people to forget to buy items on their shopping lists, to misplace keys, or to hide important documents so cleverly that they forget where they have hidden them. If an older person becomes depressed or withdrawn because of fears that such typical human behavior signals mental decline, the fear may become self-fulfilling.

The advantages of keeping the mind constantly stimulated can be seen by the large numbers of people who remain active in the business or political worlds long after typical retirement age. Senior partners in law firms, brokerage houses, and business enterprises who are in their 80s or beyond are legendary. Adolph Zukor, founder of Paramount Pictures, continued to visit the studio to give advice on projects until his death at 103. Still more common has been the number of older men found in the judicial and executive branches of government. In the United States, 85 percent of Supreme Court service has been rendered by men over 65. It is well known that Oliver Wendell Holmes was a justice until age 91, but this is still fifteen years shy of the world record held by Judge Albert R. Alexander, who remained on the Missouri bench until he was nearly 106. In the matter of chief executives, since 1940 every nation in the developed world has had at least one head of state who was 70 or older.

Anxieties over failing hearing are more justified than fear of mental lethargy. Fully 27 percent of those over 65 will suffer hearing impairment; but again, the most serious aspect of the problem is psychological. People who have hearing difficulty may withdraw into a private world because they are scorned or ridiculed when they fail to reply to unheard questions or give lucid but inappropriate responses to misheard questions. Clearly, a person living with loved ones stands a better chance of avoiding this kind of depression than someone in an overcrowded institution. Advances in hearing technology have provided less cumbersome and more sensitive aids than the old hearing horns which tended to make the user appear somewhat ridiculous.

The majority of persons over 65 will not have serious hearing loss and will continue to enjoy their fill of conversation and music. Older musicians have as impressive a list of new works as older writers do. Verdi composed *Otello* at 73, *Falstaff* at 80, and completed his *Quatro Pezzi Sacri* (Four Sacred Pieces) at 85. Wagner completed *Parsifal* at age 69, and Richard Strauss wrote his poignant *Four Last Songs* at age 85. In the period since the end of World War II there have been numerous octogenarian and nonagenarian musicians who continued to perform on the concert stage. Three of the most notable nonagenarians were conductor Leopold Stokowski, pianist Arthur Rubinstein, and cellist Pablo Casals.

Decline in the ability to see, signaled by the need for reading glasses, a norm in developed nations, is not a prelude to blindness. Few of the old become blind, and most of these cases are caused by cataracts, which could have been operated on if diagnosed early. Like so many physical declines, problems with eyesight appear to be due less to simple aging than to environment, which in this instance means reading and working under artificial illumination. Dramatic evidence of how important this factor may be is available in studies of Eskimo culture, in which it was found that individuals who lived in the traditional manner experienced little eyesight decline, while those who installed light bulbs in their dwellings developed high rates of myopia in less than a generation.

Professional artists, like hundreds of thousands of amateurs, usually find that failing eyesight is not a barrier to creativity. Pablo Picasso did an ongoing series of erotic works in his 80s, and Titian worked on mythological paintings until his death at 99. Active nonagenarian graphic artists on the contemporary scene include Marc Chagall and Georgia O'Keeffe. Among the most notable achievements by visual artists of advanced age is the work done by Michelangelo, who was carving the Rondanini *Pieta* almost to the day of his death at age 89. During the last two decades of his life, he had worked as a painter and architect, designing the Piazza del Campidoglio, painting the frescoes in the Cappella Paolina, and designing the apse and dome of the Basilica of Saint Peter.

Many misconceptions about the old stem from that widespread habit of commenting that a person does or does not look his or her age. As there is no way that visual observation, even by an expert, can determine the ages of people from 60 to 100 years old, this kind of statement is meaningless. It simply associates ill health and a neglected appearance with advanced chronological age. More errors accumulate when impressions are based on the appearance and behavior of the 5% of the population over 65 who are institutionalized rather than on the 95% who are not. Many are in institutions because of ill health, poverty, or abandonment. Their responses to survey questions and their scores on achievement tests might be considerably different if they were living at home in relative health. In view of this, all statistical data derived from institutionalized populations must be considered as presenting partial rather than aggregate portraits of the abilities of the old and longevous.

A look at longevity that excluded persons in institutions was offered by Dr. Stephen Jewett in 1973.[8] Over the years, using informal means of contact, Jewett had managed to locate and keep track of 70 persons between the ages of 85 and 103. The majority of his subjects had remained active throughout their lives and were independently employed, being mainly farmers, professionals, or owners of small businesses. They were moderate eaters, their diets being light in fat and heavy in protein. They were not overweight, used little medication, and reported few colds. As a rule, the few who drank and smoked did so moderately. There was a high rate of marriage and excellent sociability. Most reported they were not prone to worry and slept well. Their nonstressful style of life included taking periodic brief vacations and occasionally experimenting with new foods.

Findings similar to those described by Jewett appear in a survey completed in the 1960s of 402 Americans over age 95.[9] These nonagenarians had had moderate habits, had worked at jobs they liked, had not been big eaters, had enjoyed plenty of physical exercise, and had retained their zest for living through activities ranging from hobbies and money management to participating in extended families. While both this survey and Jewett's were too small and random to be more than supportive of other more comprehensive studies, the profile they describe corresponds more closely to realizable possibilities for humans than do stereotypes of old-timers vegetating on the nursing-home veranda. These studies are also in line with physical-fitness programs in which men in their 70s and 80s are brought up to the performance levels of men in their 40s and 50s.[10]

The activist longevity profile is repeated by authors on longevity who, following their own precepts, lived to at least a tenth decade. Five of the most celebrated of this group are Luigi Cornaro, Sir Hermann Weber, Sir James Crichton-Browne, Dr. Alexander Gueniot, and Scott Nearing. Cornaro and Nearing sought to share their vision of how life could be better for all the species, while Weber, Crichton-Browne, and Gueniot were physicians interested in promoting general health concepts.

By far the most celebrated of the quintet is Luigi Cornaro, who is generally believed to have been born in Venice in 1467 and to have died in Padua in 1565. Some authorities think he may have been born a few years earlier and did not die until 1566, making him a centenarian. Accepting the birth date of 1467, it can be said that Cornaro wrote his major treatise on longevity at age 83 and then revised the work at ages 86, 91, and 95. The discourse has been translated into every major European language. One early American edition which appeared at the beginning of the nineteenth century carried an endorsement by George Washington.[11]

Until the age of 40, Cornaro had suffered from various maladies, such as gout, stomach fever, chills, and generalized pain. His physicians held out little hope for his survival. At this juncture, Cornaro decided to become his own healer, embarking upon a regimen that was to carry him through more than another fifty years of life. He had become convinced that his ills, like those of the human race in general, were due to a life of intemperance, to homage to "the belly gods" and the "nervous" life they commanded. He reformed his living habits, gradually cutting back on his eating until it came to only 12 ounces of solids, mainly eggs and flour products, and 14 ounces of young wine—a total of about 1,000 calories—a day. His body grew extremely lean, yet his health began to prosper.

Aside from his dietary experiments, Cornaro's life was typical of the upper-class male of the Italian Renaissance. He had a country estate, to which he frequently rode on horseback. More than casually interested in his property, Cornaro had swamplands drained and personally supervised the management of his crops. When in Padua, he participated in the intellectual currents of the day and spoke about the joy of long life. His many works include a comedy written in his 80s to challenge the opinion that old age is dreary. His granddaughter, a nun, wrote that to the end of his life, when a meal might consist of a single egg yolk, Cornaro still liked to sing and possessed a strong, clear voice.[12]

The apparent dichotomy between the vigor of Cornaro's life and the meagerness of his diet has fascinated researchers for centuries. Perhaps as he grew older he exaggerated how little he ate or honestly forgot the fruits consumed in summer or the vegetables sliced into his soup. The tale of the egg-yolk dinner, like the effort to make him a centenarian, has the ring of apocrypha. Nevertheless, Cornaro's handling of a slowing basal metabolic rate and his whole approach to eating were in accord with the biological maxim developed in the twentieth century that the closer an organism comes to its minimal daily requirements, the longer it will endure. The classic experiment leading to this conclusion was made in the 1920s by Dr. Clive McCay of Cornell, who discovered that he could extend the life-span of laboratory rats from the usual 965 days to a little over 1,450 days by reducing their caloric intake to just above the starvation level.[13] For maximal benefit, it was necessary for the restricted diet to commence at birth and to contain all the nutrients required to maintain systemic efficiency. Subsequent experiments on other animals in laboratories all over the world have repeatedly brought the same general results.

Moral considerations prohibit massive tests on human subjects, but history has provided some gratuitous episodes that reproduce some aspects of the experiments linking dietary restriction to longevity. During both world wars when food supplies, particularly those high in fat content, were curtailed severely in several European countries, death rates fell.[14] As soon as the normal diet was restored, death rates rebounded to their prewar levels. Prisoners in camps where the food was minimal but not at starvation levels experienced no physical ill effects, and many reported cures of gastrointestinal ailments.

The danger in a dietary approach such as Cornaro's is that if carried to an extreme, it can lead to starvation. This is the sad fate of persons afflicted with anorexia nervosa. Otherwise, however, it is not very likely in developed nations, where overeating breeds so many health problems. Unfortunately, in nearly every culture both the folk tradition and the fine arts associate fatness with the positive human qualities. Shakespeare's Caesar trusted only the well fed, and crazed Don Quixote was thin as a reed while his jovial comrade Sancho Panza was as plump as the bon vivants of Rabelais and the genial toy makers of fairy tales. Certainly during eras when famine was a real threat, fat served the useful function of providing a reservoir of emergency fuel, and historically, bulging bellies have been signs of prosperity. It also is readily seen that people who are seriously ill will suffer drastic weight loss. Nonetheless, the folk and literary sages are wrong to link overweight to a happy and long life. As previously noted, there is a positive correlation between excess weight and susceptibility to nearly every disease; and the greater the excess, the greater the risk. It has been suggested that the longevity superiority of women is due to nothing more than that they are generally smaller and lighter than men. Whether this is a valid thesis or not, the lean and hungry look of Luigi Cornaro is standard in the longevity profile, particularly for those who live beyond the 95th year.

In Cornaro's diet, the role of wine, long called "the milk of the old," is another historical fluke that has proved to have a scientific basis. Massive statistical evidence gathered in the twentieth century shows that people who drink about half a liter of wine a day live longer than those who do not drink at all or those who drink wine in much larger quantities or those who drink alcohol in other forms.[15] It may be significant that Cornaro liked young local wine, for sulfur dioxide, which is added to make wines travel better, is suspected of being harmful to the body. There would be no reason to add it to local wines meant to be consumed quickly.

The independent spirit of Cornaro is another characteristic found frequently in the longevous. Unlike those who adhered blithely to the fashions of the age, Cornaro had the strength of character to persist in his own regimen, but with a temperament that did not alienate him from contemporaries. Like most of the longevous, Cornaro never "retired." At most there was a gradual easing in the tempo of his life after age 80, with less time spent on his estate and more on writing. Although his peers thought him extremely unusual, what people today would call a "character," his good humor, his responsible behavior, and finally his age made him one of the pillars of Paduan society. As with the Abkhasian elders, his counsel was sought and given on every subject.

Some four hundred years after the time of Cornaro, three contemporaneously famous European physicians made longevity one of their major concerns. The longevity profiles they advocated were similar to Cornaro's, but with a shift in major emphasis away from diet to physical activity. Each of the three doctors had seen numerous longevous patients as part of his practice, and they all capped their professional writing with books or essays on longevity composed or revised when they themselves were in their 90s.[16]

Sir Hermann Weber (1823–1918) was the most adamant about the role of exercise and was among the first to stress the added advantage of difficult terrain. He recommended one to three hours of walking each day and taking vacations that included climbing, hiking, and hunting. Sir James Crichton-Browne (1840–1938) reported that Cardinal de Satis, who lived to be 110, insisted on a mixture of two hours of walking and riding daily. Crichton-Browne underscored the advantages of vigorous country living and continuing projects throughout life. In Paris, Alexandre Gueniot (1832–1935) disclosed, with a light Gallic touch, that before working on his present book at age 99 he had, as usual, reached his apartment by walking up fifty-six steps.

In regard to diet, Crichton-Browne believed that Cornaro's caloric intake was inadequate for the average person, although he conceded that it must always be related to the caloric output demanded by one's occupation and lifestyle. Expressing similar views, Weber estimated that 2,500 calories was sufficient for the vast majority of people—a level about a thousand calories lower than Crichton-Browne's recommendations. As opposed to longevity *per se*, Weber argued that his regimen promoted a life span in which death, whenever it came, would not be preceded by a prolonged period of suffering. Massages and deep breathing exercises were highly thought of by Weber and Gueniot, respectively, as means of stimulating vital systems, and both favored a lactovegetarian diet. All three physicians were advocates of moderation in all things and were contemptuous of those who allowed themselves to fall ill at such tender ages as 60 and 70. Serving food at room temperature, keeping active throughout life, attending to personal hygiene, consuming wine, and fostering an easy-going personality were other shared recommendations.

The American heir of this tradition is Scott Nearing (1883–1993), who, like Cornaro, became a legend in his own lifetime. The impetus to his concern for a healthy life style was a world outlook that encompassed controversial views on many basic social issues. Alone or in co-authorship with his wife Helen (1904– ), Nearing wrote prolifically about his pacifist, vegetarian, and socialist beliefs. As a young man he had been blacklisted for his activism, and by the end of the 1920s he decided a better way to reshape world values might be to live in a manner that already reflected as many of his values as possible. In 1932, he and Helen bought a farm in Vermont, where they embarked on a way of living that anticipated the alternative-culture life styles that were to become extremely popular among young people some thirty years later.

The Nearings' views on longevity are scattered throughout their writings, but form an integral part of both *Living the Good Life*, an account of their nineteen years of homesteading in Vermont, and *Continuing the Good Life*, a report on the succeeding twenty-five years of homesteading in Maine. The core of the

Nearing life style is to plan daily and seasonal chores in a manner which allows for the greatest amount of time available for activities not required for survival—what the Nearings call "bread labor". Built into this approach are concerns for exercise, diet, and social involvement.

Having farmed mainly with hand implements for the better part of fifty years, the Nearings considered formal exercise a kind of folly, holding that one can always do productive work to accomplish the same end. In their case, this included digging, hoeing, weeding, composting, and hauling. In addition, Scott was fond of sawing and chopping wood for their wood-burning stove, an activity he found more enjoyable than any sport. An indication of the Nearing's lust for activity is that among their favorite pursuits was building stone structures according to a plan devised by Ernest Flagg. The couple constructed fifteen stone buildings, including two impressive stone houses, on their two homesteads. They designed the structures, quarried the stone, dug up the materials needed for cement, and erected the buildings with minimal outside assistance or machinery. Scott referred to them as one-man/one-woman projects, and Helen has written that he became so involved in the Maine house that she personally selected and placed every stone. That home was completed in 1977, when Scott was 84 and Helen was 73.

Scott Nearing's lactovegetarian diet was 50% fruit, 35% vegetables, 10% protein and starch, and 5% fat. No candy, tea, coffee, alcohol, soft drinks, pastry, or tobacco were used. When food was not served raw, it was lightly steamed, boiled, or baked to be served at room temperature in wooden utensils which were easy to clean and prevented metallic poisoning. Most of the food came from the Nearing organic gardens, where synthetic chemicals and artificial substances of any kind were banned. Although animal manure was used in Vermont, the Nearings used only "green compost" in Maine. This practice was based on their moral premise that no living creature should exploit another and on the dietary belief that animal products are harmful when consumed by humans. Scott also liked to say that keeping animals was an enormous chore that would make far more difficult the travel he and his wife thrived on. Nearing was most insistent that only part of the day be given to bread labor. The rest was to be used for pleasure, which for him meant writing, studying, and publishing.

Helen was a full partner in these enterprises and their various books, some written independently, some jointly, were published by commercial presses, while others came out under their own imprint. This latter activity involved coediting, overseeing typesetting and printing, and doing distribution by mail order. They traveled a great deal to gain new experiences and to teach in various settings, including universities, book clubs, fairs, and international health congresses. Other parts of their non-bread-labor time were devoted to local social activities, such as town meetings or musical evenings at home. New ideas and projects were the manna of their lives. After a visit to China in his 80s, Scott adapted some of the agricultural techniques he had seen to his Maine garden. A film made in 1978 shows Scott explaining his ideas with consistent wit and humor[17] and a photo story a year later in *The New York Times* identified him as the oldest author at that year's Fifth Avenue Book Fair.

Living to the age of one hundred had been one of Scott Nearing's ambitions. Shortly after his birthday, Scott told his wife that he felt his life's work had been completed. In the year or so preceding his birthday, his health had been waning, and he thought the time had arrived for a dignified death. He stopped eating and died within a short period, much as a leaf drops from a tree. Helen has continued to live in the style they espoused, writing new books and devoting considerable energy to music. As of this writing, she is an active nonagenarian.

The preferred life styles of Cornaro and Nearing were far more severe in their specifics than those of the three long-living physicians. What truly unites them is their passionate involvement with life in all of their considerable years. Such longevous individuals, however, are viewed as exceptional primarily because they have been in a position to write about their own lives and credos. There are tens of thousands of others who lived just as vigorously who remain anonymous, the marvel of their lives known only to a few close associates and relatives.

Many stories about the longevous come to public attention accidentally. In the early 1970s, for instance, a video team seeking an unusual angle on black history discovered Mrs. Lula Sadler Craig, age 101, living on the Colorado prairie with her daughter and sister.[18] The crew filmed her reminiscing about black pioneers in the Old West and covered a reunion in which hundreds of the matriarch's descendants converged to celebrate her 102nd birthday. Among the neighbors who dropped by to offer congratulations was a centenarian rancher. Similarly, Sula Benet's writings refer parenthetically to her friend Arthur "Chammy" Spurling, age 102, whom she met on vacations on Cranberry Island off the coast of Maine.[19] In 1978 the public relations department of American Telephone & Telegraph announced that its oldest known stockholder was Dolly Warren, age 106, who was still living at her own home in Washington D.C. A year later the New York metropolitan newspapers wrote of Dr. Walter Pannell, born July 31, 1879, who was still walking to work and seeing patients at his East Orange, New Jersey, office. The centenarian physician had been practicing medicine for seventy-five years! Similarly, Frances Steloff, founder of the Gotham Book Mart, New York's most famous literary bookstore, was still an active bookseller at age 100. She had sold Gotham when she turned 80, but continued to live in a third floor apartment above the store, socialized with literary figures, and came down to the main floor to help out in the busy afternoon hours. The famed Broadway director-producer-writer George Abbott stated, at age 100, "I love to work." He was as good as his word, celebrating the century mark by working up to six hours a day casting and rehearsing actors for a revival of a show he had written more than fifty years earlier.

Such stories could be multiplied to fill volumes without doing justice to more than a fraction of the octogenarians, nonagenarians, and centenarians who have lived their final years with gusto. I offer them here only as samplings of the tremendous range of creativity, satisfaction, and adventure that can be savored at an advanced age. They are the best riposte to those who protest, "Why would anyone want to live to be a hundred?"

NEW YORK PUBLIC LIBRARY PICTURE COLLECTION

Luigi Cornaro (1467-1566) thrived on and wrote about his restricted diet of about a thousand calories a day.

CANAJOHARIE LIBRARY AND ART GALLERY

Delina Filkins (1815-1928) of Herkimer, New York, one of the longest-lived females ever fully documented.

RICHARD KAPLAN PRODUCTIONS

Lulu Sadler Craig, age 102 at the time of this photo, spoke eloquently of the Old West in a television documentary, "Happy Birthday, Mrs Craig!"

JUDY JANDA

Mikhail Kaslantzia, age 104, and his wife looking at photographs of centenarians in other parts of the world.

ALL PHOTOS: JUDY JANDA

Dan Georgakas toasts Vanacha Temur, then age 110, and identified by Abkhasian authorities as one of their healthiest centenarians. Temur's two-story house is built in the style typical of the region.

A person must be at least 70 to be eligible for membership in this choir.

This Soviet photograph is used in a poster to encourage people to work as hard as their elders did.

Shirali Mislimov of Barzavu, Azerbaijan, died in 1973 at the reputed age of 170.

Kaslantzia home with photo of deceased son on second floor terrace.

Shigechiyo Izumi (June 29, 1865-Feb 21, 1986) of Japan is recognized as the longest-lived human being by the *Guinness Book of World Records.*

The Dales belongs to a category of homes in Britain operated for seniors who can manage most of their daily tasks unaided.

At age 104, Frederick Cornelius of Upper Sheringham traveled alone by bus and taxi.

Elizabeth Archer celebrated her 100th birthday at a seaside holiday camp in Norfolk.

Alice Empelton continued to garden until she was nearly 106.

CAMBRIDGE EVENING NEWS

While traveling in the Cambridge area, James Chapman, age 103, had tea with Alice Empelton, also 103 at the time of the photograph.

Welthy Fisher, shown here at age 90, traveled to China at age 99 and at age 100 was helping her secretary update her biography.

UNIVERSITY OF WASHINGTON LIBRARY/PHOTO COLLECTION

Mother Jones argued for her causes throughout her long life, marching in her last May Day parade at the age of 100.

WIDE WORLD

UPI

Talbert Hill celebrated his 100th birthday by calling an end to a 76-year medical practice.

Basco Belasques, age 92, and two co-workers set a world's record by sorting 8,200 metal bars in an 8-hour shift at the Bethlehem Steel plant in 1973.

WIDE WORLD

UPI

Maude Andrews, age 100, performing an exercise routine she has followed for decades.

Leonard Shore, age 96, showing good jogging form.

UPI

COURTESY OF AT&T CO

Martin Mack, age 105, uses his bicycle to deliver groceries.

In 1978, Dolly Warren, age 106, was celebrated as the oldest of the three million owners of American Telephone & Telegraph stock.

UPI

WIDE WORLD

Fred Broadwell, age 95, taking a turn at bat.

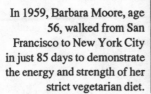

In 1959, Barbara Moore, age 56, walked from San Francisco to New York City in just 85 days to demonstrate the energy and strength of her strict vegetarian diet.

Julius Kahn, age 99, kissing his wife, Della, as they celebrated her 100th birthday on August 16, 1978, in New York City.

JACK MANNING/THE NEW YORK TIMES

# PART TWO  *The Longevity Agenda*

# 9. The Longevous Personality

*In every consideration of the medical art, the nature of the body must be regarded as a whole.—Hippocrates*

No COMPONENT OF THE LONGEVITY AGENDA is more intriguing or controversial than those mental attitudes, behavioral patterns, and moral values that compose the individual personality. Gerontologists who are strongly inclined to theories of biologically programmed aging generally consider personality issues to be decidedly secondary in importance. At the other extreme are theorists who believe that mental energy is so powerful that it can induce otherwise inexplicable healing and even slow down the aging process itself. Further complicating the debate is the fact that exponents of each view readily acknowledge that the opposite perspective has some validity in specific situations.

However one wishes to judge their importance to longevity, some personality traits and emotional patterns constantly appear in biographies of long-living people. Making the decision about how many and exactly how they can consciously be cultivated in any given person will always be more of an art than a science. Few of these traits can be objectively measured in the way food can be judged for its vitamin, caloric, and fat content or the way physical exercise can be related to heartbeat, lung capacity, or muscle

153

density. It is also apparent that many different behavioral and mental constellations can be prolongevous as long as they share the common characteristic of at the least not aggravating and possibly mollifying the unavoidable physical and emotional stresses imposed by outside forces.

One silly notion the longevity aspirant can dispose of at once is that the longevous are kindly, serene souls just this side of sainthood. They happen to be as caustic, self-centered, and jealous of their prerogatives as any other age group. Their lives will show the same incidence of marital discord, shrewd financial manipulations, and questionable moral judgments as those of the friends they have survived. Instead of having turned their backs on the world, the longevous have succeeded in overcoming, through one means or another, its most lethal challenges. If only by virtue of having lived to see their way of life vindicated by advanced age, they are likely to be unusually opinionated and strong-willed.

Not surprisingly, a key element in the longevous personality is the attitude toward time. The longevous have a marked preference for jobs that accommodate orderly, regular, and somewhat rhythmic daily patterns, and they have a distaste for those which involve constant anxiety. The longevous like to break down their work into achievable segments of relatively short duration, allowing for periodic plateaus of accomplishment as well as vantage points from which to judge overall progress. If that progress is unsatisfactory, the schedule is apt to be shifted to the pace of work rather than the work speeded up to fulfill the original plan. Guided by entrenched personal standards and focused on well-defined goals, the longevous generally place a premium on quality of performance over speed or appeals to passing fashion.

The orderly routines preferred by the longevous tend to minimize bodily wear and tear while holding down the time lost to confusion, false starts, and panic. Breaking the work into achievable segments means that there will be monophasic behavior—one major project an any given time receiving full concentration—rather than polyphasic behavior—a number of projects constantly competing for attention and inevitably pushing the body toward exhaustion in a pattern in which more and more energy is needed to accomplish less and less. Similarly, those who work late into the night or on split shifts have been shown to be among the least productive workers in terms of quality and total output. By far the best model is one that is tuned to the natural cycles of the day and year, the prime example being the daily and seasonal schedule followed by farmers. Such routines mesh with the subtle biological rhythms of various bodily systems, such as the rising and falling of internal temperature and the pace at which various hormones are released.

An immediate benefit of a regularized rhythmic life style is that it should produce good sleep, a condition essential for the body to refresh itself and to make internal repairs and adjustments. Invariably, longevous people report lifelong patterns of regular and satisfying sleep. Because of the same biochemical individuality that affects individual nutritional needs, there is such a wide variation in sleeping needs that it is best to ask not how long one has slept but how well. Most humans will be rested by from six to eight hours of sleep a night, with a few doing well on as little as four hours and a few requiring up to nine. People who take siestas in the middle of the day usually need fewer total hours of sleep. Otherwise, there is no apparent difference between those who take all their sleep at one time and those who divide it. Except for individuals recovering from an illness, regularly sleeping beyond nine hours should be as much a concern as insomnia or waking with a tired feeling. All three conditions may be symptomatic of serious psychological or physical illness, but more commonly they are the result of inferior scheduling or unresolved polyphasic behavior.

Reaching for sleeping pills or stimulants only puts off a genuine resolution of the difficulty.

The antithesis of the longevous personality is the one that Drs. M. Friedman and R. H. Rosenman identified in their book *Type A Behavior and Your Heart*[1] as being highly prone to heart attack. The Type A personality is characterized by a chronic sense of time urgency brought on by factors like polyphasic activities, unrealistic schedules, and constant deadlines, often self-imposed. Daily living patterns have a jerky or irregular nature. As the day draws on, the Type A is prone to falling further and further behind schedule, calling for frantic bursts of energy or resignation to working overtime. On a broader time scale, he or she works on weekends and holidays, and feels guilt about time taken for play. A corollary attitude involves general insensitivity to aesthetic values and little appreciation for certain things just being in the world, like a redwood forest with trees centuries old.

Frequently the Type A is thought of as a doer or a mover, the perfect competitive type suitable for the business world. This confuses mere motion with accomplishment, the wheel spinning in place with one that can propel a vehicle forward. The irritability and impatience of the Type A usually alienate fellow workers to such a degree that although a fit of bullying or an impassioned outburst may get short-term action, in the long run lack of cooperation, lack of interest, and even hostility from others become increasingly damaging to projects undertaken. One consequence of not breaking up work into doable segments is the creation of a perpetual do-or-die crisis ambiance that may culminate in emotional disaster. The clenched fist, banging on the table, and shouting are signs of a sinking psychological ship. More often than not, the Type A has made the additional error of equating efficiency with speed and quantity.

Numerous attempts have been made to measure the damage

done to the body by psychological and physical stress. The most systematic work has been done by Hans Selye, who has investigated the local and general adaptive processes of the body. This has included examination of the chemical alarm systems and responses in the central nervous system and in glands such as the pituitary and adrenals. Specific biological changes within the body are thought of as barometers of how much the body is being stressed and how successfully it is adapting.[2]

Selye believes physical stress is easier to cope with because the cause is usually identifiable. The initial response mechanism can be judged for effectiveness, and if it does not work there is a renewed search for something that does. The cause of psychological stress can be more elusive. Symptoms like insomnia, stomach pains, or muscular tension are not easily traceable to their psychological causes. While most people will understand that fighting rush-hour traffic in a car or being sandwiched in a crowded bus is likely to be stressful, fewer will appreciate that idleness can be just as dangerous. The body was made to work, and when it is idle, pent-up energy may cause a pervasive feeling of loginess. If this leads to more inactivity, the condition worsens. Finally, there are instances which are of a positive emotional nature but which require biological adaptation. Enrolling in a new school is one example. Momentary relief from stress of any kind can be obtained through various depressants, but in the long run they may only guarantee that when the stress reaches an intolerable level the residual damage will be far more severe than if the cause had been attended to sooner.

Strokes, ulcers, and migraines are only the visible tip of the stress iceberg. Selye believes that stress, influenced by dietary and exercise habits, is the leading cause of premature aging. The less change in the tissues and vital organs brought about by an adaptive response and the less stress to begin with, the slower the aging process. While not all stress can be avoided, and while there is a finite amount of adaptive capacity in the genetic bank, Selye is convinced that the average life span could be increased tremendously if people lived in better harmony with natural laws. His suggestions for life-extension mesh with the kind of moderation so often discerned in longevous profiles. For example, Selye writes that although the body must work vigorously in order to prosper, it is not constructed to take too much pressure on any one part, so that it makes prolongevous sense to diversify physical activity and to avoid pushing the organism to exhaustion. Muscular or mental activities that lead to definite solutions, such as those in monophasic behavior, prepare the body for sleep, while efforts that set up self-cycling tension or that lack a resolution promote stress.

Chronic stress can be caused by a major life pattern, such as the kind of exertion, eating, traveling, and sleeping dictated by one's occupation. Jobs that involve crowded facilities, sensory deprivation, constant crisis, or extreme isolation are not likely to be prolongevous. If eating is hurried, sleeping irregular, and travel a chore, there is need to question the basic life style.

Alleviating such personal stress may require drastic solutions like changing jobs or living conditions. Less drastic responses could include formal relaxation techniques such as deep breathing, biofeedback, yoga, or meditation. Not a few longevous people use prayer to buffer stress while others insist that a long walk at the end of the day can work emotional wonders. The possible options are truly as varied as the human imagination and individual personality. Of course, destructive responses like the illusionary relief offered by narcotics, alcohol, or tobacco are counterproductive, speeding up rather than retarding premature aging.

The difference between what is stress and what is stimulation is often a matter of attitude. An illustration can be drawn from something as trivial as solving a crossword puzzle. Stress is set into motion if one imposes a time goal on the task and works at the solution as if it were a test of mental competence. Unable to find a Latin word that intersects with the name of an Egyptian deity, a stress-prone person may get into a frenzy of dictionary research or phone the local librarian or friends for assistance. Physicians have observed that some persons become so emotionally distraught over crossword puzzles that their blood pressure rises to dangerous levels. As a result of these observations, many heart patients have been told to avoid activities of this kind. Yet gerontologists know that many longevous people regularly do crosswords and that the exercise helps keep their minds alert. The difference is that the longevous rarely impose a time limit on solving the puzzle and they get satisfaction from solving a quadrant of the puzzle or finding some difficult definition during any one sitting. They may take several days to complete the whole puzzle. If blanks occur where foreign words meet the names of mythological figures, the longevous are likely to see it as a failure of the puzzle maker as much as any lack of knowledge on their part. And if the puzzle doesn't appeal to them from the start, they can ignore it without feeling any threat to their self-esteem.

Related patterns can be found in attitudes toward play. The longevous play in order to relax, while personality types most prone to stress turn play into tension. This is not to say that the longevous do not enjoy winning or skill building. The Abkhasians love to race their horses and to play a form of polo. But they also enjoy breeding their horses, parading them, trading them, doing tricks with them, and just riding. The stressed are likely to favor sports with one-to-one competition, to insist on the finest equipment available, and to seek out professional advice on honing their skills. Practice and playing of the sport become more items to stuff into the already crowded daily calendar. When drawn to jogging, they will be attracted by the marathon aspect, setting up complex training regimens in a new cycle of deadlines, tests, and anxiety. Getting up to marathon standards or winning at competition replaces recreation as the goal of the activity. Often the only emotional relief is that the sport is seen as part of a business or social commitment and thus is not wasted time and most certainly not idle play.

Individual response can determine whether or not a situation is stressful in many other ways. The predictability of the stress, the social context, and the amount of control involved affect the adaptive response. Most people who live near an elevated railway come not to "hear" or at least not to "mind" the rumble of the passing trains, even though some neighbors and almost all visitors may find them irritating. A child who needs to be disciplined may be extremely annoying to a father who insists on comparing his child with others who seem better behaved, or the incident may be viewed as a creative part of parenting. A dripping faucet may ruin one woman's equilibrium if she is inept at home repairs, while another may see it as an opportunity to demonstrate mechanical skills not traditionally associated with her sex. Selling the family home may be heartbreaking to an elderly couple forced to the action by economic pressures or the sense that the structure is too large for them to keep up properly. The same situation may be viewed more positively by another couple who use the move as an opportunity to find housing that is less of a drain on resources, is closer to their children, or is better suited to their new pattern of social activities.

Many aspects of the prolongevous personality are thrown into high relief by the attitude toward retirement. In traditional agricultural societies like those of Soviet Georgia or in fishing towns like those on the Norfolk coast, it was the received knowledge of society that there would be no lessening of physical strength until some time in the late 70s. From that point onward, the experience that had been gained by individuals was thought to qualify them as learned advisers to the family and community. In Sheringham this new counseling role was roughly equivalent to the former activist role, while in Abkhasia it had even higher prestige. For Abkhasian women, there was the added advantage of the erosion of restrictions based on sex. The assumption of long life in both societies put an age like 60 nearer to mid-life than to oncoming old age. In some parts of Abkhasia a ceremonial cane was awarded to individuals when they reached 90—not to aid them in  walking, but to symbolize that they had finally become official elders.

Individuals in developed nations respond to entirely different expectations. Usually the work ethic is so pervasive and family networks so frail that individuals, particularly males, feel that they are what they do. They come to feel that there is not much purpose to life if they cannot work. Thus, there is a high death rate in the years immediately following retirement. The psychological crisis is further intensified in societies that put a very high premium on youth, speed, and competition. Unlike the longevous Abkhasian, who embodies the highest virtues of the culture as taught by its opinion makers, the longevous American is likely to be a maverick, denying many of the values prized by contemporaries. In practical terms, longevous persons never truly retire. Either they have chosen jobs that do not require it, or they shift to new activities that are just as physically and intellectually demanding as their formal work had been.

The modern concept of retirement is based on economic, not biological, considerations. Since 1870, when the first national retirement program went into effect in Germany, the voluntary retirement age has drifted lower and lower, while the mandatory retirement age has been a matter of intense controversy. In some occupations, retirement is possible after a specific period of service, such as twenty or thirty years, so individuals entering the field at a young age may retire in their 40s or 50s.

The idea of insisting on mandatory retirement not linked to health or ability has been increasingly under fire in most nations. In the United States retired executives have been called upon by the government to act as advisers to novices trying to set up businesses with federal loans, and there has been pressure to allow those receiving Social Security to be able to work without losing any benefits—a practice followed in many other nations. The number of Americans who refuse conventional retirement continues to grow.

A change of interest is usually more beneficial to older people than rest. Three well-known contemporary Americans with widely different interests illustrate the new directions possible after age 70. Maggie Kuhn, at age 69, founded the Gray Panther organization to act as a political lobby for senior citizens. Now at 89, she appears regularly in the media and attends conferences on aging all over the country. George B. Saunders, at age 68, founded a franchise system for fried chicken, using his private formula. It became one of the most successful fast-food outlet chains in the nation, and the distinctive white suit, goatee, and Southern charm of "Colonel" Saunders became familiar to millions of Americans. And I. F. Stone, a much-honored journalist, turned in his mid-70s to the translation of ancient Greek poetry.

If the longevous are atypical humans in their adamant refusal to retire from work even when they are financially able, they are prototypical in their living arrangements. The overwhelming majority have lived the greater part of their lives in a family unit. In the United States, at every age past 20, death rates are lower for those who are married than for those who are single, widowed, or divorced, the mortality for unmarried men living alone being the highest. Comparisons of Protestant and Roman Catholic clergy show that the Protestant clergy, who are allowed to marry, live longer.[3] The longevity factor, however, does not appear to be marriage itself so much as living in a situation that provides companionship and feelings of self-esteem. Returning to the Roman Catholic Church, researchers found better-than-average life spans among 115,000 nuns who, although unmarried, lived in communal settings, had a high sense of social responsibility, and continued to work after age 65.[4] Cardinals of the Roman Catholic Church, like U.S. Supreme Court justices, have unusually long life spans. Their zest for living is usually attributed to the power and honor associated with their high ecclesiastical office.

The companionship aspect of living arrangements is underscored by findings that feelings of loneliness often precede death and that long life among the old is usually associated with having at least one intimate friend of long standing. The loss of this friend often leads to the early death of the survivor. Retirement communities suffer from this phenomenon, as they are constantly recording deaths without having the full range of generations, which would include births, to redress the emotional balance. But such communities have the advantage of keeping their inhabitants in touch with a wide social circle with many regularized community activities— quite a contrast to the usual nursing-home situation, where dependency and abandonment are the rule. Even in nursing homes, it has been found that the introduction of pets or arrangements for visits by young people greatly buoy individual and community spirits. By far the most prolongevous living arrangement, however, is a multigenerational household or community in which all adults have personal control over their private affairs.

The phenomenal marriage rate of the longevous sheds some light on their sexual practices—an area that has been little investigated, partly because of the modesty of older people in traditional societies and partly because even in modern nations, the subject has long been thought to be an improper one to bring up with women or the old. The puritan hangup about sex persisted in strength in the United States until the onset of the 1960s. Since then it has been easier to get data, but the materials remain sketchy. One study conducted by Duke University which covered over 200 men and women between the ages of 60 and 94 disclosed that 50% of them were enjoying sexual relations. Among octogenarians the rate was between 10 and 20%, with many stating that it was lack of suitable partners rather than lack of desire which prevented them from being sexually active. Other studies have indicated that the aged have far more liberal views on sexual matters than might be expected from stereotypes of the old or from the fact that anyone over 60 during the post-World War II period would have had his or her views shaped in a far less sexually permissive era. In general, frequency of sexual relations, while diminishing with age, was consistent with the strength of the sex drive throughout the particular individual's life; and couples usually did not totally cease having sexual relations until the health of one of them precluded it.[5] It was a common observation throughout the 1970s that the sexual activity and living arrangements found in retirement communities and at senior-citizen centers were not unlike those of other adults.

Despite claims of some men to sexual performance after 90, and of some women to have given birth after 60, attempts to link old age with unusual fertility have been unsuccessful. Nonetheless, given the unusual physical and psychological vigor of those who become longevous and their marked penchant for marriage, it is logical to assume that their sexual activities are extended along with other vital interests. Longevous individuals frequently say that successful marriages are the secret of their long lives.

The self-esteem, flexibility, independence, and planning ability so marked in longevous persons are often tied to education. Statistics show that for white American males who were 22 years of age in 1900, a seven-year advantage in average life span was enjoyed by those who graduated with honors from universities, and for most of the century, among white males, college graduates have usually outlived the eighth-grade dropouts by an average of five years.[6] The significance of the first finding is all the more dramatic because by age 22 the entire group of male babies born in 1878 yet still alive in 1900 had already survived the high mortality rates of infancy and childhood. This is slightly less important for the comparison between the college graduates and the eighth-grade dropouts. One factor at work, of course, is that the less educated are likely to have more hazardous occupations, but the spread is too large and too pervasive to be accounted for solely on that basis. By and large, men and women in professions have longer average life spans than other workers. The major exceptions are farmers, who are long-living, and such professionals as journalists, air-traffic controllers, and accountants, whose work habits are either too stressful or too sedentary to promote long life. A survey of 6,000 males listed in the 1950-51 *Who's Who in America* found that male professionals outlived other males handily.[7] Another study found that a thousand corporate executives employed by the five hundred firms ranked by *Fortune* magazine as the most powerful in the United States were also long-living.[8]

One of the positive correlations found in all these studies was the association of long life and high measurable intelligence. This indicates that long life is not linked to isolation from or rejection of conventional society. The degree of formal education an individual attains is certainly not the only measure of intelligence any more than a prestigious occupation or high income are the only sources of feelings of self-worth. If that were so, then women, generally excluded from higher education and better paying occupations for the greater part of recorded history, would not be longer lived than men. In fact, most longevous men and women, whatever their occupation, derive their self-esteem from having lived according to whatever ethical principles they hold precious. The higher income and social standing linked to higher education generally enhance the sense of having led a productive and worthy life. The better educated are also more likely to keep abreast of current health standards. In the 1970s, for example, a huge decrease in cigarette smoking among the college educated took place with an accompanying boom in the passion for jogging and physical fitness. Both of these trends served to lengthen the average life span for this particular educational group.

Another characteristic of the longevous is preference for quality of experience over quantity. A longevous person is not likely to accept a travel plan that crams seven countries into a nine-day tour. Nor are the longevous likely to be the kind of social butterflies who make numerous phone calls, quickie visits, and attend obligatory social events to maintain a wide spectrum of acquaintances who will never develop into friends. By focusing on a limited number of experiences deemed highly desirable, the longevous often succeed in doing, seeing, and feeling more than those who pride themselves on constant motion and keeping every option open. Those who refuse to be selective about social options often end up like pebbles skimming off the surface of a pond. They are unable to make more than superficial contacts anywhere, and everywhere they find only mirrors of the places they have just left.

In terms of geography, the most prolongevous locales are rural areas, with cooler climates having a slight advantage over warmer ones. The difference in average life span between rural and urban areas in the United States is about five years. The investigation of 402 Americans over the age of 95 conducted by pollster George Gallup found that 74 percent of those participating had lived most of their lives on farms, in villages, or in small cities. Quite a few lived within a few miles of their birthplace.[9] These findings are consistent with samplings taken in other nations. But the historic longevity advantage of rural locations has been declining in the twentieth century. The introduction of complex agricultural machinery and the massive use of pesticides, sometimes sprayed from low-flying aircraft, has taken away many of the health benefits agricultural workers used to derive from rigorous physical work done out of doors in a relatively serene environment. Many rural areas are further disadvantaged by having a paucity of doctors and inadequate health care facilities.

Perhaps the least understood aspect of the longevous personality, yet one that is tremendously important, is the expectation of health as the normal condition of life. While thinking won't make it so, it seems to help. Minimally, prolongevous convictions are needed to muster the determination to follow beneficial dietary, exercise, and living patterns. At age 75, it is imperative to consider the years that stretch to 100 as another quarter of life to be savored, not as the last sand in the time glass.

Just how powerful the benefits from a prolongevous mind-set may be is a matter of intense scientific scrutiny. The major practical focus has been on how mental attitudes affect the development of or recovery from specific diseases. An impetus to this line of investigation has been Hans Selye's work on stress which has already been referred to. It is speculated that if the physiological responses to stress are not resolved they may cause a disease, weaken the body's immunological system, or lessen the body's ability to fight a disease already contracted. Conversely, other physiological responses induced by positive psychological input might be able to increase the body's immunity to disease or aid it in resisting a disease already contracted. Setting up strict scientific measurements for this kind of research is extremely difficult, yet the field is promising, and the implications for longevity are tremendous.

The clearest examples of mind interacting with matter are the kind of purely psychosomatic diseases that psychology has made familiar. A related phenomenon seen in all hospitals is that some patients on hearing they have a serious disease or must undergo painful treatments seem to lose their will to live and fail to respond to treatment. The high mortality rates among people who have recently retired, who have just lost a spouse, and who live alone are in much the same category. Although the physical process by which negative emotions weaken the body is not precisely understood, there is little question that the interaction exists.

That the mind may be able to affect health positively is a more tenuous possibility, but there is some supportive statistical evidence. Numerous studies have shown that death rates fall before major holidays. It appears that many individuals who are extremely ill are somehow able to rally for one more major celebration or family reunion. It is also common to find death occurring some time after a birthday or important event rather than shortly before it. In the area of "miracle" or "faith" cures, found in all major religions, investigators have discovered that after the ecstatic moment during which the first breakthrough to a cure takes place, a moment such as a lame person's suddenly walking, there will be a long period of recuperation in which recovery proceeds along predictable and gradual lines. A sore will not immediately disappear but will heal over a span of weeks or months. It is most significant to note that among such cures there is no recorded incident of regeneration of limbs or correction of a genetically caused disease or condition.

Even more interesting than religious cures (which are not easily verifiable) are controlled tests in various medical facilities which show that in many situations 30 to 40 percent of patients given placebos are cured or show significant improvement. The conclusion that could be drawn from these and similar findings is that the mind may be able to influence the body's ability to self-heal, either by rallying the natural curative mechanism already identified or by tapping as yet undetermined resources. It's been theorized, for example, that the endorphins, the body's own pain relievers, are released in response to placebos. Placebo cures also raise questions abut drugs deemed chemically curative. To what degree is their effectiveness also due to the placebo phenomenon? Are they more helpful when the patient is enthusiastic about their use and less helpful if the patient is wary? Or does it not matter what the patient thinks or feels?

Approaches that attempt to deal with the response of the entire person have been grouped under the category of holistic medicine. Among the pioneers in that field is Dr. O. Carl Simonton, whose specialty is cancer, one of the most dreaded of all modern diseases. Simonton was intrigued by the spontaneous remissions found in some cancer patients and in "cures" that resulted from drugs known to be generally ineffective. He wondered if some psychological profile might not make people more prone to cancer in the way a stressful life style made people more prone to heart disease. A comprehensive summation of his views appears in *Getting Well Again*,[10] a book coauthored by Stephanie Matthews-Simonton and James Creighton. The authors present an impressive summary of placebo cures effected by different institutions and outline a theoretical model of how stress might cause malignancies. Another long section is devoted to mental techniques that might be used to fight cancer or to relieve the kind of stress they believe can lead to it and other maladies. The authors see their psychological work as a supplement to rather than as a replacement for standard cancer treatments. Simonton is a radiation oncologist.

A better-known example of how psychological attitudes may effect the cure of a difficult illness is the experience of Norman

Cousins, editor for many years of *The Saturday Review*. In 1964, Cousins was struck down and crippled by ankylosing spondylitis, a severe collagen disease thought to be irreversible and incurable. Working closely with his physician, Cousins cured his ailment with an incredible will to recover and 25-gram daily doses of vitamin C. Pursuing the hypothesis that positive emotions might help in the curative process, Cousins chose to concentrate on laughter. He began by screening the films of the Marx Brothers and episodes of *Candid Camera*. His physician found that after hours of viewing the films, there were measurable positive physical reactions in the body. In order to continue with the unorthodox laugh therapy, Cousins had to move from the hospital to a hotel room, where he found the atmosphere much more congenial. Later he was to learn of a British study which showed that the survival rate of heart patients being treated in an intensive-care unit was no higher than that of those being treated at home—possible confirmation that a crisis atmosphere can nullify the impact of sophisticated technological support systems.[11]

Cousins first wrote about his recovery in *The New England Journal of Medicine* (December 23, 1976). After reprints of the article and follow-up essays had appeared, he published a full account of his experience, its aftermath, and possible implications in *Anatomy of an Illness*. Still later came *The Healing Heart: Antidotes to Panic and Helplessness*. The original article of 1976 produced over three thousand letters from doctors commenting on every aspect of his recovery. This outpouring of professional concern indicated the enormous interest in the kind of issues Cousins, like Simonton and the holistic school, had raised. One might argue that it was the vitamin C which brought about the cure. In this respect, it is important to note that doctors who have used C to treat cancer patients generally believe it to be most effective in combination with standard treatments and that its impact is enhanced by the patient's belief that it will help. Cousins also described a study referred to by Dr. Jerome D. Frank of the Johns Hopkins University School of Medicine in which 176 cases of cancers were remitted without surgery, radiation, or chemotherapy. Cousins speculated, "One wonders whether a powerful factor in those remissions may not have been the deep belief by the patients that they were going to recover and their equally deep conviction that their doctors also believed they were going to recover."[12]

The ability of the mind to affect physical health was given renewed popular exposure in the 1990s by a Bill Moyers investigatory series on public television. Moyers later published interviews with the fifteen physicians whose work was featured on the programs in a book entitled *Healing and the Mind*. Those interviewed represented a variety of medical specializations and were often affiliated with prestigious institutions. Moyers' introductory comments to the section on the art of healing summed up much of the holistic credo by stating that he felt it was time for the nation to consider a new medical paradigm in which the present "body parts" orientation was replaced by "mind/body" medicine.

A consciously holistic approach to health most certainly sheds new light on some of the personality traits associated with the long living. Rather than constituting a life style of sacrifices, these characteristics activate the most natural, creative, and satisfying responses of the organism. Among these may be powers of healing and health maintenance that we've only begun to understand.

# 10. DOCTOR TWO LEGS

*I have two doctors, my left leg and my right. When body and mind are out of gear (and those twin parts of me live at such close quarters that the one always catches melancholy from the other), I know that I shall have only to call in my two doctors and I shall be well again.—Sir George Macaulay Trevelyan*

STRENUOUS PHYSICAL ACTIVITY THROUGHOUT THE course of life is the most common thread in the biographies of longevous people. Nonetheless, every winter people will die from the exertion of shoveling snow, and every summer a fair percentage of tennis players and golfers become victims of heart-attack and heatstroke. In the United States, many high school athletes will develop degenerative diseases by mid-life, and as a group, male professional athletes have life spans below the national averages. These paradoxes demonstrate that physical exercise, perhaps the single most important item in the longevity agenda, can be a cruel double-edged sword that must be approached as objectively as one approaches the age claims of supercentenarians.

The physical fitness of the longevous has traditionally been associated with work. For many, this involved some form of manual labor, often in a rural setting. With the introduction of labor-saving devices in the workplace and the home, everyday life presents most people with far fewer physical demands. More than ever, maintaining physical fitness has come to require conscious planning, including an understanding that not all forms of exercise are prolongevous and almost all when carried to excess are harmful. The exercises that best meet prolongevous criteria are those built around the most natural movements of the body. These actions promote oxygen efficiency, skeletal durability, and muscular strength without jeopardizing the body with unnecessary strain or tension. They also must be congenial enough to be part of everyday life and pursuable in some variation to the hundredth year and beyond.

The exercise which most fully meets these criteria is walking. Among its virtues are that walking can be accommodated to daily routines with ease, is the safest form of exercise, requires no special equipment or setting, and can be undertaken for hours on end with the body continuously gaining benefits. It is the exercise overwhelmingly preferred by people over 70.[1] Most persons who reach their hundredth birthday have literally walked most of the way.

Although more and more people have adopted walking as their primary form of exercise, a greater number are drawn to the various exercise regimens that have become omnipresent in American culture. Exercise videos and books are big business, and health clubs dot the civic landscape. Worthy as many of these enterprises are, few posit longevity as their goal. They are mostly about muscle building, aesthetic ideals, weight reduction, and socializing. Not a few inadvertently encourage antilongevous habits. In view of this reality, individuals who have longevity as their goal need to be clear about the physical effects they want and do not want to flow from their chosen exercise routines.

A prime prolongevous exercise goal is to maintain and strengthen the respiratory and cardiovascular system. Forcing the lungs to work strenuously over a protracted period of time is the only way to maintain their overall capacity to pull in the oxygen essential for all bodily functions. The vital capacity of the lungs of sedentary people diminishes in direct proportion to their sloth, progressively causing them to feel short-winded or out of breath with the slightest exertion. By contrast, the lungs of active people will show no significant decline over many decades. The same exercises also strengthen the muscles around the lungs so that the amount of oxygen available on short notice can be greatly increased. Meanwhile, the arterial system which carries the oxygen to waiting cells and organs is being assisted. The arteries expand and are kept junk-free by the burning off of waste products, which otherwise might accumulate as dangerous plaque. Simultaneously, new vessels are created. Some of them will go around blockages that have already formed, and others will improve circulation in neglected parts of the body. These new vessels take some time to construct and come into play only as complete networks, accounting for the sudden surge of strength an individual will feel after being on a program for a few weeks.

The net result of the improvement of the cardio-respiratory system is that every cell and organ of the body operates at increased efficiency. The "high" often reported by joggers is the immediately invigorating impact of oxygen-rich blood on the brain cells, and a feeling of power is partly related to the impact of oxygen on the vital organs. A major long-range benefit is that the conditioned heart at rest beats less rapidly in order to maintain the body's support systems. Furthermore, as various materials can be taken from and added to the bloodstream with reduced effort, the blood itself flows at lower pressure, reducing dangers that could come from hypertension. The heart, having become fully oxygenated, is less prone to damage from fibrillation, a frequent cause of heart attacks.

Equally dramatic changes occur in the muscular and skeletal systems. New muscles are created, and old muscle tissue, instead of hanging free from the skeletal frame as happens in inactive people, remains taut. Thanks to the rhythmic patterns of movement, the muscles become lithe and elongated, giving the body the wiry strength characteristic of the longevous. The same movements stimulate bone marrow, so that the density of bone is either maintained or increased. This is essential to combat the high incidence of hip fractures which afflict older people. Muscles in the digestive tract are also stimulated, which aids in evacuation and has an overall relaxing effect. Secondary benefits include regulation of sleep, control of appetite, prevention of minor aches, discouragement of varicose veins, tightening of loose skin, and, of course, burning off of stored fat.

These gains occur only when the activity takes place over an extended period without being carried to the point of fatigue. Prolongevous activities must not be confused with somewhat similar activities which may be fun to do but are either neutral or negative in their longevous effects. Usually, these sports or exercises emphasize a single aspect of the body such as form, stamina, coordination, speed, or strength. Frequently, they involve dubious diets, supplements, and movements. Because the aims are usually linked to athletic competition or aesthetic ideals rather than overall health, they may be considered longevity sidetracks. Examining a few of them helps to define what is prolongevously desirable and what is not.

*The skill sidetrack.* Ballet students undergo extremely long and physically arduous training programs. Their caloric output is high and they achieve incredible muscular control, yet because of the stop-start nature of the dancing and extreme stress on various parts of the anatomy, ballet dancers have no longevous advantages and frequently experience joint disease. Those fascinated by the challenge of golfing or bowling are in a related category. They may be having a good time, but the longevous impact of hours of play is not much greater than that for stationary sports like skeet shooting, billiards, or shuffleboard. More strenuous games like tennis, handball, and squash may develop excellent hand-eye coordination as well as other skills, but the stop-start pattern of play, the jerking movements, and the fatigue induced by playing in the sun or in stuffy enclosures neutralize most possible benefits.

*The speed sidetrack.* Running very rapidly over a short course or swimming several laps at top speed is debilitating. Projecting how many calories would be expended over an hour is misleading, for the pace could never be maintained that long. Rather than promoting the steady oxygen efficiency that is of benefit in daily life, racing is a severe test which swiftly draws extraordinary amounts of oxygen from the lungs. This sudden oxygen withdrawal is so enormous that the stress can trigger a heart attack. This rarely occurs in athletes who have trained methodically for racing competition and who understand their capacities, but even they must sit quietly, gulping down fresh oxygen to restore their strength as soon as the event is completed. The dangers of oxygen depletion can be fatal for otherwise sedentary people who suddenly have the urge to dance all night, shovel snow, or take part in a game of touch football. Another danger from speed events is that they may put severe pressure on the joints and organs because of the momentum involved. This drawback is multiplied when leaping or jumping is involved.

*The misnomer sidetrack.* What most people refer to as jogging is actually running. True jogging involves a pace just a bit faster than walking. Its only advantage over walking is that it achieves the same cardiovascular benefits in a shorter space of time. Its danger is that jogging usually turns into running which is longevously problematic due to the stress it brings to the joints. Another important longevity consideration, whether one runs or jogs, is using a soft running surface like grass. Hard surfaces, such as concrete, significantly intensify long-term wear-and-tear damage.

*The muscle-building sidetrack.* Working any particular group of muscles will stimulate their growth. When weights are kept light and strength is built mainly through repetition, there are longevity benefits, but when the buildup comes by using extremely heavy weights there are problems. This is most evident if one considers the physique of the professional body builder. In order to lift extraordinarily heavy weights, the lifter must have layers and layers of fat to support the overdeveloped muscles. The jerking motions involved in the actual lifting place sudden and possibly traumatic demands upon the heart. Muscle can become so unnaturally developed that the joints and connective tissues do not function normally. Professional muscle men do not enjoy long life spans and manipulating any muscle group beyond the point needed for survival activities may be a gross distortion of bodily design. What constitutes "the body beautiful", of course, is a matter of aesthetic taste. Bulging muscles, however, are no more inherently desirable than feet withered through binding or necks made long by being stretched by rows of metal braces.

People caught up in longevity sidetracks usually begin to alter their diet so that it may better support their exercise. This often involves misplaced faith in animal protein, mineral supplements, megavitamins, sugar, and steroids. Even when this is not the case, the diet is deflected from the goal of supporting overall health to supporting a peculiar activity, such as swimming across the English Channel or lifting 200 pounds of iron above one's head. In contrast, the normal prolongevous diet is sufficient for carrying out exercises that are also prolongevous. Other difficulties that may arise are the stresses resulting from distorting the daily schedule to fit in more and more exercise time and those created by trying to meet ever-rising performance expectations. The runner arising at dawn to get in a few extra miles in preparation for a marathon or the swimmer constantly competing with a stopwatch is not on a prolongevous wavelength.

Most long-living people incorporate strenuous activities into their habitual routines to the highest degree possible, have regular daily patterns, and monitor their health and exercise informally. Without falling into the rigidity of those caught up in longevity sidetracks, anyone embarking on a longevity agenda will want to have regular checkups. At the outset of any program it is wise to get blood-pressure, heart-efficiency, and cholesterol/triglyceride readings at a doctor's office. During the first year or so of the program, keeping track of these on a semiannual basis is useful. Once desired levels have been reached, the checkups can be extended to once every two or three years without any harm. There also exists an extremely simple, cheap, and reliable measurement of the body's longevity potential which can be made at any time: total body weight.

Every longevity study cited so far has noted the spare somatype of the longevous. These observations find startling statistical confirmation in records compiled by various life-insurance companies in the United States. The companies keep track of the weight of their clients at the time of death. Their analysis, which is crucial to the decision-making of multi-million-dollar enterprises, reveals that light body weight provides one of the most reliable predictors of longevity at any given age. Obese persons are virtually precluded from longevity. A few overweight individuals, most of whom have become heavy relatively late in life, may be seen at age 90, but they are very scarce past 95. The operating principle is not that low body weight will produce longevity, but that longevous life styles will produce low body weight.

Longevously desirable body weights are much lower than those popularly associated with good health. An impressive illustration of this is a desirable weight chart created by the Metropolitan Life Insurance Company based on the mortality statistics of 4 million clients of various insurers. These guidelines indicate that the most longevous body weight for a man of 6 feet having a medium body frame is between 150 and 167 pounds. These findings are based on death from all causes, including accidents.

The Metropolitan Life chart has been challenged by theorists who base their reservations on the Boston Longitudinal Study which found slightly overweight men living longer than those who were underweight. I've discussed the flaws in that analysis in my introduction. While always bearing in mind that weight is only one of the longevity factors, hundreds of studies have established the correlation between excessive weight and increased rates of disease and death. That opting for heavier weight is just so much wishful thinking is demonstrated by considering only three very different weight/health studies.

A long term study of 19,000 Harvard graduates compared the thinnest 20% with the heaviest 20%. The thinnest, among other advantages, enjoyed a 60% lower risk of heart disease and 40% lower risk for death.[2] A follow-up on the Framingham Study estimated that for each pound of excessive weight the risk of death increased by from 1 to 3%.[3] Looking at weight in a specific age group produced similar results in Sweden. A study followed 850 men, age 50 on the onset of the project, for ten years. At age 60, compared to the thinnest, the heaviest had a dramatically higher incidence of heart disease, clinical diabetes, kidney stones, and gallstones.[4]

What specifically constitutes small, medium, and large frames is subjective, but the weight ranges of four million Americans tabulated for life span are an extraordinarily large and persuasive data base. From a longevity standpoint they indicate that over 85% of all Americans are overweight. The antilongevous fat in most years comes to five billion pounds. While the extent of the overweight phenomenon may be surprising, its existence is not. Concern with

## Desirable Weights*: Age 25 and Over[5]

| HEIGHT (WITHOUT SHOES) | WEIGHT WITHOUT CLOTHING (POUNDS) | | |
| --- | --- | --- | --- |
| | SMALL FRAME | MEDIUM FRAME | LARGE FRAME |

### MEN

| HEIGHT | SMALL FRAME | MEDIUM FRAME | LARGE FRAME |
| --- | --- | --- | --- |
| 5 ft. 1 in. | 104–112 | 110–121 | 118–133 |
| 5 ft. 2 in. | 107–115 | 113–125 | 121–136 |
| 5 ft. 3 in. | 110–118 | 116–128 | 124–140 |
| 5 ft. 4 in. | 113–121 | 119–131 | 127–144 |
| 5 ft. 5 in. | 116–125 | 122–135 | 130–148 |
| 5 ft. 6 in. | 120–129 | 126–139 | 134–153 |
| 5 ft. 7 in. | 124–133 | 130–144 | 139–158 |
| 5 ft. 8 in. | 128–137 | 134–148 | 143–162 |
| 5 ft. 9 in. | 132–142 | 138–152 | 147–166 |
| 5 ft. 10 in. | 136–146 | 142–157 | 151–171 |
| 5 ft. 11 in. | 140–150 | 146–162 | 156–176 |
| 6 ft. | 144–154 | 150–167 | 160–181 |
| 6 ft. 1 in. | 148–159 | 154–172 | 165–186 |
| 6 ft. 2 in. | 152–163 | 159–177 | 170–191 |
| 6 ft. 3 in. | 156–167 | 164–182 | 174–196 |

### WOMEN

| HEIGHT | SMALL FRAME | MEDIUM FRAME | LARGE FRAME |
| --- | --- | --- | --- |
| 4 ft. 8 in. | 87–93 | 91–102 | 99–114 |
| 4 ft. 9 in. | 89–96 | 93–105 | 101–117 |
| 4 ft. 10 in. | 91–99 | 96–108 | 104–120 |
| 4 ft. 11 in. | 94–102 | 99–111 | 107–123 |
| 5 ft. | 97–105 | 102–114 | 110–126 |
| 5 ft. 1 in. | 100–108 | 105–117 | 113–129 |
| 5 ft. 2 in. | 103–111 | 108–121 | 116–133 |
| 5 ft. 3 in. | 106–114 | 111–125 | 120–137 |
| 5 ft. 4 in. | 109–118 | 115–130 | 124–141 |
| 5 ft. 5 in. | 113–122 | 119–134 | 128–145 |
| 5 ft. 6 in. | 117–126 | 123–138 | 132–149 |
| 5 ft. 7 in. | 121–130 | 127–142 | 136–153 |
| 5 ft. 8 in. | 125–135 | 131–146 | 140–158 |
| 5 ft. 9 in. | 129–139 | 135–150 | 144–163 |
| 5 ft. 10 in. | 133–143 | 139–154 | 148–168 |

*For weights with ordinary indoor clothing, add 5 pounds for women and 8 pounds for men to the above figures.

excess poundage has long supported an American weight reduction industry, replete with diets, exercises, and devices of all kinds. Most of the weight reduction plans popularly advertised are doomed to failure in the long term because they are not concerned with overall life styles. It has taken years for the overweight body to reach whatever dimension it has attained. Under the chin, around the belly, and in every nook of the body, there are veritable fat cities making constant demands upon the feeding, policing, and sewage systems of the body. Attempts to tear down the fat cities in a crash program further clog all vital networks, throwing the body into confusion and causing more stress than the stored fat had. The weakness, fatigue, and headaches experienced by people on trick or starvation diets are signs that the body is protesting its ordeal. Many diets increase these dangers by encouraging potentially dangerous chemical reactions within the body. In place of this kind of chaos, the fat cities need to be torn down methodically, with the muscles rebuilt and the body toned as an integral part of the process. The answer lies in prolongevous exercise.

From a longevity prospective, the ideal exercise for a moderately active person is one hour of brisk walking a day. Doing this while making no changes in diet will burn off three pounds of weight each month, more than is lost in most weight reduction programs. The difficulty, to be sure, is maintaining the same caloric intake and actually walking the full hour each day, whether in 60 minutes, or shorter segments of no less than 20 minutes. Each week will have its own pattern, but it is always better to do something every day rather than bunching up longer periods two and three times a week.

The weight to aim for is at the lower end of the weight ranges in the insurance chart. Once at that level individuals can consider loss of more weight but that would be a matter of fine tuning. Achieving the lower range weight goal will probably take years for most people, and maintaining it once it is achieved is a lifelong process. These realities make it essential that whatever the exercise routines may be they must be seen as attractive rather than as a chore.

The pace of longevity conditioning can always be accelerated by lowering caloric intake or by increasing exercise time, but under no circumstances should weight loss become an end in itself. Internal body-management systems will gradually reshape the body along the lines most natural for a particular person. The quickest spur to this process comes from exercises that provide gentle but constant toning of the muscles and skin. These exercises need to be differentiated from motorized exercise machines that are worthless for muscle rebuilding, and machines that stimulate the body with rollers and belts that may cause internal bruises and other damage. Saunas, steam baths, and massages have a relaxing effect that may combat stress, but they do not lead to weight loss or body shaping. Almost all schemes for spot reduction are futile, because the body takes fat from all cells when seeking energy, not just from those in the area directly agitated. High impact aerobics such as those made popular in the early video tapes of Jane Fonda, exercises in which both feet leave the floor, should be avoided due to their jolting effect and joint stress. Low impact aerobics are acceptable, but individuals need to be wary of health club classes. The instructors are not medically trained and most of the routines they favor involve movements that are antilongevous in their speed, stress, and intricacy. The same can be said for most exercise tapes put out by movie stars and other celebrities.

Scattering prolongevous activities throughout the daily and weekly schedule is the surest way of getting up to a daily average that can be maintained for a lifetime. An excellent starting point for activity is one's method of transportation. Those living within five miles of their place of employment could walk or ride a bike instead of taking a car or a bus. The suburban pattern in which one spouse regularly drives the other to the train depot could be replaced by having the commuting spouse walk or bike to the station whenever weather permits. In the city, one could get into the habit of getting off public transportation a few blocks early in order to walk the remaining distance or, if feasible, walking from a point where transfers are usually made. An advantage of the latter is that over-all time spent getting to work may come out about the same, as part or all of the period formerly spent waiting is spent walking. Those who work in office buildings might forgo the elevator and climb stairs. Additional walking can be done at lunchtime and after work, especially for shopping that does not require carrying heavy loads. The short car hop to the neighborhood store is also expendable. However brief the walk, it provides more stimulation than sitting in an automobile.

Within the household itself, many tasks can be reprogrammed for longevity value. Mopping, sweeping, and waxing become pro-longevous when they are done at a brisk tempo. From one-half to one full hour of any of these activities, or a combination of them, provides the equivalent of walking for the same period. In the country, sawing wood with a hand tool or splitting logs is unbeatable. Whatever the household task, if it can be done vigorously and continuously with fluid motions it becomes beneficial. Transformation of essential labor in this manner has particular psychological comforts for those who do not enjoy formal exercise or who consider it frivolous.

Any number of specific recreational activities are longevous. Unbeatable for its overall toning by virtue of working every muscle in the body is swimming. Any stroke is prolongevous as long as the swimming is continuous. The major drawback to swimming is that doing laps in a pool or swimming back and forth across the same lake may become tedious as a daily enterprise. More often than not, swimming serves well as an alternative or adjunct to walking. Other water-related longevous activities would be long walks in the surf, and watercraft that require muscle power instead of motors or wind. Causal beach games like volleyball are more valuable for their social role than for physical conditioning. Whenever activity is undertaken in the sun, there should be as little cooking of the skin as possible. Tanning is a defensive reaction of the body to the attack of the sun's ultraviolet rays. Consciously seeking a tan is to consciously age the skin prematurely and raise the risk of cancer, so umbrellas, sunscreens, and broad-brimmed hats are part of the prolongevous arsenal.

Sharing many of swimming's prolongevous benefits is hiking, which may be thought of as walking in nature. Once basic conditioning of the body has taken place, the activity may go on for hours without fatigue. Whether with a backpack for overnight camping or just a knapsack for snacks, hiking—thanks to the challenge of terrain and the need to climb or scramble over rocks—accelerates the buildup of muscular strength and overall vigor. It is slightly less safe than walking because of the greater possibility of falling or becoming exhausted, but limiting hiking to well-marked nature trails greatly reduces even these minor risks.

Cross-country skiing is a kind of hiking on snow. While it does not involve climbing as hiking does, it burns even more calories, because of the equipment involved and the winter temperatures, and is an excellent muscle builder. The sport is extremely popular in Scandinavia, a region with some of the longest average life spans found anywhere in the world; a study of 396 Finnish champion endurance skiers born between 1845 and 1910 revealed that they outlived their long-living fellow citizens by five to seven years.[6]

Sports activities of any kind are almost always preferable to no exercise at all, but some activities are longevously superior to others. Biking, horseback riding, and roller skating rank high;

bowling and golf do not. In colder climates, sledding, tobogganing and ice skating are prolongevous, while downhill skiing and hockey are not. The benefits of sledding and tobogganing, of course, are not so much in the slide downhill as in the climb up. If mechanized means are used for this, the longevous advantage is lost. Downhill skiing flunks out on this score, and even when there are no accidental spills that break bones, it can easily abuse the body with its various jolting and straining movements. Hockey is only a little less antilongevous than football due to the body checking involved. Snowmobiling is neutral at best.

Sportslike activities ranking high on the prolongevity scale would be modest weight lifting, Asian systems like *t'ai chi chuan*, and water aerobics done in heated pools. Dancing is still another pleasurable activity that is prolongevous when done in extended time segments. The only disadvantage is that many dance environments are filled with smoke or are quite noisy. The contemporary American nightclub with its brainwrenching flashing lights and overamplified music is a longevity chamber of horrors.

Any workplace procedures requiring physical movement should be grouped into continuous segments for the longevity bonus. Those who work at desk jobs will find that if they get up at least once every hour to stretch and move about, they will become more clear-headed and will feel much more energetic. Although exercise time and gym facilities as fringe benefits are a new concept, major corporations have found that providing a full-scale gym for clerical, manual, and managerial workers to use at various times during the day raises productivity and cuts down the number of days lost to illness. Even in the most conventional setups, there are likely to be opportunities for prolongevous activities both during work and afterward. Schoolteachers who hurry home after a tough day to relax with a cigarette, martini, or coffee would be better off using their school gym for an hour.

The relaxing effect of exercise is particularly significant in a nation in which tension is a major health complaint. A number of tests have pitted walking against the most common tranquilizers and other drugs to see which relaxant is the more effective in lowering blood pressure, relieving nervous tension, and combating tightened muscles. Walks of approximately fifteen minutes proved more effective in both the short and long term, even without factoring in possible side effects from chronic use of medication. This principle was understood in ancient Greece, where Aristotle, among others, taught that people should walk as they carried on a discourse or attempted to think out a problem. A more familiar example is the image of the expectant father walking off his anxiety by pacing outside a delivery room.

Gardening, with its multiple demands on the body, scores extremely well on the longevity scale. When briskly done, movements like hoeing, digging, and raking for an hour at a time are equivalent or superior to jogging. Bending to pull weeds, staking up plants, tugging at sacks of manure, and other strenuous chores tote up numerous pluses for the musculo-skeletal system. One can lose oneself for hours in gardening, a kind of physical exertion which seems more effortless than most activities. The ultimate production of food or flowers provides a unique and satisfying reward for the energy expended.

A certain personality type will be more comfortable with a formal set of exercise routines and a system to measure bodily response. Such individuals can develop their own routines using tables found in the Canadian Air Force program,[7] the aerobic system of Kenneth Cooper,[8] or the exercise mode of the Pritikin Plan.[9] The major caution in using these plans is that they are aimed primarily at promoting cardiovascular health rather than longevity *per se*. As such, they are somewhat less sensitive to long-term wear-and-tear problems than they should be. As the prolongevous person wants to be walking fast and hard at age 90, the effects of exercises on ankles, tendons, bones, ligaments, and joints are major considerations. Plans like these also have a tendency to demand less time commitment than is really needed to pile up longevity gains.

Particular exercises may be appealing because of the little time involved. Ten minutes of skipping rope in the style of a professional boxer can equal an hour of walking. Yet this exercise is not prolongevous because it jolts the body, depletes oxygen, and stresses joints. When faced with exercise choices, one is best advised to be cautious at all times, and if warm-ups are required, they should never be dismissed as unnecessary. It is also important to bear in mind that one doesn't have to sweat to get longevity benefits.

Eliminating the risk of unnecessary wear and tear once more puts walking in the longevity spotlight. Given a choice between running in place and taking a walk, the walk is superior on at least three counts. First, it is much easier to upgrade one's routine to a walk of an hour than it is to reach the equivalent exercise by running in place. Second, natural movements are always easier and more benevolent to the body than artificial ones. People who run in place frequently experience stiffness or cramps in their legs. Third, when approaching a walking pace of five miles an hour, the body usually yearns to set off into a jog, and a walk/jog pattern may develop. Increasing the speed, however, is less important than continuing the activity for at least an hour. A walking program may be thought of as a revival of the old American habit of a daily constitutional. President Harry S. Truman was an avid walker whose brisk gait often left reporters panting behind him. When still a senator, Truman had noted that his fellow senators were dying of heart disease at an alarming rate. He asked a doctor what preventive measure he should take and was told to start walking.

No exercise agenda, whatever its particulars, should be rigid.

While the program is best followed each day, when the weather is uncooperative or when the air quality is adverse, a shift to indoor activities or even inactivity may be best. The same holds true when walking or jogging can be done only alongside busy motorways. There's no longevity gain in having the lungs inhale large amounts of poisoned air which the body will have to contend with for hours.

The long-term ability of exercise to hold off premature aging can be seen in some extraordinary athletic feats by older people. At age 71, Edward Payson Wetson, for example, walked from New York to San Francisco in 123 days. At age 81, walking backwards, Plennie Wingo covered the 451 miles between Santa Monica and San Francisco in 85 days. Accounts of almost every marathon race of any size usually include the participation of at least one non-agenarian. In the land of the marathon's origin, Demetrious Iordanidis walk/jogged the 26.2 mile course in six hours and 42 minutes when he was 95. Three years later, he needed seven hours and 33 minutes to finish. Asked why he needed an extra hour, he replied, "I was younger before."[10]

Even more to the point is the story of Mrs. Eula Weaver as recounted by her physician, Nathan Pritikin.[11] At age 67, Weaver had suffered from angina; at age 75, she was hospitalized with heart disease; and at age 81 she suffered congestive heart failure. Her circulation became so feeble that she had to wear gloves in the summer months to keep warm, and she was so weak that she could not walk more than a dozen feet without collapsing. Desperate to regain her health, Weaver put herself in the care of the Pritikin longevity center. She began a program of gradual walk/jogging and shifted to a prolongevous diet. In a year she was off medications. In two years she was able to walk three miles at one time and could chalk up ten miles a day on her stationary bicycle. She continued her improvement and at age 85 began to set running records in the 800- and 1,500 meter events for octogenarian women.

The prolongevous lesson to be drawn from these kinds of stories, and there are many of them, is that after conditioning of the body takes place, people in late maturity and beyond can expect active lives. Exercise programs that are valid for people aged 30 to 80 need not alter significantly thereafter. Changes would be of degree, not kind. As for restriction based on sex, it is safe to say that the males should be able to keep up with the sturdier females as long as the usual precautions are taken against exercising to the point of fatigue.

The paramount point of reference regarding exercise is that one is not living in order to exercise well (much less break athletic records), one is exercising in order to live well. The slim, wiry prolongevous somatype is not to be sought obsessively. It will form automatically from a combination of prolongevous eating and exercise habits. Prolongevous exercises, characteristically rhythmic in nature, should be movements the individual enjoys, sees as valuable and finds easy. They should be planned to be done alone if necessary, although group involvement can be strongly reinforcing. Exercise schedules must remain flexible, and as long as there is genuine progress toward reaching clearly defined goals, a gradual change is best. By far the best pattern is one which integrates vigorous physical activities into everyday life routines.

The exercise component of the longevity agenda constantly rebuilds and maintains the body, from its humblest cell to its most complex organ. Without this daily stimulation, the vital systems will decline far more rapidly than they have been genetically programmed to, bringing on premature aging and its fatal companion. Nothing can take the place of exercise. Exercise, in fact, will minimize the need for special diets, supplements, and medications. The key skill involved is a natural movement normally mastered by the end of the first year of life: walking.

# 11. Food as Fuel

*If we lived entirely on raw, fresh plant foods, as our*
*ancestors did millions of years ago, there would be no need*
*for concern about getting adequate amounts of the essential*
*foods such as vitamins.* —*Linus Pauling*

IT HAS BEEN CORRECTLY OBSERVED THAT we are what we eat.
Contemporary gerontologists have added the equally correct observation that we are what we choose *not* to eat. Both perspectives
are essential in determining how often we eat and what quantity,
type, quality, and preparation of food is most conducive to max-
imizing the life span. Although the diets of longevous people and
the health guidelines of medical authorities are very much in
confluence, most of us remain prone to wishful thinking and faddish
behavior regarding diet. This is largely because of the many non-
nutritive functions food serves in our lives.

Primary among these functions are food's role in various
ceremonial aspects of life. Feasts are the centerpieces of many
holidays and some foods are synonymous with national and ethnic
identity. Often people overeat to show that they appreciate the
special delicacies prepared by mothers, aunts and grandmothers.
There can be a tremendous psychological boost in being a wine
connoisseur, gourmet cook, or consummate host. Food also plays
a symbolic role in religious rituals and is often thought to have
curative or rejuvenative powers when blessed. Asked the secret

of long life, centenarians frequently mention food. Typical is Mrs. May Lauchuck of Poughkeepsie, New York, age 104, who advised, "Take a teaspoonful of vodka laced with garlic twice a day"—a different formula from that of Signora Paolina Pichi of Borgonesia, Italy, also age 104, who recommended eating spaghetti three times a day.

An insight that may be gained from even the most flippant recommendations of the longevous is that they really enjoy their diets and that these diets can be quite diverse. Due to biochemical individuality, no single diet can ever be designed to meet the needs of all people. A food that is beneficial to one person may be harmful to another. The caloric needs of a construction worker are not the same as those of an accountant. A pregnant woman will of course have special nutritional requirements. Despite these wide variations in individual needs, the lifelong eating habits of the longevous contain some constants applicable to everyone.

The major characteristic of the diet of longevous people is low caloric intake throughout life. As opposed to the average American daily caloric intake of 3,000 to 4,000, the longevous average from 1,500 to 2,000 calories. In addition, the typical American diet contains 40 to 45% fats, 15 to 20% proteins, and 35 to 45% carbohydrates, while the diet of the longevous contains about 10 to 15% fats, 10 to 15% proteins, and 70 to 80% carbohydrates. Otherwise, the kind of food eaten by the longevous is not greatly different from that consumed by others, with the exception that longevous people tend to eat far less meat.

Three components of this dietary scorecard have powerful laboratory backing: low caloric intake, minimal meat consumption, and a low percentage of fat. Unfortunately, the immediate psychological response to these realities is that health is a matter of deprivation. This is not true. As is often the case with the longevity agenda, less actually means more. That is, less meat, less fat, and fewer calories mean more health, more vigor, and more years of healthy life. The major "deprivation" is a greatly lessened chance of needing open-heart surgery, chronic medication, and physical rehabilitation.

Despite these statistical probabilities, most Americans resist cutting back on meat, lowering caloric intake, or reducing their consumption of fat. That many consider a predominantly or exclusively vegetarian diet to be artificial, nutritionally inadequate, and even faddist is not surprising. In the 1950s the American government began to promote the four-food-group concept which insisted that meat and dairy products should make up 50 percent of the daily diet. Few Americans understood that those recommendations were the work of agricultural lobbyists promoting economic interests rather than recommendations of medical authorities promoting public health. Not until the 1990s did the federal government devise new recommendations with some linkage to health priorities. The new "food pyramid" put the nutritional spotlight on fruits, vegetables, and grains while lowering meat and dairy intake to 25 percent of the diet at best. Decades will pass before even these modest revisions become cultural norms, but one immediate benefit is that they make anyone with a longevity agenda based on a vegetarian diet appear reasonable, rather than a health extremist.

Far more persuasive than government edicts on what constitutes good fuel for humans is the physical design of the human body, particularly its digestive system.[1] For starters, the fingers are wonderful tools for harvesting fruits, nuts and vegetables. Lacking strong claws, they are not well adapted to killing other creatures. The teeth, in turn, are better designed to gnash vegetables than to tear flesh, the so-called canines being puny instruments for ripping when compared with those of most true carnivores. Human saliva, which breaks down food in the mouth, is alkaline, as in herbivores, containing ptyalin, an enzyme that predigests starch from plants. Farther along the digestive tract, the stomach, which can accommodate a dazzling variety of foods, does not have the powerful acids needed to digest raw game, such as the freshly killed mouse that a cat's stomach handles perfunctorily.

The most dramatic indication of the largely herbivorous nature of the human digestive system is its overall length and shape. The digestive tract of a carnivore is usually three times the length of its torso, as measured from mouth to anus. This shortness allows for quick processing and rapid evacuation so that meat does not decay within the intestines and give off toxins. The human digestive tract is about twelve times the length of the torso—four times as long as that of carnivores but only one-fourth longer than that of most herbivores. This system is comprised of a very long, convoluted small intestine followed by a larger, smoother one, indicating its affinity with digestive systems of herbivores.

Looking at secondary traits, human systems continue to resemble those of mammals such as gorillas, which feed mainly on fruits, nuts, and grains. Like these creatures, humans drink by sucking rather than lapping, sweat through the skin rather than through the tongue, and produce alkaline urine. Whereas true carnivores are instinctively aroused by the smell of bleeding raw flesh, humans are repelled. Conversely, true carnivores are indifferent to the aroma of ripe fruit, while humans are attracted by it.

The scientific resolution of these facts has been to classify the human species as omnivorous, but this classification does not indicate what percent of the total diet should be meat. Anthropologists working with prehistoric skeletal remains have determined that originally humans were primarily fruit eaters. Even after flesh consumption entered the diet, the ratio of plant foods to flesh foods was about 3 to 1—the reverse of the pattern in many contemporary diets. The gradual shift to meat was a consequence of the improvement of hunting technology, the domestication of some animals, and the development of agriculture. Meat ceased to be a food of opportunity, and the range of plant foods eaten dwindled considerably. The mere fact that eating meat is gastronomically possible and economically convenient does not, however, make it desirable, especially if meat is a daily staple.

All available studies indicate that exclusively or predominantly vegetarian diets result in the lengthening of the average life span by five to ten years. To be sure, some of these studies have focused on organized groups, such as the Seventh Day Adventists, or informal movements such as that of grain-oriented macrobiotic advocates, in which there is tremendous social support for many prolongevous habits. This type of support makes it impossible to credit the diet as the decisive factor in their longevity agendas; but even cautiously interpreted, the studies indicate that vegetarianism is clearly supportive of long life. Vegetarian groups also have an extremely low incidence of many of the diseases associated with premature aging. In contrast, populations with the highest rates of beef intake have the highest rates of cancer, particularly of the breast and colon.

More powerful support for a primarily vegetarian, low-fat, and low-caloric diet is found in the work of physicians who have used diet to treat plaque-clogged arteries. Nathan Pritikin first brought public attention to this non-surgical approach to heart disease (America's number one cause of death) in the 1970s, and Dean Ornish has done similar work in the 1980s and 1990s. A common element of their work is lowering patients' fat intake to no more than 10% of the diet while supervising a mild exercise routine based on walking, fortified with a low-caloric diet. Using angiograms and other conventional diagnostic tools, Ornish proved that his program could reverse as well as halt clogging, a claim Pritikin had also made but never fully established. Ornish also uses stress reduction techniques such as visualization, deep breathing, meditation, progressive deep relaxation and stretching, to augment diet and exercise in what amounts to a prolongevous health triad for those severely ill from heart disease.[2] This dietary and exercise approach is a far cheaper and much safer method of dealing with clogged arteries than bypass surgery. It has the additional decided advantage of dealing with the cause of the condition and preventing its recurrence, which bypass surgery does not.

A predominantly vegetarian diet is also the main feature of the most daring longevity experiment now in progress. Roy Walford, one of America's most honored gerontologists, adheres to a diet of severe caloric restriction and superior nutrition to make a personal bid to become a supercentenarian. His plan derives from countless studies which have shown that caloric restriction in life forms as diverse as protozoa, fleas, fish, and rats has greatly increased their life spans, sometimes nearly doubling them. The greatest effect occurs when caloric restriction is initiated at birth. The subjects tend to be somewhat smaller in size than usual but otherwise normal. Caloric restriction in later stages of life is also effective in extending life spans, but not as dramatically. Walford believes caloric restriction will have the same results in humans.

The diet Walford follows involves five days a week of eating from 1,500 to 2,000 calories and two days of fasting. The percent of fat is from 2 to 5. By staying on this diet perpetually and using exercises like swimming, Walford hopes to bring his weight down to some 30 pounds below the lightest weights in the Met Life tables referred to earlier. To maximize the nutritional value in his limited food supply, Walford fed data into a computer about the chemical qualities of his food, his caloric limits, and his nutritional needs, including specific limits on fat and cholesterol levels. The combination of foods that the computer determined best met all criteria was predominantly vegetarian.

Walford has spelled out the rationale and details of his diet in numerous writings. A good popular text is his *Maximum Life Span*.[3]

In that book he also evaluates popular American diets such as the Scarsdale, Atkins, and Pritikin plans. He judges the first two effective for prompt weight loss but controversial in respect to long term health. In contrast, he believes anyone following the Pritikin plan over a lifetime will achieve a modestly extended life span. Walford's own program clearly is of a different nature. His is a maximal effort to break all established age records. Although its specifics are too severe for any but the most experimentally minded, its general pattern embodies the basic longevous dietary agenda.

Because of their sensitivity to the nutritional value of food, health-conscious vegetarians enjoy another longevous benefit. They rightly believe that the less a food has been tampered with and the more quickly it arrives from the earth, the more nutritious it is. Most vegetarians, therefore, will try to live in situations in which they have access to garden-fresh vegetables, and would consider the Abkhasian habit of eating freshly-picked greens for breakfast a reasonable one. Those who include cereals in their meals eat only whole grains, understanding that milling away the germ or seed robs the grain of its most nutritious part as well as its brownish hue.

The worldwide infatuation with white rice, white pasta, and white bread is one of the most absurd and tragic of human follies as countless hours are wasted lowering the quality of food. In the United States, the devitalization of grain takes bizarre twists. Commercial bakeries with national distribution will advertise that they have added a dozen or more vitamins to breads when in fact the overall processing has taken away many more nutrients than are returned. Some firms will use caramel coloring in their dough to make their products look like whole-grain loaves. The superiority of whole grains is so indisputable that anyone mildly interested in longevity should use them whenever possible.

The most basic tampering with food, however, occurs in the

cooking process. A diet nearest to that afforded by nature would concentrate on raw foods—nuts, seeds, greens, fruits, and berries. Food that must be prepared or softened will suffer the least nutritional loss if steamed, boiled, or baked. The broth left over from steaming or boiling can be consumed as a soup to recover most of the loss. The form of cooking to be avoided most is frying. Whether frying oil begins as a saturate or an unsaturate, when heating commences, the oil becomes saturated, and fat permeates the food. Vital elements like enzymes are destroyed by frying, and the food is made more difficult to digest, placing extra burdens on all parts of the digestive system. Many otherwise excellent foods, such as the potato, become antilongevous when turned into French fries or potato chips. By contrast, a baked potato, spared a butter-and-salt bath, is extremely nutritious and easy to digest.

The perennial debate on the advisability of including dairy products in the diet has been given a new dimension by the controversy over the possible harm done to the cardiovascular system by a high cholesterol intake. Numerous vegetarians abstain from dairy products on the ground that humans are the only known creatures to consume milk after infancy and that many adults cannot tolerate lactose. Others argue that dairy products are rich in protein and contain many key nutrients such as calcium.[4] For them, the only danger is in excessive consumption. The matter cannot be resolved on strictly statistical grounds, as there are no studies comparing vegetarians who use no animal products with those who do.

With these considerations in mind, the decision whether to include dairy products in the diet becomes largely one of individual taste. As long as the entire fat content in the diet remains low, there is no observable harm in consuming some eggs, cheese, yogurt, cream, or butter. Dairy products with low fat content can be treated like any other food, and case histories of longevous people show that many, including Delina Filkins, used dairy products extensively throughout their long lives.

A predominantly vegetarian diet automatically provides many health bonuses. One of them is that vitamin and mineral content will easily exceed the minimum daily requirements set by the Food and Drug Administration. Another is that raw foods, a large component of vegetarian fare, cause minimal strain on the body, as they take only eighteen to twenty-four hours to go through the entire digestive process from ingestion to evacuation. Cooked and processed foods need from eight to one hundred hours to accomplish the same journey and may give off poisons while languishing for long periods in the lower intestinal tract. Development of constipation and hemorrhoids, chronic complaints in developed countries, is usually prevented or minimized by vegetarian diets because of the foods' high fiber content. Vegetarian foods produce large but soft stools that cleanse the tract and stimulate regular evacuation without strain.

An objection frequently raised to a vegetarian diet is that it provides insufficient protein. This view is based on at least two fallacies: that the body needs a large quantity of protein daily and that meat is the best source of protein. There can be no question that protein is crucial to bodily well-being. Protein provides twenty-two essential amino acids, including eight which the body cannot synthesize. It is needed for growth, and it regulates the body's fluid balance. The minimum daily requirements for adults established by the Food and Agricultural Organization of the United Nations are about 30 grams for the average adult female and 38 grams for adult males. The National Academy of Sciences in the United States recommends an additional 20 grams as a safety margin.

The American diet far exceeds these standards.[5] From 1900 to the end of the 1970s, with almost no change from year to year, the average American consumed between 88 and 104 grams of protein daily. Much of this came from meat, although protein is found in eggs, nuts, lentils, grains, brewer's yeast, beans, dairy products, seeds, and other foods. The danger of eating an otherwise nutritious and varied vegetarian diet and not automatically receiving sufficient protein is nil.

The mystique of animal protein is nurtured by the fiction that it is needed to build muscle, an idea going back at least to ancient Greece, where Olympic athletes were taught to eat flesh if they wished to be champions. Contemporary football players and boxers, operating under the same principle, often train on diets featuring steak two and three times a day. Yet the protein from vegetable sources provides the same acids as protein from meat, and the actual working of muscle to build new muscle requires energy that is best furnished by carbohydrates and fats.

Vegetarian animals are the world's sturdiest creatures. The endurance of the camel, the strength of the ox, and the longevity of the tortoise are proverbial; and the bird with the longest life span happens to be the parrot, a fruit and seed eater. In contests staged at the turn of the century in France and the United States, vegetarian athletes who were pitted against non-vegetarians came out ahead in most categories, including endurance and strength.[6] Numerous world and Olympic records are held by vegetarians, some in weight lifting. Anyone doubting the strength-building powers of vegetables might try to arm-wrestle a gorilla or put a flying tackle on an elephant.

If vegetable versus animal protein were a matter only of six of one versus half-a-dozen of the other, the choice could be left to individual taste; but there is mounting evidence that high protein consumption is another case in which more of a food is not only not better, but decidedly harmful. Coaches have discovered that athletes who are on a protein-heavy diet and train vigorously are particularly subject to dehydration and heat stroke. This occurs because high protein consumption increases the need for fluid to wash out the byproducts deposited when the protein is metabolized. A diet consistently high in protein puts a chronic burden on the kidneys and, to a lesser degree, the liver. High protein intake reduces the body's calcium and has been linked to various cancers and heart diseases.

Intensifying all of these danger factors is the adulteration of the animal products now sold in the marketplace. Any similarity between meat provided by the modern cow, chicken, or turkey and meat provided by them in the nineteenth century is purely coincidental. Modern animals are forced to grow faster and fattier through chemicals. A notorious example of these chemical hazards is exemplified by diethylstilbestrol (DES), which, although proved in 1947 to be carcinogenic, was injected directly into animals for another twenty-five years before being prohibited by federal mandate. DES is only one of fifteen sex hormones presently being used, ten of which are proved or suspected carcinogens. Some, like DES and dienestrol diacetate, are so clearly linked to vaginal cancer that the Food and Drug Administration warns against their use. A number of scientists, not linked to the government, have speculated that the soaring rate of breast cancer in women may be related to the different hormones routinely pumped into animals slated for human consumption.

To this health concern may be added the dangers posed by scores of antibiotics and other drugs that are known to have a negative effect on the human organism. Some are injected directly into animals, and others are added to their feed. Virtually all turkey feed, 60% of cattle feed, 30% of chicken feed, and 80% of feed given to swine and calves have these additives.[7] Still other additives, including sodium nitrite used to preserve and color luncheon meats, are such firmly established carcinogens that several nations have banned their use, following the lead of Norway. Government reports indicate that 14% of all meat and poultry contain illegal residual levels of drugs and pesticides. Yet another hazard is posed by the seventy transmissible diseases carried in animals which are eaten by humans. The chance of infection is primarily guarded against by an antiquated and understaffed meat-inspection system which came into existence only after widespread abuses by meat-packers were publicized at the turn of the century.

Cattle, probably more sacred in the United States than in India though for quite different reasons, have been re-engineered to provide fat marbling throughout their bodies, giving beef its distinct taste without regard for the added burden on the human heart. That grand old American bird, the turkey, has been similarly altered, reduced from six native breeds to one, a reshaped White Holland. The self-basting frozen creature widely sold at Thanksgiving and Christmas gets a significant portion of its weight from a cheap fattening injection of water and oil. More brutalized than either cattle or turkeys are chickens, many of which are diseased and have cancer.

How meat is prepared, including "down home" favorites like fried chicken and barbecued ribs, creates more problems. Frying has already been identified as a peril to digestion. Deep-frying is worse. Barbecuing on a grill is somewhat easier on the digestive system, but the portion of the meat coming into contact with the grill can become carcinogenic, as can all charred meat. People using chemically manufactured charcoal cubes instead of wood briquettes add more toxins. Unfortunately, few people can or will connect their heavy meat consumption with premature aging or degenerative diseases.

Fish, crustaceans, and mollusks generally are treated as meat in terms of dietary components. They have fewer inherent drawbacks if they can be found in uncontaminated waters; but this is increasingly difficult, as many streams, lakes and parts of the ocean have become polluted through chemical leaching and dumping. The most dangerous poisons in American waters are mercury and PCBs—polychlorinated biphenyls. Their threat is so immediate that many lakes have been closed to commercial fishing. Just examining a fish does not reveal whether it is contaminated. The buyer is left to trust in the fish seller's honesty, and more often than not the seller is without the means to certify the fish safe for consumption.

The history of PCBs illustrates the magnitude of the toxic problem.[8]  Since they were first made in 1930 by Monsanto Chemical for use as coolants and lubricants, 1.4 billion pounds of PCBs have been produced in the United States alone. Although questions about their harmful effect on the health of chemical workers were raised in the 1940s, it was not until the mid-1960s that PCBs seeping into the environment began to show up in the dead bodies of birds, fish, and animals. The alarm was first sounded in Sweden. Among the problems traced to PCBs were bone deformities, cancer, and stillbirths. After the environmental movement made their production a political issue, the manufacture and sale of PCBs were banned under the terms of the Toxic Substance Control Act. Meanwhile,  an estimated 150 million pounds remained in the soil, water, and air, with another 290 million pounds in dumps and landfills. PCBs have been found in the Atlantic Ocean at depths below 10,000 feet.

Chemical adulteration of food reaches its zenith in the processed and packaged food industries, where additives artificially flavor, color, and preserve foods. The only purpose of these additives is to increase the product's profitability. The artificial flavor substitutes for expensive natural flavor; the artificial color cosmetically disguises what has happened to the food during processing; and the preservatives extend the product's shelf or warehouse life. How successfully the body can handle these additives is a matter of bitter dispute. But no one can argue that few of the additives appeared in any food before 1930 or that they convey any discernible prolongevous benefit.

Additives acknowledged to be toxic or carcinogenic are common. Arguments which border on being criminally irresponsible have been developed to the effect that the use of poisons in small quantities is harmless or an acceptable risk in view of the marketing advantages. These arguments are invalid. Different body chemistries have different tolerances for a poison, so there can be no foolproof safety threshold. Furthermore, chemicals interact when combined, so that taking in several different additives, even those considered safe when taken in isolation, can have unpredictable and possibly adverse chemical consequences. Whether the additives hold down prices is questionable as well. Successful mass marketing existed before additives became widespread, and the most expensive foods on the market are exactly those prepackaged and processed products with the most additives and chemical alterations.

A person with a good background in chemistry and lots of time might conceivably go through all the chemicals used in foods to determine which are safe, which are dubious, and which are definitely harmful. This would require inquiries to each manufacturer to find out what general terms like stabilizers, emulsifiers, and artificial flavors (or colors) mean in specific chemical terms. Frequently, artificial substances are given clever names which obscure their true nature. Hence, the artificial flavor "vanillin" is easily misread as the natural flavor "vanilla." Artificial products carry names like "Dairy Creme" or "Dairy Creamer" even though they are non-dairy products.

The Food and Drug Administration is mandated to deal with adulterants in food, but it has been understaffed and underfunded for decades. Despite the impression given by the media that it is extremely difficult to get new additives onto the market, the FDA faces a nearly impossible job trying to monitor the new chemicals constantly being proposed. In practice, rather than the manufacturer's having to prove or even guarantee the safety of additives, the FDA must prove their possible ill effects. Despite these handicaps, the FDA has established a guideline for using additives that no one who seeks long life dares to ignore. Time and again, substances originally believed safe are proven to be extremely harmful. No fewer than fourteen of the sixteen food dyes approved in 1946 were banned in 1980 on the grounds that they were carcinogens. It seems clear that consumers are being asked to jeopardize their health in order to improve corporate balance sheets. One can only speculate on how much of the nation's staggering annual medical bill might be attributable to "cost-saving" additives.

Processed foods are so low on the nutritional scoreboard to begin with that the risks posed by additives make them virtually unacceptable. One can only hope that consumer rejection of such products will reach a high enough level to discourage producers from using them. The health-food boom has been something of a corrective to the trend in which more and more foods are tampered with; but terms like "natural" and "organic" must be legally defined to prevent abuse. Legislation spurred by health activists has brought about better food labeling and strengthening of laws affecting product safety, but much more remains to be done. It would be helpful if manufacturers were held financially and even criminally liable for suppressing negative findings about the safety of what they sell as food. There are so many excellent foods readily available that there is no validity to the argument that some risks are acceptable or necessary. The argument sometimes heard that any food eaten in sufficient quantities causes cancer is simply not true.

Fresh fruits and vegetables are not automatically safe either.

Although DDT and other dangerous pesticides once widely used are now banned, there are still more than five thousand approved pesticides, waxes, and colorings. The safest way to avoid them, apart from having a personal garden, is to patronize stores that sell food grown without chemicals or spraying—the way all food was grown before the twentieth century. While more expensive than regular produce, such natural foods, used exclusively in vegetarian meals, are cheaper than a typical meal with meat and processed food. A second option is to patronize a farmers' market. Small truck farmers usually employ more traditional growing methods, and they can be asked what pesticides they may have used. Very rarely will they wax or color their products. Untreated dried fruits and nuts are available in most areas, but one has to examine the packages carefully or ask questions about the use of preservatives. Simply shopping at a health-food store or choosing a package marked with health-food claims is no guarantee of safety. Many companies have tried to take advantage of the fact that quality food is more expensive, but they have not really provided the promised quality.

Fortunately, most pesticides, as claimed by their producers, do not penetrate the skin of plants, so thorough washing adds a considerable margin of safety. Even when a shopper is thrown back on produce grown by agribusiness, the danger of consuming toxins is much less than with processed foods and meats. The least chemical contamination occurs at the lower end of the food chain. Thus, root vegetables and grains have only a fractional retention of pollutants, but meat products can have high retention. Legumes, fruits, and vegetables of all kinds have relatively low retention. Dairy products fall midway between the various meat and non-meat categories.

Sugar poses another dietary problem. Most American consume about two pounds a week, one-fourth directly and three-fourths as part of processed foods. The excess pounds burdening many people's bodies are caused by this sugar overload. Some degenerative diseases have been traced to a high sugar intake, but the most insidious effect of sugar is that it debases the palate. When there is no strong addiction to sugar, what tastes good is usually nutritious, but as one develops a sugar habit, only what tastes sweet is thought to taste good. Overweight but undernourished sugar junkies are not uncommon.

When cutting down or eliminating sugar from the diet, one has to be wary of the various names manufacturers use for sugar. Sucrose, corn sweetener, fructose, dextrose, and sorbital are all sugars. The sugar found in natural food is sufficient for bodily functions, so it is nutritionally unnecessary to use additional sugar. Wholly refined white sugar is the most difficult sugar for the body to handle and should be avoided. Partly refined brown sugar, the staple of many health-conscious households, is not much better. Honey or molasses, both of which contain minerals and vitamins, pose fewer digestive difficulties, but should never be thought of as health foods, and their use should be held to a minimum. The most easily handled and most useful sugars are those found in fruit. An apple or orange in the morning will give one a better start than a sugar-coated bakery product. Sugar taken as fruit has the advantage of being in a bulky form which makes excessive consumption less likely.

Artificial sweeteners such as cyclamates and saccharin place one in double jeopardy. Independent scientific organizations have shown both to be carcinogenic, and both keep alive one's acquired taste for sweets. An irony of saccharin consumption is that because of the way saccharin chemically reacts with fat cells, it may increase the desire to eat in overweight people. Saccharin's use by heavy smokers is especially dangerous because of a synergistic reaction which intensifies the harmful effects of tobacco.

Salt, formerly used mainly as a preservative, shares many of the characteristics of sugar as a palate debaser. Some recipes that now feature large quantities of sugar and salt can be traced historically through cookbooks to recipes requiring neither flavoring in any significant amount, if at all. Although it is not understood how sodium influences blood pressure, studies of more than twenty cultures show no hypertension where salt consumption is limited. This and other evidence has led physicians to caution high-blood-pressure patients, among others, to reduce their salt intake or eliminate salt from their diet altogether. For the prolongevous, salt, like sugar, should rarely be added to food. Processed foods are sodium disasters about which the 34 million Americans with high blood pressure must be particularly concerned.

Liquids should be judged by the same criteria as solid foods. Healthful drinks include unadulterated fruit juices, vegetable juices, mineral water, milk (skim or buttermilk preferred), and plain water. The body's appestat will indicate the desirable quantities unless there is artificial stimulation from salt or sweeteners. Soda pop is to be avoided because of its many chemical additives, colas being the worst because of their high caffeine and sugar content. A twist of lime or a dash of freshly squeezed lemon juice in naturally carbonated mineral water provides a thirst quencher whose only additives are a trace of vitamins and minerals.

A peculiar situation pertains to alcohol. Heavy consumption seriously damages various parts of the body, particularly the brain and the liver, and alcohol in any quantity accelerates the body's ability to assimilate fat. Alcohol also interacts with cigarette fumes in a way that increases the carcinogenic effect of smoking. In spite of these negative effects from heavy consumption of alcohol or consumption in combination with smoking, moderate drinkers who do not smoke are less likely to suffer heart attacks than abstainers.[9] Consumption of alcohol is relatively common among centenarians: one may recall the jigger of applejack taken every morning in Abkhasia, the daily half-pint of potato brew enjoyed by Shigechiyo Izumi, the wines consumed by Luigi Cornaro, and the occasional brandy favored by the ladies of Cambridgeshire.

The benefits of alcohol, especially for older people, are linked to its ability to arouse the appetite, stimulate the heart, and expand the arterial walls. One study of wine-drinking in eighteen developed nations concluded that its protection for the heart might be linked to some ingredient other than alcohol, but most researchers believe the benefits are at least partly due to an increase alcohol causes in the number of alpha lipids. Although news reporters like to write stories about hard-drinking old-timers, it must be emphasized that the advantages of drinking are not so grand that a taste for alcohol should be deliberately cultivated. But if alcohol is part of the diet, moderate consumption may have some prolongevous benefits. "Moderate" is defined as about nine shots of distilled spirits, a dozen cans of beer, or fourteen glasses of wine a week. Higher consumption should be avoided; and it is advisable to eat some food when drinking.

Mixed drinks are a poor way of taking alcohol, because of the sugar and additives which give them their distinctive flavors. Traditional beer made with heavy malt tended to be rich in Vitamin E, but modern brewing methods have pretty much de-nutritionalized the drink. In any case, heavy beer drinking is inadvisable, as the excessive water intake stresses the kidneys and other organs.

The modern passion for caffeine is another example of using a counterproductive fuel. Among the numerous effects of caffeine are a depletion of the B vitamins and irritation of the urinary and anal tracts. The major source for American adults, of course, is coffee, but caffeine also appears in cocoa, chocolate, cola drinks, and some teas. A small glass of cola has about half the amount of caffeine in a cup of coffee, and a chocolate bar about a fourth. This means that when overall body size is considered, a child drinking two glasses of cola a day and eating two chocolate bars has a caffeine intake equivalent to eight cups of coffee for an adult. Taking caffeine as a means of "settling down" is, biologically speaking, nonsense, for one of its chief effects is to irritate the nervous system and stomach. Even drinking caffeine to stay awake while driving is somewhat self-defeating, because the body will suffer depression about an hour after taking in the caffeine, calling for a new hit.

Drinking tea is not necessarily a good alternative. Many teas, particularly those thought of as brisk, contain nearly as much caffeine as coffee. Tea also may contain catechin tannin, which has been shown to cause oral and esophageal cancer. This danger is avoided if the tea is taken with milk, which binds the tannin. Herbal mixtures are not the health miracles often advertised either. A few contain carcinogens, and many that yield medicinal benefits do so because of an unusual concentration of acids. Using such brews on a regular basis is like taking penicillin daily. Anyone determined to use tea as a regular drink needs to study the particular leaves involved, Chinese green tea being among the better options.

While caffeine has no positive input in the diet, its consumption in very moderate quantities may not be particularly harmful. As long as a person can limit caffeine intake from all sources to the equivalent of two cups of coffee a day, it is far more important to concentrate on reducing the intake of fats, sugars, sodium, and artificial additives. This emphasis is particularly advisable for those who find it difficult to stop drinking coffee at once. Decaffeinated coffee also could be used for psychological support, but since the harmful effects of coffee are not limited to its caffeine content, decaffeinated coffee is not a good long-term solution. As the body becomes chemically tuned to an ungraded diet, coffee will usually cause headaches, consciousness of the heartbeat, stomach upsets, and other unpleasant reactions which will help one to give up drinking it for good.

Some health manuals advocate that the variety of food in the total diet be limited, with only a few foods eaten at any given meal. Although this idea has a poetic appeal because of its simplicity, a mono-diet does not make nutritional sense. Primitive peoples ate a much wider range of plants and fruits than people in modern societies do, and the diversity of foods the stomach can accommodate with ease suggests that variety was genetically intended. Singling out a narrow range of food to be the fuel of the body causes one to run the risk of excluding an adequate amount of known and unknown essential nutrients. Other than the commonsense avoidance of foods that in combination produce volatile chemical reactions, there are no particular advantages to eating only one or two foods per sitting.

How often one should eat is a more pertinent concern. A nibbling pattern would seem to be the most natural, as that is the way most animals in nature eat, but there is no evidence that a limited number of regular meals is harmful. The three-major-meals-a-day pattern, which is based on the economic organization of modern society, is acceptable. Far more important is that the largest caloric intake occur early in the working day. Borrowing an often-used group of similes, it is best to breakfast like a lion, lunch like a squirrel, and dine like a bird. The rationale is that food not burned for energy during the day will be stored as fat or excreted. The more calories taken late in the day, the more the body is forced to work needlessly. Although psychological dependencies have been built around late eating or midnight snacks, the physical consequences can be extremely negative. The prolongevous should fuel up early, use the fuel during the course of the day, and go to sleep without forcing new internal housekeeping chores on the tired body.

Another need allied with regular eating habits is regular evacuation, the subject of more jokes than almost any other bodily function. While great individual variations are possible, even light eaters should expect one bowel movement each day. However, only when one feels bloated or uncomfortable should less frequency be a matter for concern. In that case, within the context of highly regularized eating times, there should be an increased consumption of raw foods, foods with high fiber content, and liquids. Exercises that put pressure on the lower abdomen also can be done, as long as one follows the usual exercise precautions. Should these responses fail to achieve regularity, then it is much wiser to consult a physician to see what might be the trouble than to get into the laxative habit, which has long-term negative effects.

The pivotal prolongevous meal is breakfast, for it is here that the day's eating cycle is established. What is considered a proper breakfast food is just a matter of convention, a doughnut and coffee hardly being more natural than a plate of vegetables or a fruit salad and soup. As a prelude to a vigorous day in the fields, many traditional farming families used to have mammoth breakfasts comparable to modern dinners. Lumberjacks packed away piles of pancakes before going into the woods to work. Complex carbohydrates, such as those received from cereal and breads, that will release energy throughout the day at a regular pace, are superior to the momentary lift of sugar and coffee. Fruits, nuts, and preserves can be used for immediate energy, but any food that is prolongevously rational is fine. To be avoided in most cases is an extremely light breakfast, which tends to set up a delayed-eating cycle culminating in a late dinner.

The temperature and speed at which foods are consumed are secondary factors, yet worthy of some consideration. A fast meal is nearly always a poor meal. Everyone has burned the inside of the mouth by eating something too hot, or has gotten a headache from eating something too cold. These extremes are hints from the body that, by and large, food and drink are best consumed at the temperatures at which they are most commonly found in nature. This does not preclude hot drinks, frozen desserts, soups, or chilled fruits, but it does suggest that they be consumed sparingly. Slowing down does more than prevent burned mouths and headaches. Digestion commences in the mouth, with chewing and salivation. If this part of the process is bypassed by bolting food or washing it down with liquids, more work is required later in the system by parts of the body less suited to the task. Fast eating also can outpace the stomach's ability to signal the brain that enough fuel has been ingested—one reason second helpings often feel less satisfying. Once again, the folk customs of Abkhasia are pertinent; the Abkhasians believe it is impolite to eat rapidly or to eat large portions.

Taken item by item, few of these dietary changes are extreme or difficult. As a totality, however, the diet is quite distinct. Unlike faddish plans which promote rapid weight loss by temporarily upsetting the normal chemical relationships within the body, the prolongevous diet aims to provide the variety, quality, and quantity of foods that will sustain the most efficient and beneficial reactions. The systematic reduction of fats, salt, sugars, and additives will produce innumerable chemical adjustments within the body. Gradual weight loss will be the most visible side effect. Rushing these changes would be a grave error. In addition to the organism's dislike of abrupt changes, because of the internal chaos they cause, there are many psychological and social pressures to contend with.

The shift to a prolongevous eating pattern begins with the reduction or elimination of the highest-risk foods. While these are being dealt with on a priority basis, other poor but less destructive habits may continue. A period of more than a year may be needed to work through all the major required changes, with the pace dictated by individual personality and the quality of the diet one starts out with. Time will be needed for friends and acquaintances to accept new habits. Among the most difficult problems to deal with may be those caused by close relatives or parents who insist that their brand of home cooking, however flesh-and-fat oriented, is essential to good health, and who feel insulted if it is declined. A disingenuous but effective strategy for maintaining a prolongevous diet without giving offense to others is to say that one is following doctor's orders. Another option is to eat strictly prolongevously at home, but to be more flexible in business or social settings.

A major reference work is needed by most people to get an idea of the caloric and nutritional values of the most common foods. *The Wellness Encyclopedia* published by the University of California is particularly good for this purpose because its editors provide a disease prevention program that includes exercise and stress reduction components. Guides like this need not be consulted very often, but even the best-informed will need to research particular foods from time to time. One should check on foods one eats regularly when one has a problem with weight control or insufficient energy. The following twelve points can serve as prolongevous dietary guidelines:

1. Set a caloric intake that will maintain body weight at the desired prolongevous level or that will move one's weight toward that level at the rate of no less than a quarter-pound and no more than a full pound a week. For most people this can be done on a diet ranging between 1,500 and 2,500 calories daily. The caloric intake, however, will be greatly influenced by the amount of daily physical exertion.

2. Work toward a dietary balance of 10-15 percent fat, 10-15

percent protein, and 70-80 percent carbohydrates.

3. Emphasize high-quality foods, such as fresh vegetables, fresh fruit, and whole grains.

4. Minimize meat, fish, or poultry consumption. These are best served in combination with vegetables, as in a stew, or as a garnish, as in Middle Eastern and Asian cooking.

5. Eat raw foods whenever possible. Otherwise, steam, boil, or bake food. Avoid frying.

6. Whenever possible avoid all preservatives, artificial flavorings, artificial colorings, and other food additives.

7. Take in the largest of amount of calories early in the workday. Keep all late eating to a minimum, and never eat just before going to sleep. Try to regularize mealtimes.

8. Hold salt consumption to a minimum. Be aware that salt can be a significant ingredient in many prepared foods.

9. Hold sugar consumption to a minimum. Be aware that sugar often slips into the diet under different names.

10. Drink only moderate amounts of alcohol.

11. Minimize or eliminate the intake of caffeine.

12. Eat slowly.

The achievement of a prolongevous diet is a long-term process, not a single revolutionary act of the will. At any given point, it is sufficient just to be replacing some nutritionally negative items with more positive ones. An unavoidable period of trial and error will be necessary to find new food combinations, eating habits, beverages, and other dietary components that are truly satisfying, for it is essential that the new diet be enjoyable. If the diet is viewed as a sacrifice of good living, then it is not likely to be maintained. Indulgences like ice cream and pastry do not have to be altogether eliminated, and reducing their frequency to satisfy caloric and fat guidelines is immensely facilitated by the gradualist approach.

The process has one built-in advantage which is that as the diet becomes nutritionally superior, there is a corresponding surge in general health and a tendency for the body to react poorly to improper fuels. Perhaps there will never be a hundred-percent consistency, but the more one's actual diet and one's ideal diet come into confluence, the better the longevity prospects.

# 12. BIOCHEMICAL INDIVIDUALITY

*The sensitivity of various people to our artificial drugs
seems to be fairly uniform. Not so the sensitivity to
vitamins. There seem to be people who are unable to absorb
or store them, and such people may develop symptoms of a
vitamin deficiency on a diet which is completely satisfactory to others. —Albert Szent-Gyorgyi*

THE BIOCHEMICAL INDIVIDUALITY OF EACH human being is as
distinct as a fingerprint. The differences in basal metabolic rates are
of specific importance to longevity since slower rates have been
found to have a prolongevous effect. One spectacular difference
is the fact that while two-thirds of all humans have three arteries
branching from the aorta, the remaining third may have one, two,
four, five, or even six. Similarly, the weight of the liver in relation
to the rest of the body varies by sevenfold. Such differences in
structure and mass are found in virtually all organs and systems of
the body and greatly influence specific nutritional needs for each
person.[1]

Nutritional needs are further affected by a myriad of other
factors. Illnesses almost always require at least a temporary
increase in essential nutrients, because of the damage done by the
disease and by the drugs used to treat it. Pregnant women, older
people, and those living in areas with poor soil may require additional mineral intake, while urban dwellers coping with foul air
and potent virus strains may require extra vitamin protection.

217

Awareness of realities of this kind has led many to add supplements and medications to their diets. Their process of selection, however, is often foolhardy.

Instead of consulting professional sources, most people put their trust in popular health books or articles in health magazines. Although literature like this can provide a useful theoretical introduction to nutrition as well as a grasp of the nutritive value of specific foods, it cannot be relied on for making serious decisions about health. The major problem is that the data is usually offered in breezy simplifications of experimental research. The tentative nature of the conclusions, or the narrowness of the sample base in the original research, is often overlooked by the reader. The secondary author also rarely stresses the unknown long-term effects of increased use of a vitamin or mineral or fails to emphasize that, as with alcohol, what is sometimes beneficial in small doses may be quite harmful in larger ones. Nor do such authors appreciate the risk that the increased intake of one vitamin or mineral can necessitate increased intake of others. The better health writers, who do try to account for this phenomenon, often propose a supplementary balancing act that leaves most people dizzy and is much too finely tuned for the present state of medical knowledge.

Recommendations on supplements tend to run in faddish cycles. Claims are rephrased with increasing enthusiasm in much the way the Hunza myth was propagated. The result is that some substances become widely used before basic research on them is conclusive. In the 1970s, selenium was optimistically heralded as a possible cancer preventive because of some preliminary research and statistical data relating low rates of cancer to cultures with a relatively high intake of the mineral. But later research indicated that selenium in large doses might cause cancer, could damage the central nervous system, and probably was responsible for some dental problems. The continued uncertainty about selenium is not unique. Because some supplements are discussed widely and sold over the counter, consumers have been lulled into using them, regarding their safety with a suspension of disbelief they would never grant to the synthetic chemicals found in processed foods.

The starting point for judging the need for any vitamin or mineral supplement is the minimum daily requirement set by federal health agencies. Below these requirement levels, a specific disease of malnutrition will develop in almost everyone. Meeting the minimum daily requirement, however, does not necessarily rule out the possible need for higher amounts or considerable variations based on specific body chemistries or living conditions. One can decide whether one needs to add a vitamin or mineral supplement to the diet by learning about the most widely used: vitamins E and C and iron and calcium.

Vitamin E has been extolled as a youth-giving substance because of its role as an antioxidant. By keeping cellular garbage from clogging the bloodstream, E promotes healthier skin tissue and better circulation. Less visible is its activity against free radicals, atoms that have broken off from other molecules, and careen through the system like cue balls on a billiard table. They split other molecules, creating more free radicals and disrupting orderly cellular life. Vitamin E halts this destruction by binding free radicals. It works similarly against substances like lead and ozone breathed into the body through polluted air.

Gerontologists have long used E in devising experimental diets and programs. Unlike BHA and BHT, synthetic antioxidants used in packaging materials, or the natural mineral selenium, even in high doses E has no discernible negative effects. Among the best natural sources for the vitamin are whole grains and green leafy vegetables. One health writer has remarked that a rather poor Londoner of the nineteenth century who drank a few pints of malt beer and ate brown bread took in far more E than his or her present-day counterpart.

Yet it is precisely in the polluted modern metropolis that the need for E is greatest. This appears to be one situation in which an unnatural environmental condition may call for an unnatural quantity of a vitamin as a countermeasure. Determining the minimum daily requirement for E is difficult, because no particular disease seems to result from its absence. Until research is more conclusive, increase in the consumption of E should be made choosing mainly natural foods, with a possible intake of from 100 to 400 international units daily as a supplement in environments where air quality is poor or there are high levels of background radiation.

There is thus some controversy about using E, but much more exists over the use of ascorbic acid, better known as vitamin C. The minimum daily requirement set by the U.S. government is 60 milligrams for adults, the dosage necessary to prevent scurvy. But the best-known advocate of vitamin C, Dr. Linus Pauling, who won a Nobel Prize in 1954, has argued that the dosage most adults should be taking is between 2 and 4 grams.[2] A difference of this magnitude among scientists is startling, to say the least. Almost as startling are the claims advanced on behalf of the vitamin. Ascorbic acid is said to prevent colds, combat the harmful effects of carbon monoxide, improve circulation, aid in the healing of wounds, and promote health in various organs. In addition, it has an undeniable synergistic effect when combined with E, making that vitamin far more potent than when it is taken alone.

Pauling believed that getting proper amounts of C into the diet would add from four to six years to the average life span—two to three from the prevention of the damage done by colds and another two to three from the improvement in general health. These gains would result from the use of ascorbic acid as a food supplement, a role that must be differentiated from its possible utilization as a medicine. One of the justifications offered by Pauling for his recommendations was based on a diet we have already identified as prolongevous. Pauling calculated that a diet of 2,500 calories coming only from fresh natural plant foods would provide 2.3 grams of C. Such a diet, of course, is not possible for most people today, because vitamins are destroyed by modern farming and packaging methods. The C content of crops is greatly reduced because they are picked green so that they can ripen on the way to market; and there is thus a long delay between field and table. Processing wipes out most of the vitamins in prepared foods, as does cooking at high temperatures, particularly when certain trace metals are present.

The optimal dose of C depends upon the biochemical makeup of each person, as is the case with all nutrients. Pauling believed that a few people may get on quite well with as little as 250 milligrams daily, while others might require as much as 10 grams. He emphasized that all available evidence shows C to be one of the least toxic substances consumed by humans. Although minor side effects sometimes occur when megadoses are taken, there has never been a case of serious illness or death resulting from consuming too much C. There have been intriguing speculations about why the human body cannot manufacture its own C and whether C is properly classified as a vitamin. But the worst consequence of oversupplying C would seem to be that it is passed out through the urine without being used or induces bowel movements.[3]

Some scientists have hypothesized that C may be a kind of general or universal antitoxin which rallies bodily defense mechanisms. Researchers have been using it in combination with E in their longevity programs, and work is under way in various nations to see if ascorbic acid has a role to play in the treatment of gallstones, arthritis, diabetes, atherosclerosis, senility, and other ailments. In several countries, massive doses of C have been used to treat terminally ill cancer patients. The results have been more positive than those obtained by more conventional therapies.[4] In relation to cold prevention the findings are indeterminate, but advocates claim that an intake of about 3 grams a day will prevent colds in most people. They note that even if far more of the vitamin is consumed than is needed, the danger is infinitesimal compared with the dangers known to accompany continued use of non-prescription cold fighters such as analgesics and antihistamines. Compared with C, aspirin, one of the most widely used drugs, is dangerous. Regular use of aspirin will lead to internal bleeding, and in doses of 20 to 30 grams it is lethal.

Without necessarily accepting the most positive views of the qualities of C, it makes longevous sense to include large amounts of it in the diet, either through choice of foods or in combination with a supplement. Bodily reactions should be the prime method of determining how much to take, with the 2.3 grams suggested by Pauling a better starting point than the 60 milligrams needed to prevent scurvy.[5] Any factors that may deplete intake of the vitamin or increase its need would suggest temporary increases in the supplement. Most certainly, ascorbic acid should be the preferred method of dealing with colds and headaches and, because of its synergistic effect, should be used as a defense in combination with E against environmental toxins. Foods rich in C can be found in any nutritional chart, but some with the highest concentration are broccoli spears, black currants, kale, parsley, and peppers.

Minerals are inorganic substances of a quite different nature from vitamins. Although some of them, usually in extremely small amounts, are essential to bodily functions, in high quantities most minerals become harmful and will cause depletion of other nutrients. A diet featuring plant foods and some dairy products will easily satisfy all the known mineral requirements of the body. Nonetheless, the pressures of advertising and health gossip have made mineral supplements a highly profitable industry.

Probably the most commonly supplemented mineral is iron. The "tired blood" syndrome and the higher iron needs of women and children have been widely publicized. Pregnant women, due to the demands of the fetus, and women who menstruate heavily need to be particularly attentive to their iron intake. Real iron deficiency, however, is largely the result of the high percentage of refined foods in the typical modern diet. If more iron is needed, far better than any supplement would be an increase in the intake of natural foods rich in the mineral. If that fails to produce the desired results, the problem is likely to be not the amount of iron available for use but the body's inability to use it—a matter for a doctor, not an over-the-counter salesperson, to deal with.

Calcium, the most prevalent mineral in the body and the main component of bones, is another widely supplemented mineral. Yet there is little chance of calcium deficiency in people who use dairy products. If those foods are restricted for any reason, a conscious effort should be made to ensure that the required daily intake of 800 milligrams is being met. This is far from difficult. Three ounces of sardines (with bones) provide 372 milligrams, and a cup of shelled almonds provides 332. Servings of dandelion, mustard, turnip, or collard greens are nearly as good. Any comprehensive nutritional chart will yield combinations of calcium-bearing foods that will negate the need for supplements like bone meal or dolomite.

Calcium deficiencies are quite often only tangentially problems of supply. High intakes of fat hinder the body's ability to absorb calcium, while high intakes of animal protein result in excessive calcium losses through urination. Likewise, when large amounts of other minerals such as phosphorus are ingested, the need for calcium increases accordingly. More importantly, vitamin D must be present in the body for calcium to be absorbed through the intestinal wall. Thus, anyone who is low in vitamin D for any reason must make appropriate adjustments. This may mean supplementation or more exposure to sunlight, which is necessary to stimulate the body's production of the vitamin. Studies in Scandinavian countries, for example, indicate that one reason for that region's high rate of bone fractures may be that Scandinavians do not get enough exposure to sunlight during most of the year.

Whenever the body's immediate need for calcium falls below the daily minimum, the body will borrow it from the bones and the teeth. A chronic deficiency will produce deformed bones in children and soft bones in adults. Conversely, although a moderate oversupply of calcium can be usefully stored in the bones, continued overdoses create health problems of their own. Many people, recognizing that a mineral is necessary, but that at the same time there can be too much of a good thing, will avoid supplementation unless the need is established through testing and the effect of supplementation is monitored by a physician. In the case of calcium, many adults will probably want to supplement with a calcium-magnesium combination to bring the dietary intake to at least one gram of calcium per day. As in the case of iron, women have been found to be more likely to need supplementation.

Seeking medical advice on supplements opens the whole question of the role the practicing physician should play in the longevity project. The ideal practitioner would regard the physician-patient dynamic as a partnership. The emphasis would be on the maintenance of health rather than on the prevention or cure of disease. One historical precedent for this kind of relationship can be found in ancient China, where a healer was paid only as long as the patient remained in good health. Unfortunately, today's focus is on treating disease, not preventing it. Furthermore, medical schools place such a strong emphasis on surgical procedures and powerful drugs that they all but ignore nutrition and other means that might allow the body to maintain good health using its own resources. Once a doctor goes into practice, pharmaceutical and medical-equipment companies continue the orientation begun in medical school. This system is further reinforced by patients who put off seeking assistance until they are seriously ill, patients who want quick cures, and patients who lack self-discipline, like those with high blood-pressure who won't lose weight or those with heart disease and emphysema who won't stop smoking.

The search to find the right physician requires more effort than allowing one's fingers to meander through the professional pages of the phone book or simply using doctors who have treated friends or family. Even a physician known to have a nutritional perspective may simply prescribe supplements with the same abandon with which other physicians dispense penicillin or Valium. The more realistic approach to securing good medical advice is to find a traditional but sensitive physician who can be convinced that the would-be longevous individual offers a positive change of pace from usual patients and an opportunity to observe the long-term effects of naturalistic health practices. Such a physician should be prepared to answer many questions and to have in-depth consultations with the patient.

One of the first things prolongevous patients need to do is determine whether any organic problems will prevent them from undertaking the longevous agenda, especially the exercise component. When going over test findings, it is not enough to be informed that the results are normal. Exact numbers should be obtained, and they should be related to longevous, not conventional, standards. During and after the transformation to a prolongevous profile, some people will feel more comfortable if changes going on in the body are monitored periodically. A suitable checklist and timetable can be worked out with the physician. The patient should make it clear that he or she is willing to pay for the time, testing, and expertise involved, just as others would pay for surgery, medication, or bedside consultations.

Prolongevous ground rules should be established firmly during the initial diagnostic period. For example, the annual checkup advised by many health professionals can be a physical ordeal. Doctors working with older patients have questioned the desirability of many of the procedures involved, because they greatly fatigue or discomfort their patients. Such doubts should be extended across the entire age spectrum. Especially dubious are tests that inadvertently cause pain, although that is not the sole criterion.

That a test is standard procedure is no guarantee of its safety. The diagnostic X-rays routinely ordered by doctors, dentists, and chiropractors provide a chilling example. Using language designed to make science accessible to the average person, Dr. Priscilla Laws has written an analysis of the dangers posed by X-rays.[6] She has shown that diagnostic X-rays currently constitute the largest source of humanly created radiation exposure and that a person who undergoes a complete series of abdominal X-rays may easily exceed the annual occupational safety limit. Moreover, what is considered a safe dosage has been revised spectacularly downward for more than eighty years. In the 1910s and 1920s, 10 rems a day was considered an acceptable exposure. By 1936 an advisory committee had lowered the rate to 30 rems a year. In 1957 the National Committee on Radiation Protection and Measurement lowered the acceptable amount to 5 rems a year. Alarmed by the steady rise in background radiation and the increasing incidence of cancer, many public health activists believe the present standards are still too generous.

In the introduction to Law's study, Dr. Sidney M. Wolfe of the Health Research Group summarized the alarming conclusions in reports on radiation safety made by the Department of Health, Education and Welfare. These studies found that 20% of all X-ray units inspected were not in compliance with state laws, the result being that patients were exposed to excessive and illegal amounts of radiation. Over 90% of all medical X-rays were being given without proper shielding, and about 50% overexposed the patients because the beam was much larger than needed. Dentists who had completed their professional training prior to 1940 were found to be exposing their patients to twice as much radiation as dentists who graduated after 1965. A subsequent study completed by the Food and Drug Administration's Bureau of Radiation Health in 1979 was just as disturbing. The survey, which covered forty-five states, showed that of 35,224 dental X-ray units inspected, 36% used exposures that were "excessively high," and even among the 3,152 new units inspected, 61% were not in compliance with federal regulations.[7] These findings have not resulted in any significant upgrading in government regulations.

So many other medical practices are associated with hazards that the term "iatrogenic disease" has been coined to indicate mental or physical disorder caused by these procedures. Some of the major contemporary iatrogenic reactions stem from ineffective vaccines, laboratory errors, faulty diagnostic devices, overdoses of medication, and useless treatments. Medical schools are concerned about these hazards, which are as old as the profession and as predictable as human fallibility. Even under the best of circumstances, favored techniques often inflict pain, poison the body, or take other caculated risks.

Considering the stakes involved, before agreeing to any medical intervention the patient must insist on detailed information about how that intervention affects the body, any known risks, and viable alternatives. Any procedure which involves a serious invasion of the body is particularly suspect. If faced with a disturbing diagnosis or proposed course of treatment, the patient should seek a second or third opinion before making a final decision. Although chemical or surgical remedies may not be avoidable, if reasonable alternatives are available they should be seriously considered, whatever the apparent inconvenience.

The methods used to treat high blood pressure in the past forty years provide an insight into why the newest and easiest treatment isn't always best. During the 1940s it was established that sodium intake had an adverse effect on hypertension. Restricted-sodium diets became the treatment of the day. In 1957 various medicines that acted directly on the nerves and blood vessels, without requiring sodium restriction, were developed and quickly became the favored treatment. By the 1970s these new drugs were found to be creating negative side effects, and many physicians returned to the sodium-restriction approach, especially in cases where medication would have to be taken for a substantial period of time. Of further concern was the growing tendency in the 1980s and 1990s to treat mild or borderline cases of hypertension with drugs, subjecting the patient to needless risk.

In addition to direct negative effects on the body, medication may also deplete the organism of minerals and vitamins. Digitalis, used by many heart patients, affects potassium and thiamine levels. Diuretics affect vitamin B, vitamin C, calcium, magnesium, potassium, and zinc requirements. Mineral oil and commonly used drugs like aspirin, barbiturates, antacids, and antibiotics cause nutritional depletions. Occasional use of such substances is hardly cause for alarm, but if they are used habitually, mineral and vitamin supplements of some kind may be in order. The negative effects of many drugs were first observed in older patients who had used them for a considerable time or whose restricted diets or failing health made them susceptible to deficiencies.

In short, no supplement or medication should ever be taken without demonstrated need, established by bodily symptoms which have been judged against professional medical literature or by consultations with a physician. Exceptions to this are situations in which the need has been demonstrated before any symptoms can develop. For example, because iodine deficiency in the soil is known to encourage goiter, it would be foolish for persons living in iodine-deficient locales to wait for signs of the disease before adding some iodine to their diet. Those living in industrial areas can determine whether to use C and E supplements by similarly evaluating the quality of their food and environment. At some future time, when nutritional science is more fully developed, it may be possible to pinpoint specifically prolongevous nutritional requirements and adjust the diet accordingly. Even then, and most certainly until then, it is best to get vitamins and minerals from natural foods, in which the combination of nutrients, their form, and as yet unknown factors are more likely to be positive than in commercial pills produced for profit. A rule of thumb for identifying how much of any given nutrient is needed would be to determine how much of it would be available in a 2,500-caloric diet made up of raw foods. Unless there are symptoms of deficiency, much more than that amount is not likely to be useful to a healthy person.

In regard to all these matters, popular health literature has an important gadfly and informative role, but a very minor prescriptive one. By consulting such sources, a reader can keep abreast of the latest machinations of agribusiness, the drug firms, and the food industry. Readers can find guidance and useful tidbits on the nutritional value of a particular food; an article may point out that pink grapefruit contains vitamin A while white grapefruit does not, or that the nutritional value of brown and white eggs is the same. But when a nutritional cure is advocated for some condition, it is time to be wary. If the vitamins and minerals to be added to the diet can be obtained through a reasonable choice of natural foods, there is little danger involved in following the suggestion. When this is not possible because of the huge amounts called for, the footnotes to the article must be consulted to locate the original research.

Professional journals can be obtained through almost all state university and public-library systems; they are not as difficult to read as one might think. Often the recommendations will be found to be based on speculations arising from little evidence. However, any treatment that appears promising can be brought to the attention of a physician. If such a research effort seems too much of a chore, then the original malady cannot be very serious and the risks of ingesting unusual quantities of dietary supplements are not justified. The long-range effects of megadoses of some supplements may be just as calamitous as the effects of medications. Only time will tell. The era of massive vitamin intake is still in its infancy.

Another guideline to consider is that there are at least three distinct reasons for using any supplement: on a long- or short-term basis because the diet cannot provide it in adequate amounts; on a short-term basis as a medicine to treat a specific condition; and on a regular basis because of demonstrated need related to biochemical individuality.

Some health seekers, disgusted by supplements, medications, and technological gimmickry, turn to folk remedies which they believe are somehow legitimized by virtue of their historical survival. Certainly much work remains to be done in systematizing knowledge developed in various folk traditions. Chemical analysis of plants used by folk healers has shown that some of these plants have genuine curative properties. Techniques like Chinese acupuncture are increasingly being integrated into medicine. But these are matters for highly trained professionals. By and large, sentiment aside, folk medicine has always been a trial-and-error procedure dependent on specific psychological, social, geographical, and dietary frameworks that cannot be easily replicated. It would be reckless to suppose that any single treatment come upon haphazardly and out of its original context is likely to effect a cure, particularly of a serious disease, that has eluded modern scientists.

Throughout the world, the longest-living populations are precisely those which enjoy the most modern health services and the most advanced theoretical sciences. To believe otherwise is to delude oneself with faith in primitive folk wisdom that never existed.

The polar opposite of putting additional vitamins, minerals, and foods into the body is fasting—the temporary suspension of all fuel intake. Its advocates believe that fasting is ideal for periodically detoxifying the body. They argue that just as an animal that has been wounded will refrain from eating in order to allow the body to marshal all its reserves for healing, so cessation of eating will allow the body to concentrate on elimination of unwanted materials in the cells and arterial passages. Fasting is differentiated from starving in that starving connotes a breakdown in healthy tissues and vital organs, while fasting means that only fat reserves and nonessential tissue are affected.

A strong argument against fasting is that the longevity agenda will accomplish the same housecleaning benefits without fasting's several disadvantages. The foremost of these is that a few days of fasting will produce reactions of weakness, headache, and nausea. Even the ability to read comfortably is usually affected. There are serious dangers to maintaining the proper glucose level and threatened impairment of functions requiring water-soluble vitamins, minerals, and protein not stored in the body. Consequently, most long fasts are conducted under supervision in hospital-like conditions, and they are marked by considerable periods of inactivity. Most religiously motivated fasts are candidly anti-health in that one of the objectives is the penitential mortification of the flesh.

Accepting the logic of the fasting advocates for a moment, there are a number of experiments which indicate that a semi-fast of about 500 calories a day is preferable to a total fast, since the breakdown of unwanted bodily deposits proceeds without the accompanying trauma of the closing down of major systems.[8] A comparison can be made to steel mills, which are rarely shut down totally because of the enormous energy output needed to restart operations. On two major points there is no serious medical dispute: fasting is one of the most ineffective methods for long-term weight reduction, and prolonged fasts without proper supervision are dangerous.

Fasting appeals mainly to those who want a kind of quickie health fix that doesn't require surgery or medication. Denying the body its daily fuel also plays to the notion that instead of being the normal condition of the body, health is attainable only through discomfort and deprivation. Accounts of fasting for more than a day or so at a time (usually for religious reasons) are rarely encountered in biographies of the longevous or massive studies of those over 90.

People seeking to improve their health often resemble scorpions consuming their own tails. Beguiled by feats of modern medicine, too many overdiagnose and overmedicate their most trivial ailments. Others, aware of their poor diets, get lured into a complex balancing act of vitamin and mineral supplements. Still others seek out exotic foods and treatments. But most such measures to improve health actually imperil it. Taking into account the qualifications outlined earlier, a predominantly vegetarian diet with a high concentration of raw foods remains the best all-around bet for getting the proper amount of essential nutrients. The front line of health maintenance for those who have actually achieved longevous life spans has been the nearest garden, greengrocer, or farmers' market.

# 13. THE TOXIC SOCIETY

*Most scientists agree that the overwhelming majority of cancers are environmentally caused. As such they are largely preventable. But the failure by the public, industry, and government to recognize this fact and act on it is why we have a cancer epidemic today, and why that epidemic may become even worse in the years ahead.*
*—Robert H. Boyle for the Environmental Defense Fund in Malignant Neglect*

AN ACIDIC RAIN HAS BEGUN to fall. The nitrogen and sulfur oxides released into the atmosphere by various petrochemical processes have made snow, hail, sleet, and rain in some places as acidic as vinegar. The American industrial Midwest has spawned acidic rains in New England and northern Canada, while the great industrial basins of Germany and Britain have caused acidic rains in the forests of Norway and Sweden. The Athenian Acropolis, symbol of Europe's loftiest aspirations, is so badly corroded by air pollutants that the Greek government is considering encasing it in a massive glass dome. Yet domes would hardly be practical for the fifty thousand high-altitude lakes in the Adirondacks and Canada that have been so poisoned that some plant life and entire fish populations have been decimated or totally eliminated. Snakelike domes stretching hundreds of miles would be needed to shield the meandering streams of Norway and Sweden that are now lethal to salmon. As yet, the menace to human life from acidic rain remains minimal, but the phenomenon is a sinister foretaste of environmental dangers to health and life that are uncontrollable by national, class, or individual action.[1]

Like poor eating habits and lack of exercise, environmental poisons may take decades to work their havoc. None are more fearsome in this respect than carcinogens, whose destructive force may gestate silently for ten to forty years before imperiling the host. With new synthetic chemicals and new sources of radiation being manufactured pell-mell, the developed nations are engaging in an ecological brinksmanship whose slightest miscalculations could bring on terracidal reactions. If these threats to health and life continue to rise or even remain at present levels, the best-laid longevity plans will be seriously compromised. Self-interest dictates that the longevity minded strongly support the various movements aimed at environmental detoxification. At the same time, there are preventive measures to be taken which can modify the immediate personal dangers considerably.

As recently as the 1860s, the United States could rightly boast of the quality of its environment. The industrialization which began in earnest shortly thereafter adversely changed this situation, but massive environmental deterioration did not commence until the introduction of petrochemicals in the 1930s and the dawn of the nuclear age in the 1940s. The body of every American now contains residues of some of the quarter-million industrial chemicals in use. Every one of the thousands of synthetic chemicals is a substance that cannot be found in nature and whose interaction with life forms remains a guesstimate.

The center of toxicity is the industrial workplace.[2] Irrefutable research has established the link between cancers and working with substances like vinyl chloride, asbestos, industrial dyes, chromates, nickel, uranium, and glass fibers. More specifically, previously rare cancers can be tied to precise substances. Mesothelemia with asbestos, angiosarcoma of the liver with vinyl chloride and polyvinyl chloride, and oat-cell carcinoma with bis-chlormethyl ether are three examples. The linkage of black lung with coal mining and brown lung with textile weaving is also beyond scientific dispute. Where such clear and present dangers exist in the workplace, prolongevous persons have no option but to switch to other industries and move house away from toxic workplaces. A drastic response of this kind is dictated by the unwillingness of companies to face up to the danger of the processes they have set in motion and by the slowness of government to establish adequate safeguards for workers or the public.

The negative properties of the most dangerous substances usually were known decades before there was any effective regulation. Vinyl chloride's link to cancer was first suspected in the late 1940s; the dangers of industrial dyes were known in the 1890s; and the various effects of asbestos, established conclusively at the turn of the century, were described by physicians in ancient Greece. In spite of this history, all three substances were used with abandon until well into the 1970s; and although the amount of exposure considered safe has been consistently lowered, corporate managers and their medical experts have stubbornly defended the adequacy of each new and lower safety threshold. In most instances, regulation would not have been imposed if unions representing the affected workers had not financed their own medical studies and publicized the results in the mass media. Arguments over acceptable standards of exposure have dragged on for decades while the substances continue to cause incalculable numbers of premature deaths, painful diseases, and sterility. The burden of proof has always been on the victims, and even when they have proved to be aggrieved parties, the responsible manufacturer has rarely made financial settlements—even though no payment can ever compensate for loss of life or catastrophic illness.

Given these realities, workers dealing with chemicals of any kind stand in danger of developing cancer as one of their "fringe benefits" of employment. To prevent this, they must have their unions finance independent studies of every substance to which they are exposed. When there is any doubt about safety, the margin of error must be on the side of prudence. If safety equipment and special procedures are suggested by the manufacturer, they should be followed to the letter. Legislation also must be developed to make corporations liable for environmental damage and personal injuries, even if the problem stems from honest miscalculations. If there is conscious deception regarding health hazards, criminal charges of the kind that would apply to any premeditated poisoning should be imposed. A responsible step in this area was taken in 1979 when the Nuclear Regulatory Commission proposed to fine Consumers Power Company of Jackson, Michigan, $450,000 because the utility neglected for eighteen months to close the valve on a 4-inch pipe leading into its reactor containment building.[3] No radioactivity escaped, but if there had been an accident of the type that occurred at Three Mile Island, the results would have been catastrophic. The fine was the largest in NRC's history and served as a warning of the public's growing intolerance of negligent safety procedures in industry. Only such stringent measures can make compliance with environmental regulations cost-effective for affluent polluters, and absolutely imperative for managers, researchers, and other responsible individuals. When the acidic rains become lethal to human life, it will be too late to ask which firms or individuals were responsible.

Industrial planners habitually save money for their firms by using the environment as a garbage dump. They release dangerous by-products into waterways, push them out of smokestacks into the air, and allow them to seep into the soil. The eventual victims of this pollution may be hundreds or thousands of miles downriver or downwind, making it difficult to pin the pollution tail on the responsible donkey. The public needs to understand that when there are continuous insults to the body by noxious chemicals, the result is cancer. Even minute quantities may cause the disease, but the risks definitely increase with the amount and time of exposure. Thus, it does not seem purely coincidental that wherever there is a concentration of petrochemical industries there is a cancer hot spot. The most prominent example is the infamous cancer alley of New Jersey which coincides with the industrial complex bordering the New Jersey Turnpike. In addition to the phenomenal cancer rates found in some factories located in that corridor, communities on Staten Island and in Brooklyn, separated from the source of contamination by miles of water, also are affected because of the prevailing westerly winds.

Risks from the air, however, are most serious in metropolises where industrial wastes are trapped by skyscrapers and where automobile exhausts add to the toxic overload. Although the petrochemical smog of Los Angeles is prototypical of this, numerous cities have similar problems. One defensive measure has been for health bureaus to alert the public when the air quality is inferior. If such an alarm is given, no prolongevous person and certainly no one with a chronic heart or respiratory disease should be out of doors more than absolutely necessary. At such times strenuous work or exercise does not demonstrate hardiness so much as foolhardiness. The best course of action is to gain the protection of air conditioning, which filters out many pollutants. Should one's city of residence have many days with unsatisfactory air quality, relocation must be considered. Air is not a luxury like a banana cream pie; it contains the oxygen that is vital if cells are to maintain the organism for the one-hundred-plus years of life for which it is intended.

Far more dangerous than air pollution is exposure to tobacco smoke. Although the smoker is the primary victim, any small room with even one person smoking in it will have a higher level of carbon monoxide, carcinogens, and toxins than the entrance to most factories. The dangers to longevity are acute. According to a follow-up report of the Surgeon General released in 1979, a two-pack-a-day habit will reduce the smoker's lifetime by from eight to nine years and will increase the overall death risk at every age by about 70%. A survey issued later the same year by the State Mutual Assurance Company of America independently confirmed the government's conclusion. Based on research concerning 100,000 policyholders, the insurance report found that at every age after 20, smokers had at least double the mortality rate of nonsmokers and that for certain diseases such as lung cancer the risk was as much as 15 times as great. The average life span of the policy holders who smoked was from seven to eight years less than for non-smokers. Insurance companies backed these findings by offering lower premiums to nonsmokers. The reports of the Surgeon General and State Mutual were in line with worldwide health research on smoking that had been ongoing for at least twenty years; the first scientific paper linking tobacco and cancer dates to British studies done in 1761.

One effect of smoking not widely appreciated is its devastating synergistic effect in combination with toxins. An asbestos worker has 16 times as great a probability of developing cancer as the average American, but if the asbestos worker also smokes, the probability leaps to 60. Analysis of death rates among urban dwellers indicates that those who do not smoke do not have a significantly higher incidence of various respiratory diseases than those who live in rural areas, but urban dwellers who do smoke do. One explanation for this is the synergistic interaction of air pollutants and tobacco smoke. This interpretation is supported by findings that the most polluted cities do not have the highest rates of lung cancer and that there is not much difference between life-long residents of cities and recent arrivals. In all cases, the incidence of respiratory disease is higher in those who smoke; but in addition, men who smoke have a higher incidence than women, and manual workers than professionals.

Other negative aspects of smoking can be seen in American Cancer Society studies which show that if one smokes only a pack of cigarettes a day, in addition to the chance that lung cancer will increase by 684 percent, the chance for cancer of the mouth increased 890 percent, cancer of the larynx 709 percent, cancer of the esophagus 317 percent, cancer of the bladder 100 percent, and cancer of the pancreas 169 percent. The use of filter tips and low-tar cigarettes reduced the odds, but such gains were lost if the number of cigarettes smoked increased because of the illusion of safety. Pipe smokers and cigar smokers also ran lower risks, but compared with nonsmokers the chances for cancer of the lung were 120 percent higher, for cancer of the mouth 150 percent, and for cancer of the larynx 200 percent. For cancer of the bladder, the risk was 100 percent greater for pipe smokers and 400 percent greater for cigar smokers.[4]

At least eight carcinogens have been found in tobacco smoke, and there is a positive correlation between higher doses and higher probability of disease. The Surgeon General's reports further indicate that coronary disease is an even more likely result of smoking and there is a much higher risk of lung disorders such as emphysema. The one bright note is that the body is capable of overcoming some of the damage. If even a heavy two-pack-a-day smoker quits, in the course of fifteen years the average life expectancy and the chance of developing degenerative diseases gradually move to those of nonsmokers.

In spite of this overwhelming evidence, the United States, like other nations, has refused to treat tobacco as it would treat a dangerous microbe which murders more than a million people every decade. Tobacco firms are allowed to propagandize their wares in mass media, and the government continues to subsidize many marginal growers who might otherwise be forced into bankruptcy. Regulation of smoking in public places is vigorously opposed by a combination of economic interests and addicts who believe smoking is one of their inalienable rights. It is hard to remember, at times, that smokers are not only a minority of the adult population, but a declining minority.

Some smokers are comforted by the idea that breathing city air is equivalent to smoking. This error is based on misinterpretation of studies such as the one which found that a person standing in Manhattan's Herald Square for twenty-four hours would be exposed to the same amount of pollutants as found in two packs of cigarettes. One must realize not only that no one would stand in Herald Square for twenty-four hours, but that the intersection is far from typical: it is the crossroads of three major traffic arteries (34th Street, Broadway, and the Avenue of the Americas); there are many tall structures (including the Empire State Building) in the vicinity, and it is affected by the adjacent garment district and department stores, which have an unusually high concentration of idling truck traffic. Even so, the pollutants in this atypical area would be randomly distributed throughout the air, while the pollutants in a cigarette are highly concentrated, being heaviest exactly in that portion which enters the mouth.

The dangers for a Herald Square pedestrian are potential; those for a smoker, actual. Moreover, when breathed through the nose, the natural filtering system of the body, some pollutants will be kept from entering the lungs. In contrast, tobacco smoke is deliberately inhaled directly into the lungs. Because of this, exhaled smoke, which has left many of its poisons inside the smoker's body, is less dangerous than undiluted smoke from a burning cigarette. Smokers still enamored of the Herald Square study must face the fact that whatever dangers do exist in such locations are geometrically higher for them because of accelerating risks that result from an increased total intake of carcinogens. In short, given that 85% of lung cancer occurs in smokers and a good portion of the remainder is linked to identifiable workplace risks, it's clear that the disease which kills approximately 100,000 persons annually is primarily caused by tobacco, with air pollution acting mainly as a synergistic factor.

No one remotely concerned about his or her longevity will smoke because smoking is so deadly it undermines all benefits from an otherwise longevous life style. Nor is eliminating the dangers of smoke simply a personal matter. Secondary smoke is so lethal that living with or working beside a chronic smoker is as dangerous as it is unpleasant. To compromise on this issue is to forfeit a chance for reaching even the average life span in good health. Although prohibition of smoking in the work environment and in public places has increased impressively in the past two decades, few smokers truly comprehend that what they call their right to smoke amounts to a right to kill not only themselves, but others. Dr. Elizabeth Whelan has put it succinctly in *Preventing Cancer*:

> Ironically, many people who are worried about the adverse effects of air pollution overlook the most obvious form that we come in contact with: one cigarette smoker, in a matter of minutes, can fill a closed room with higher concentrations of the carcinogen benzo (a) pyrene than are found in the most polluted city air in the world. If you are worried about the effects of air pollution on your lungs, your best bet would be to ban smoking in offices and public places.[5]

Dr. Whelan offers an interesting analysis of the spread of cancer in the United States during the twentieth century. She calculates that when respiratory cancers, which were extremely rare in 1900, are eliminated from the statistics, the overall cancer rate for men has declined and the rate for women is nearly stable. Whelan then points out that breast and colonic cancers are highly influenced by the fat-heavy American diet. Though we may not necessarily accept her contention that it is fat consumption *per se* and not toxic substances *plus* fatty foods which are the nexus of the problem, we can conclude from her reasoning that the major contributing causes to the top three cancer killers for women (breast cancer, colonic cancers, and lung cancer) and the two for men (lung cancer and colonic cancers) are tobacco smoking and fat-laden diets. This analysis offers substantial support for two pillars of the longevity agenda: no smoking and a low-fat diet.[6]

That dietary and environmental factors are strongly linked to cancer is proved by numerous studies which show that the sites and types of cancer occurring in humans shift with geographic location even when there is a genetic relationship between the two populations. Thus, Japanese living in Japan have one set of cancers, but Japanese who have emigrated to the United States have another. Sexual differences show the same pattern. Women living in cultures with high breast-cancer rates have one incidence curve while women in societies without high breast-cancer rates have quite another.[7] Studies of isolated groups with high cancer rates usually report a specific type of cancer associated with a specific cause, a pattern like the one found in workplace cancer. Biological aging, however, does not appear to be a significant factor. Cancer is a leading killer among Americans under age 20, the years when biological defenses are at their strongest, but after age 80, when biological defenses are increasingly weaker, cancer rates drop.

Public awareness of environmental health hazards is not new.

The popular 19th century author Lewis Carroll referred to the fact that hatters were subject to brain damage because of the mercury used to tan furs and Charles Dickens pointed out that chimney sweeps were subject to respiratory diseases. A host of writers have addressed the maladies found among miners. What is unusual in the twentieth century is that distinctions between workplace risk and general risk are being obliterated. The high rate of cancer among naval-yard employees working with asbestos took on new urgency when do-it-yourselfers trying to improve their living spaces found themselves confronted with asbestos insulation or when parents disturbed by alarming cancer rates in grade-school children found them linked to asbestos materials used in school construction. Millions more were shocked to discover that many hand-held hair dryers were lined with thin asbestos shields which could easily flake into the stream of hot air being blown around their faces or that some brands of electric toasters had asbestos liners in proximity to the bread being prepared for breakfast. Automobile mechanics could only wonder if the asbestos used in brake linings wasn't as dangerous to them as to the original production workers who assembled them at the cost of extremely high rates of lung disease.

Asbestos is not an isolated example. Other household manifestations of workplace toxins include the petrochemical insect-killing strips which work by poisoning the atmosphere, glass-fiber draperies which may release splinters into the air, and miracle cleaners, paint strippers, and glues which do their work through chemical reactions that may injure the body. Considerable controversy also surrounds the use of various plastics to wrap and store food because of the possibility that petrochemicals may leach into the food. It has been found, for example, that lemon and tea will interact with a polystyrene cup in a manner which dissolves the container and releases carcinogenic material into the tea.[8] Keeping abreast of these hundreds of disputes is a hopeless task for any individual. Reliance on as many natural materials as possible for household wares and furnishings is an excellent defensive measure, but ultimately the only long-term solution is the regulation of petrochemicals at the point of production.

The need for social rather than individual response is illustrated in the relatively well-publicized issue of fluorocarbons. Although they pose no immediate individual danger, fluorocarbons threaten planetary health. After being released into the air from a spray can, refrigeration unit, or air conditioning system, fluorocarbons make their way into the atmosphere where they deplete the ozone layer. Even though worldwide restrictions on the production and use of fluorocarbons have gone into effect, the fluorocarbons already released have created holes in the ozone layers in the Arctic and have lessened the entire ozone layer by some 10 to 15%. Unless the world sanctions hold and the phasing out of fluorocarbons continues unabated, the incidence of human skin cancer could skyrocket and the stage be set for unpredictable climatic changes.

A dangerous escalation of environmental dangers is occurring with the introduction of nuclear power as a major energy source. Three hazards are involved: the possibility of explosions, the probability of accidents, and the certainty of radioactive waste. Any exposure to radiation is harmful to the human body. As Nobel Laureate George Wald has said, "Every dose is an overdose . . . A little radiation does a little harm, a lot does more harm."[9] Natural sources of radiation are not exceptions to this rule. Navajo Indians working as uranium miners suffer epidemic-level cancer rates, and Yemenis who live near radioactive thorium sands have 25% higher rates of mental retardation than their neighbors. On the military front, major nuclear powers are so aware of the dangers of atmospheric poisoning that they have voluntarily limited themselves to underground testing of their nuclear weapons and have tried to make this a universal practice. Most of the developing atomic powers have not yet seen fit to follow their lead, and every time such a nation makes an atmospheric test, radioactive clouds float around the world with no one able to predict which unlucky nation will receive the radioactive fallout.

Human error, equipment malfunctioning, aging facilities, and natural disasters like earthquakes make every nuclear facility an accident waiting to happen. In 1979 as American utility companies were mailing out information kits to film critics to demonstrate that the kind of accident shown in the film *The China Syndrome* could not happen, that kind of accident took place at Three Mile Island. In 1986, shortly after Soviet scientists boasted about the safety of their nuclear industry, the most devastating nuclear accident to date occurred at the Chernobyl power plant in the Ukraine. The radiation released into the atmosphere by the Chernobyl blast was equal to ten percent of the total radiation ever released by bombs. The Faustian risk in putting nuclear time bombs in populated areas has never been more lethally exposed.

While the immediate death toll and devastation at Chernobyl were self-evident, the more subtle but fatal long-term and world-wide effects were not. In *Deadly Deceit*, Jay M. Gould and Benjamin Goldman have looked at Chernobyl's effects in the United States. In the state of Washington, some 9,000 miles distant from Chernobyl, nine days after the blast, radioactive iodine-131 was at peak values in the state's rainfall. During that month the United States experienced a 5.3 percent rise in its death rate as measured against the previous year, the highest upward spike in half a century. Milk supplies throughout the nation were contaminated. Gould and Goldman provide persuasive statistical evidence that this contamination caused a 12.3 percent increase in the nation's infant mortality rate, led by a whopping 28% increase in the South Atlantic region. The highest rates occurred in the states with the highest concentration of radioactive materials in milk and the lowest rates in the states with the lowest amounts.[10]

The larger thrust of Gould and Goldman's work is to establish that even small doses of radiation, the kind of low-level radiation the American government deems safe is, in fact, literally deadly. Part of their massive statistical analysis makes note of increasing death rates in a region after a nuclear plant begins operations. In response to the assurance given Americans that not one death resulted from the Three Mile Island accident, Gould and Goldman report that among the 159,684 residents living within a ten mile radius of the accident, there was a 64% increase in cancer from 1981 to 1985, nearly three times the national increase.[11] Most disturbing of all is their documentation of how the government has consistently downplayed—if not covered up—all nuclear problems in the half century since the Manhattan Project was launched in 1942.

An examination of almost any year in the nuclear age verifies Gould and Goldman's charges of laxity and deception. Four incidents from late in 1979 are illustrative. In Denver, workers at the Robinson Brick & Tile Company were stunned to learn that the factory where some had been working for years had been built on a former (1914–17) dump site of the National Radium Institute.[12] In the Southeast, some 100,000 dwellings were found to have been built with concrete blocks made from radioactive slag sold to construction companies by the Tennessee Valley Authority.[13] In Los Angeles, Atomics International admitted that in 1959 it had released radioactive gases over the San Fernando Valley after a serious accident at an experimental nuclear plant.[14] And in Washington, D.C., a report suppressed for twenty-six years finally revealed that 4,200 sheep that had died in Utah in 1953, after exposure to a 24-kiloton blast, had been severely radiated. Their thyroid glands showed a concentration of radioactivity that surpassed the maximum permissible concentrations for humans by from 200 to 1,000 times.[15]

Leaks, ineptitude, and the pervasiveness of low-level radiation compound the problem of disposal of nuclear wastes. Until a method is found to deradiate wastes, their radioactive life span is measurable in tens of thousands of years. At present, the most common method of control is to encase the material in lead containers and bury them in tunnels or caves. Such procedures place enormous faith in the longevity of the shielding and in the ability to safely move the wastes to dump sites. This is no one-time problem. The more nuclear plants there are, the faster the waste materials will accumulate. Assuming that there will be a continued use of radioactive substances for medical purposes and for military defense, disposal is an endless problem. Another concern is that there is a history of high mortality rates among researchers, doctors, nurses, and patients because of ignorance or overly optimistic early estimates of permissible exposure levels to radiation.

Considering all these realities, no prolongevous thinker will opt to live within 50 miles of any nuclear plant or storage area, and most certainly not downwind or downriver from either. And he or she will be concerned about the routes and methods used to transport radioactive waste to the storage areas. As with other nuclear problems, the involved parties are not to be counted on for candor or restraint. Until they were stopped by local political pressure, utilities were moving atomic wastes through the residential streets of New York City, one of the most densely populated areas of the country.

Nuclear power's advantages over fossil fuels are chimerical. Our national treasure and scientific expertise would be better directed toward developing technologies based on nonpolluting solar, wind, and tidal power, with nuclear input held to a minimum if utilized at all. Such a course would begin to make the world of technology compatible with the world of biology and provide a start for the eradication of cancer and other diseases of industrial development.

The threats to longevity posed by radiation are not limited to a few nuclear plants, any more than petrochemical contamination is limited to the workplace. It has not been much publicized that common household items have become sources of radiation. One is the microwave oven, which sits in the heart of the kitchen and may emit radiation if defective. Smoke-detector alarms with ionized particles are so perilous that the installation instructions warn that when the detector is dismantled it should not be discarded in a regular garbage dump—a warning most likely to be long forgotten by a second or third occupant of the premises. Even more common than microwave ovens and smoke detectors with ionized particles are devices with radium dials and paints that glow in the dark. The amount of radiation exposure involved from these household items is small, but as with additives in foods, a growing number of small exposures may add up to a major risk. Commonsense dictates that anyone who aspires to a long life should avoid these household appliances.

In our toxic-prone society, even toiletries must be looked at with a skeptical eye. Skin irritations frequently are the consequence of the chemicals used in cosmetics, synthetic fabrics, and soaps. Cosmetics that are applied near the eye, nose, or mouth should be chosen with extreme care; and it is an excellent practice to use undyed white facial or toilet tissue rather than colored or printed tissue. Hair dyes are the most dangerous cosmetic products of all. Almost all permanent hair dyes and most tints, rinses, and semi-permanent dyes contain carcinogens. Unless the consumer is certain this is not the case, such products should be avoided, as the carcinogens can be absorbed into the body through hair follicles. Henna, a plant product whose highlighting and tinting effects last several weeks, can serve as a noncarcinogenic substitute.

A toxin that works much faster and is even deadlier than radiation or the carcinogens in dyes is dioxin, which is used in herbicides and defoliants. This poison first came to public attention at the time of the war in Vietnam. From 1962 to 1971, 10.6 million gallons of Agent Orange, a defoliant containing dioxin, were sprayed over the Vietnamese jungles in an effort to deprive guerrilla forces of cover. Over 1,000 Americans took part in the spraying and 6,000 more were exposed to it. The number of Vietnamese exposed is undetermined, but is probably considerably higher. The difficulty with dioxin is that in addition to defoliating trees and killing pests, it has severe adverse effects on the human body, causing cancers, miscarriages, and birth defects. How long it is retained in the soil in a dangerous state is not known.

American servicemen who were exposed to dioxin have experienced extremely high rates of cancer, including rare brain tumors, high mortality rates, and high percentages of children with birth defects. After a long legal battle, some monetary compensation has been made, but the U.S. military and its dioxin suppliers have refused to accept moral culpability for what amounted to chemical warfare on the environment.

The use of dioxin in Vietnam is just one example of human exposure to the substance. Silvex, a spray containing dioxin, has been used extensively in reforestation projects in Oregon, where dioxin has subsequently been linked to miscarriages and other health problems. Power companies throughout the nation have used dioxin to keep unwanted vegetation away from their utility poles. They and the manufacturers insist that when used with the recommended safeguards, dioxin is safe.

I have had a personal experience with those kinds of assurances. One summer I noticed that the mountain laurel in my back yard were withering. Upon investigation I discovered the telephone company had sprayed a substance containing dioxin around a nearby telephone pole to keep down weeds. Many yards of soil had to be replaced to remove the contamination, and the residual effects lingered for years. No one informed me that the chemical had been used, or bothered to consider that it might poison not only the mountain laurel but the vegetable gardens a few yards away in both directions.

Dioxin's potential for catastrophe was demonstrated in 1976 when it, along with other chemicals, was released into the environment by a chemical explosion in Seveso, Italy. The danger was so great that the most contaminated zone had to be evacuated. Years later, women in the first three months of pregnancy were prohibited from living in another, less-contaminated zone, and children under 12 were barred during daytime hours. All animals in the district were slaughtered, some 600 children developed skin diseases, and the incidence of birth defects increased. Committees investigating the explosion uncovered a familiar pattern: Hoffman-La Roche, the company involved, had attempted, immediately after the explosion, to minimize the dangers, and the local health officials had not been quick to seek outside help. Eventually, Hoffman-La Roche paid $23 million in damages to individuals and companies and another $54 million to various branches of the Italian government for emergency and cleanup operations.

Still another possible toxic source is the water faucet. One of the great leaps forward in life extension during the nineteenth century was purification of drinking water, but yesteryear's source of infectious diseases may be today's source of environmental maladies. Auto plants in Michigan annually dump nearly fifty thousand pounds of phosphorus into the Detroit River, and steel mills in Ohio pollute the Cuyahoga with 137 tons of solids and 182,000 pounds of sulfur, chlorine, phenol, cyanide, ammonia, magnesium, iron, and oil. This sort of dumping occurs in every American waterway. Consequently, it is not surprising that a study of eighty-eight counties in Ohio showed that death from cancers of the digestive tract were much higher in areas served by surface water than in areas served by wells. In New Orleans, where the Mississippi flows toward the Gulf of Mexico carrying the agricultural and industrial toxins of more than a dozen states, cancers of the kidney, bladder, and urinary tract are abnormally high. From the Hudson to the Columbia the story is the same: the mighty rivers of America have become so severely polluted that the purification systems of many cities are no longer adequate to deal with the problem. From 1940 to 1960, there were 228 outbreaks of poisoning due to the water supply; but as in most pollution problems, the cause-and-effect relationship between contaminant and diseases was impossible to document with precision because of time lapses, population shifts, and multiple causes of degenerative diseases.

People who live in the country or in small towns are not necessarily exempt from these water-pollution woes. The most modest factory can affect an underground water table from which wells draw. Any strange odor or foaming in a stream or rivulet warrants immediate investigation. Assistance is available from the Environmental Protection Agency and local public-health officers. If the water proves to be less than satisfactory, one should use bottled water provided by a responsible company. If one is considering a filtration device for faucets, it is best to check with a good consumer guide, since many of these devices are useless or worse.[16]

Water often becomes contaminated because toxins leach into the soil from poorly supervised or illegal chemical dump sites. Of equal concern at such sites is the dangerous mixture of wastes. If the drums used to store chemicals should break or rust through, the resulting chemical interactions can produce fires, explosions, and release of lethal gases. Additional public risk results when haulers paid to transport wastes to legal dump sites decide to pocket the fees and dump the load into a vacant city lot or secluded country area. What the driver considers a minor infraction of the law is much closer to a capital crime; but until the punishments involved bring home the gravity of the offense, illegal dumping and slipshod supervision of dumps will persist. Dump sites, like nuclear power plants, are environmental time bombs. Although the federal government has allocated millions of dollars for toxic cleanup of hundreds of identified sites, less than a handful have seen any action.

The consequences of not taking action are visible in the disaster that occurred in the Love Canal area near Niagara Falls, New York. Here, thousands of people had to be permanently resettled and nearly eight hundred homes had to be purchased by the state. There was an undeniable immediate threat to life and health from a chemical dump. It was found that the odds for contracting cancer were as high as one in ten for anyone living near the edge of the site, and this calculation took into account only chemicals in the air, neglecting the known contamination in the soil and underground water table. Love Canal was another environmental time bomb that exploded.

Perhaps the most underrated and misunderstood environmental pollutant is noise, which usually is regarded more as a nuisance than as a health menace. While most people recognize that impairment of hearing is a danger, few realize that forty epidemiological studies in eleven nations have linked excessive noise exposure to cardiovascular disorders. The measurable reactions include decrease in gastric juices, increased intracranial pressure, constriction of muscles, skin reactions, the release of adrenal hormones, and increased blood pressure. Exposure to high noise levels can be an immediate danger to those suffering from circulatory diseases, heart problems, and high blood pressure, and it inflicts long-term wear and tear on everyone.

The unit used to measure noise is the decibel, one decibel being the lowest sound that can be heard by a human ear under quiet conditions. This measurement indicates the amount of pressure on the ear, and the numbers rise logarithmically. Serious health effects commence at about 80 decibels, and at 140 decibels there is pain. A whisper is about 20 decibels, a ticking watch 30, a vacuum cleaner 75, heavy traffic 80, a motorcycle 95, a subway car 105, amplified music 110, and a large jet engine 125 at a distance of 75 feet. Sounds in a home in the country will usually be in the 20-30 decibel range, while sounds in an apartment in New York will be in the 50-70 range, depending on the time of day and district. Factories are usually in the danger area, with considerable variation from department to department.

Just as spicy foods have to become increasingly spicier to be tasted because taste buds are destroyed, loud noises beget louder noises as hearing deteriorates. The contemporary fad for highly amplified music and delight in loud noises feeds upon itself and upon the hearing difficulties of workers who do not protect their hearing at work with earplugs and other devices. Booming night club loudspeakers put out from 115 to 130 decibels, while a riveter's gun heard at thirty feet is over 110 decibels.

In terms of life extension, the major danger from noise is the long-term wear and tear stress it causes. Hearing tests given at high schools and colleges revealed that students' hearing is deteriorating much sooner than in previous generations. To avoid the rapid aging that is associated with such a syndrome, the prolongevous will want to avoid any occupation in which unavoidable noise levels greater than 80 decibels are a condition of work, and they will arrange their lives so that noise is under control. Political activism at a local level can play a significant role in noise abatement. The difference in cost between a loud garbage truck or subway car and a quiet one is negligible and a sum saved many times over in medical expenses and human dignity.

Anyone with a shred of social consciousness or any thought for posterity must be concerned with environmental pollution. But for strictly selfish prolongevous reasons, the need for action is urgent. As the twentieth century moves to a close, environmental pollution has emerged as a major threat to long life and health everywhere in the world. Cancer, which is already the number two killer in the United States and on the increase, is bound intimately with pollution, whether the form be particulate matter, radiation, petrochemicals, or toxins. These same pollutants play an additional negative role in heart disease, many respiratory diseases, birth defects, and in other threats to life. Since terracidal technologies and chemistries are not essential for human survival, playing Russian roulette with talk of environmental "trade-offs" and "acceptable risks" is lunacy. It amounts to no more than an excuse for a monstrous greed that values short-term private profit above the cost of long-term threats to all life forms.

Individual responses can reduce many environmental dangers, but these threats need not exist at all, and there is the ever-present danger of falling victim to some unsuspected source. The only acceptable permanent solution is general detoxification of society through control of pollution at its source. Achieving such an end will be as arduous a struggle as that experienced by the nineteenth-century sanitation reformers whose efforts culminated in a near doubling of the average life span. The same combination of governmental timidity, private avarice, and professional arrogance works once again in opposition to structural change. The political trend in the 1990s toward privatization of national resources and deregulation of industry augurs poorly for the near future. We can only hope that the required political mandate for environmental detoxification will be mustered without the need of first suffering a planetary cancer epidemic or a global acidic rain.

# 14. REDEFINING THE BIOLOGICAL LIMITS

*This problem (aging) should be solved with even more resolution
than that devoted to the solving of the bomb problem a while
back, or the current problem of conquering the cosmos.*
                                        —*L. V. Komarov*

DURING THE AGE OF ENLIGHTENMENT, European scientists
began to think of the universe as being like a clock. A Creator had
fashioned the parts, wound them up, and set the mechanism
working according to fixed laws, which humans eventually could
master for the betterment of their lives. By the twentieth century
the clock metaphor had been extended to the interior of the human
body, which was often described as containing numerous individual systemic clocks, kept running by proper nutrition, exercise,
and medical treatment. It also was possible to speculate that the
clocks could be rewound periodically, perhaps a limited number
of times, perhaps infinitely. Almost without notice the ancient
dream of rejuvenation and immortality had passed from the
imaginative realm of myth into the rational methodology of the
research laboratory.[1]

Any rewinding of biological clocks entails the development of a
unified theory of aging. Strangely enough, even though aging
occurs in all times and places, proceeding through the various parts
of the human organism at a fairly predictable speed, there is no
satisfactory explanation as to why aging happens or how it is

255

regulated. Treatment for aging must address symptoms rather than causes. But if the causes of aging could be determined, aging would be reduced to the category of a disease. The prospect would then be to modify the effects of or totally eliminate causes of aging: the ultimate cure of the ultimate disease.

This staggering vision is no longer limited to science fiction. The work done in microbiology since the 1930s has been as revolutionary as that in physics during the earlier decades of the century. Just as theoretical physics culminated by mid-century in the birth of the nuclear age, the new biology is expected to make a revolutionary impact on aging. Even before a breakthrough that might redefine all previous limits on the human life span, it is likely that there will be a series of advances, each of which could add five, ten, or twenty years to the average life span. The implications for persons who will be no more than 80 years of age at the dawn of the twenty-first century are unprecedented. Instead of being at the cusp of old age, their projected life spans may be extendable by decades, with the accelerating possibility of living to enjoy new advances that make additional extensions possible.

An examination of the scientific principles and pioneering experiments of anti-aging specialists is clearly relevant to any longevity project. Most important in this regard are what changes in present life style could be safely adopted in view of the preliminary findings and what insights that work offers into the longevity components already identified. Having a basic orientation to anti-aging research also puts an individual on guard against adopting reckless measures on the basis of incomplete or misunderstood experimental research. The disposition toward fraud and wishful thinking in rejuvenation products and techniques exceeds even that of centenarian age claims.

The simplest hypothesis on aging is that there is a mechanism within the body, perhaps in the brain, hypothalamus, or pituitary, which releases an enzyme, a hormone, a substance X which signals the body to start closing down its systems. The discovery of such a mechanism, if it indeed exists, would make it possible to devise a counteraging magic bullet which would keep the substance from being released, delay its release, hamper its effectiveness, or destroy it.

Similar to the death-substance theory is the idea that aging results from coding in the basic DNA or in errors made through the linking RNA of each cell. The error phenomenon has been compared to a duplicating machine in which subsequent copies or copies made from copies are never quite as clear as the original. Eventually the dot to an "i" gets left off or a "t" is left uncrossed or a message is smudged. It is observable that as cells age, their errors multiply. Consequently, as cells are replaced through division, errors accumulate more rapidly. Part of the problem may stem from outside factors like radiation which destroy part of the DNA and RNA, but structural problems in the genetic instructions cannot be ruled out.

Whatever the source of cellular error, should genetic engineering or genetic surgery ever become a reality, a physician would be able to readjust the DNA and RNA to their original efficiency. It also might be possible to take disease-fighting cells from a person during his or her early teens when those cells are extremely vigorous, freeze them, and then reintroduce them into the body later when the cells left in the body have become weaker and less efficient. Ultimately the genetic code itself may be alterable. When this is possible, diseases based on genetic inheritance would become curable.

Another aspect of cellular error under intensive investigation is the immunological system of the body. As the organism ages, the white blood cells find it harder to distinguish between dangerous or unhealthy cells and cells that are sound. New cells sometimes are treated as hostile microbes. The body, in effect, begins to attack itself. No one has been able to understand why this occurs or how it may be prevented. Auto-immunity may be linked to the presence of a general "death agent," accumulated cellular errors, or as-yet-unknown factors. There is some hope that hormones might be able to combat this phenomenon. For example, thymosin, a hormone produced by the thymus gland, has been found effective in the treatment of some auto-immune conditions.

Cross-linkage of protein molecules is yet another of the cellular-aging theories. The term refers to the hardening of connective tissues and has been likened to cells that are glued together or toughened in the way leather is in tanning. The hardened connective tissue becomes less able to deliver oxygen, nutrients, hormones, and other substances to the cells. It is suspected that some soil-bacteria enzymes might break down cross-linkage. Thus, soil analysis of any area where there appears to be unusual longevity has become standard. Although no enzyme or other substance has yet been found to combat cross-linkage, tobacco smoking and radiation are known to encourage it.

In addition to cross-linkage, cellular interactions produce unneeded by-products sometimes referred to as intercellular sludge, cellular garbage, and clinkers. While it is not clear whether these should be thought of as causes or products of aging, they cause considerable damage. Viewed as a group, clinkers may be seen as so much corrosion or dust interfering with the delicate settings of the internal biological clocks. Various vitamins and antioxidants in combination with low-fat diets are being investigated to determine which would be most effective in preventing the accumulation of the garbage in the first place, in escorting the debris out of the body, or in chemically transforming it into more useful compounds.

A more fundamental role of cells in aging is advocated by Leonard Hayflick. In the 1950s Hayflick disproved the long-standing biological axiom that the individual human cell is capable of infinite divisions or reproductions of itself. His laboratory work showed that with the intriguing exception of cancer cells the human cell is limited to approximately 50 divisions. This discovery has come to be called Hayflick's Limit. Hayflick has continued his work on cells and has come to the conclusion that the basic cause of human aging is in the cells. He reasons that the life span of any animal is determined by the tissue or organ that ages fastest. If the aging of cells that make up that tissue or organ can be halted, then the tissue or organ will not age. If this could be done for all components of the body, there would be no internal aging whatsoever. Hayflick and his colleagues have dubbed their research as cytogerontology, the study of how cells age. The details of his theoretical approach and the experiments which flow from that approach have been offered in numerous scientific papers. Hayflick has written *How and Why We Age* in which he presents his views, all major theories of aging, and considerable longevity data in language accessible to the general public.[2]

Hayflick's work opens the possibility of nuclear cellular transplants to fight disease and extend life. Cells that have completed only some of their potential divisions could be taken from an individual and kept in cold storage. At a later date, the cells could be returned to the donor to complete their pairings. Although there would be a finite limit to this process, life spans could be extended considerably longer than is now possible. Some experiments using vitamin E have indicated that cells reproducing in cultures can be made to double a hundred times, twice the Hayflick Limit. This pushes longevity possibilities even farther, assuming of course that what happens in laboratory cultures will also happen in the human body.

Another intervention proposed at the cellular level is chemical tampering with body temperature. It is estimated that if the body's thermostat could be lowered by from two to three degrees Celsius, there would be no negative side effects, while life might be extended from twenty to thirty years. This lowering could be accomplished through drugs, genetic engineering, mechanical devices, or mind techniques. One proposal involves a sleeping chamber which could lower the temperature of the body at rest near freezing in the manner of a hibernating bear.

Looking forward a few centuries to the age of intergalactic travel, suspended animation through freezing could overcome the problem of voyages that might last a hundred or more earth years. Part of the crew could be kept alive but frozen for months or years at a time. The conscious lifetime would not be increased, but the overall lifetime would be spread out over an incredible period. One hundred crew members on a hundred-year voyage might each be awake for only ten years. If no one was over 35 at the time of lift-off, no one would be more than 45 on landing, even though a hundred years had elapsed.

A contemporary attempt to gain entry into the superlongevous future through freezing is called cryonics. This method involves the placing of a fresh corpse in a container and freezing it to the temperature of liquid nitrogen. Its advocates hope that the process will preserve the body in a state of suspended animation until such time as the diseases that killed the body can be reversed or until aging itself has become a curable disease. The problems associated with cryonics are enormous. Even its most optimistic supporters acknowledge that the present freezing technology may be so primitive that the chance of successful revival is exceedingly slim, a mere percentage of one percent. A problem less candidly addressed is that the body should not be dead at the time of freezing if positive results are to be anticipated; yet if the body is not technically dead, then the freezing itself might be legally definable as murder. Because of this dilemma, secrecy surrounds any cryonic encapsulation, but insurance policies are available that guarantee the maintenance of the cryonic chamber for hundreds of years.

In opposition to the theories which place the major cause of aging within the organism itself are theories of wear and tear, which hold that the body is aged, for the most part, by relentless outside pressures. These hostile forces include emotional factors, physical collisions, and environmental pollutants of every description. A bridge between this view and the auto-immunologic theory is that any force which weakens the body from the outside may so disorient the immunological defense system that it begins to malfunction. The process accelerates as more and more irreplaceable cells are lost, and the body's slowing ability to recover makes stresses such as noise progressively more harmful.

In *Prolongevity II*, perhaps the most readable and comprehensive popular work on anti-aging, Albert Rosenfeld points out that almost every facet of aging eventually is connected to all others and can be used to explain them. Until there is a unified law of aging, it will be difficult to separate some effects from some causes or to put aging factors into a hierarchical order of menace. Rosenfeld is also sympathetic to the view that the body may face a multiplicity of agers. Perhaps there is a substance which signals the body to slow down, but if it should fail, there are backup systems. The limitation of cell doublings or auto-immunological errors or cross linkage or cellular garbage will slow down the organism, and if they do not, never-ending wear and tear will.

A more optimistic view is that bodily programs are aimed at survival of the species, with death an irrelevant consideration. This view emphasizes that the body is coded to have its major systems in prime condition during the reproductive stage of life. What happens afterward may not be genetically programmed. Alex Comfort has used the analogy of a spacecraft designed to photograph Mars on a bypass flight. All the craft's systems will be in top operational efficiency during the most advantageous periods for taking pictures, and there will be no energy wasted on self-destruct systems. The craft may be unlucky and collide with an object in the asteroid belt. Some of its parts may fail or be damaged by cosmic rays. Or it may be trapped by the gravitational field of a planet, either becoming an artificial moon or being pulled into the atmosphere until it is consumed like a falling star. The craft might, however, escape the Solar System altogether and become an intergalactic voyager. The implications for humans are that if the body is not programmed to self-destruct, the medical problem for life extension is immensely simplified. Rather than thwarting coded death systems, the prolongevous physician will be concerned with maintenance and repair.

Thinking of the body as a machine requiring maintenance leads to the need for replacing as well as repairing worn-out parts. Automobile life may be extended for decades, but only if components are replaced as part of the general upkeep. The wooden peg leg and iron arm hook were among the first human spare parts to be widely used. Today science has provided pacemakers for tired hearts, plastic tubing for destroyed arteries, mechanical joints for worn-out bones, and transplants for dysfunctioning organs. Perhaps some future philosophers will be debating at what point an organism contains so many artificial parts that it ceases to be human and should be thought of as an android or robot. Long before that hypothetical era, however, bionic spare parts and other techniques will be making a substantial impact on comfort in old age and on life extension. Cameralike devices and miniaturized radio technology have already raised the possibility that afflictions like blindness and deafness may become as obsolete as smallpox.

A more spectacular technique mentioned in relation to providing human spare parts is cloning. To judge from procedures now possible with simple life forms, scientists may at some future time be able to use a cell from a human donor to construct a body that would be an identical twin. Futurist writers have projected the possibility of having a spare clone body for each human, which could serve as an ideal organ bank, since the identical genetic codes would eliminate problems of tissue rejection. The ultimate in this line of reasoning is that a clone could be created and kept in suspended animation without activation of the brain. When the donor's original body began to fail, the donor's memory bank could be transferred to the clone: a *de facto* self-birth. That such a scenario could ever become possible is problematic. The subject is worthy of mention only to indicate the fantastic projections that are now theoretically consistent with established scientific canon. The fact that they appear to be possible does not guarantee that they actually are possible or that they are necessarily desirable.

Contrasting with superscience methods such as cloning or bionic parts is anti-aging research that draws from traditional knowledge. As the physical effects of stress have become recognized as potent antilongevous factors, there has been a resurgence of interest in ways of reducing stress damage through techniques that promote the mental mobilization of internal bodily energy. Methods rooted in the ancient practice of yoga have been measured objectively and have been found capable of lowering blood pressure, reducing body temperature, slowing heartbeat, relieving muscle tension, and increasing the amount of oxygen in the blood. Similar benefits have been obtained by people working with biofeedback, methods by which individuals use electronic devices and graphs to listen to their own vital signs in order to regulate them through purely mental techniques. As it is unlikely that mind control could ever check the destructive effect of a force like radiation or a large dose of arsenic, mind techniques are used primarily as adjuncts to prevent or alleviate the wear and tear caused by stress.

Another anti-aging issue rooted in traditional knowledge is the search for a perfect food. Robert Prehoda has written of a future when there will be synthetic food that improves upon the chemistry of Mother Nature by providing the optimal bodily fuel in a form that causes the least amount of internal wear and tear.[4] Today's health tonics, multivitamin supplements, and hormonal injections are the initial steps in this direction, and finding the most effective antioxidants and determining the exact role of various hormones, enzymes, minerals, and vitamins remains the present focus of anti-aging dietary research. Progress must necessarily be slow, as many food elements have the double edge to them already described in relation to mineral supplements. Long-term experiments with other mammals will be needed before a diet of optimal foods can be authoritatively determined. Minimum daily requirements for many nutrients have not been established, and levels for most are in dispute.

Before a single synthetic food or dietary regimen is available for tailoring to biochemical individuality, there will be a series of modest improvements in nutrition which will steadily upgrade the diet. But the life-extension claims that have been made for some antioxidants, tranquilizers, and metals are strictly premature, having no verifiable base. To put them into the body on a regular basis is to play the guinea pig for posterity, a role that may be honorable but one that should not be taken lightly or without a clear understanding of the risk involved. Prolongevous optimists must realize that when an experiment is called "promising" the adjective is not a blanket go-ahead signal so much as a warning that the findings are tentative. Unsuspected side effects, such as the increased rate of kidney failure now linked to the heavy use of Tylenol and other brands of acetaminophen, may develop.[5] Or the procedure may prove to have only a passing effect.

Another example of the risks facing anyone too eager to experiment with new anti-aging processes is offered by the fate of some older men at the turn of the last century who sought sexual rejuvenation. They became convinced this would be possible through grafts or injections derived from the testicles of goats and monkeys. Except for psychological support, the procedures simply didn't work. What might have been another amusing, if expensive, example of human gullibility became tragic when one set of grafts inadvertently used syphilitic monkeys, transferring that disease to humans at a time when penicillin had not yet been discovered.[6]

Sexual rejuvenation also figures heavily in an anti-aging technique favored by the wealthy in midcentury—cell transplants from lambs. Developed by Dr. Paul Niehans, the method is based on the assumption that liver cells will rejuvenate the liver, heart cells the heart, kidney cells the kidney, and so forth. Treatment at Niehans' lush Swiss clinic became popular among the elite of Europe during the 1930s, and his claims got a tremendous boost when cell transplants to Pope Pius XII were followed by the pontiff's recovery from a serious illness which had resisted previous treatments. Although most of Niehans' patients preferred to remain anonymous, a few, including Somerset Maugham, have written glowingly of the effects of the cell therapy. Generally, however, Niehans has been viewed as part of the beauty-doctor clique rather than as an anti-aging scientist. He never published a list of patients who enjoyed unusual life spans or vigor, and he never published a scientific treatise explaining the how and why of his method. His critics note that Niehans did not undertake his own therapy and that when he died, in his late 80s, the signs of his enormous wealth were more visible than any signs of his rejuvenation. A number of nations, the United States among them, ban the cell transplants on the grounds that they are useless and perhaps dangerous.

A totally different anti-aging contingent attempts to determine what health effects result from climatic forces such as cosmic rays, barometric pressure, electromagnetism, and sunspot activity. Investigators have found that bodily temperatures adjust to diurnal rhythms, falling in the evening and rising in the earlier part of the day. One of the causes of the phenomenon known as "jet lag" is that when a body has moved rapidly through time zones or from the northern to the southern hemisphere, its physical responses are no longer synchronized with the new pattern of night and day or with summer and winter. The greater the distance traveled, the greater the likelihood of a period of disorientation and readjustment. Positive correlations also have been found between outbreaks of lymphocytosis and increases in solar activity; and some weather fronts seem to be accompanied by an increase in the number of hospital admissions. It is not clear whether the fronts or solar outbursts trigger a crisis about to occur in any case or whether they are causes of the ailment. Nor is it certain that the correlations so far uncovered would hold up under a longer, more comprehensive time period. Related work has attempted to determine the cause-and-effect relationship between prevailing winds in Europe and diseases that come in their wake. If definite connections were established, it might be possible to give warning forecasts such as those issued when the air quality is dangerous. Individuals found to have higher sensitivity to certain types of weather could adjust their behavior for heightened or lessened efficiency.[7]

Soviet researchers were among the first to look at the possible longevous effects of positive and negative air ions. Their work included field studies in the areas of the Caucasus with the highest centenarian concentrations, but remained inconclusive. Scientists in other countries have used negative air ions in the successful treatment of third-degree burns. Once the benefits and dangers of positive and negative air ions have been comprehensively cata-logued, it may be possible to regulate ionization in enclosed spaces like homes and offices. In addition, serious attention could be given to using natural or synthetic fabrics that most effectively mediate between climatic forces and bodily reactions.

Promising as these many facets of anti-aging research are, the work is severely handicapped by inadequate funding. If the United States ever decided to invest in a Methuselah Project in the way it once invested in the Manhattan Project to develop a nuclear bomb, a series of significant breakthroughs might be speedily achieved. But this is not likely to occur. Many government-connected scientists and social planners are greatly troubled by the social and economic readjustments that would be required in a society having considerable numbers of people over 80. Another spectrum of opposition stems from those whose religious orientation makes them uneasy about genetic tampering and even such relatively simple medical interventions as contraception, artificial insemination and abortion.

The only major area in which massive federal spending intersects with longevity research is space exploration. As plans for space platforms, moon colonies, and interplanetary travel move toward realization, the search for optimal foods, fabrics, exercises, atmospheres, and the like becomes imperative. The whole adventure of humans in space also presents the first opportunity to observe reactions of the body to various cosmic influences when it is not surrounded by a protective atmosphere developed over the millennia.

In the long run, anti-aging research remains in the domain of medicine. One could say that all medical research is a fight to extend life and delay death. Although, eventually, every doctor loses every patient, medicine continues to deny that failure, at any given moment, is necessary. Every small medical advance hastens the day when life spans will approach the genetic limits. At the same time, work such as recombinant DNA research, at once the most dangerous and the most revolutionary biology ever conceived, questions whether any genetic program should be considered a final arbiter of age. The scenario for successful anti-aging progress as we enter the twenty-first century is that even before the elaboration of a unified law of aging, incremental gains in knowledge will steadily redefine the quality and duration of life. Encouraging as this prospect is, the average person must always differentiate between methods which seek to aid us in reaching the present genetic limits and those which defy all limits. The first strategy aims to make individual behavior more harmonious with forces that have been interacting in a predictable fashion for as long as humans have observed them. The second would remake the rules of the cosmic game, creating situations for which precedents may be irrelevant. Doomsday chemicals or cellular tampering that would make present life spans appear like a paradise lost are just as possible as a future in which life is calculated in centuries rather than years. Dr. Jekyll, after all, did not anticipate Mr. Hyde. The stakes are so awesome and the ground so uncertain that societies, like individuals, had best proceed with extreme caution. The years of Methuselah and even physical immortality may be waiting somewhere along the time-space continuum, but they are not around any foreseeable gerontological corner. And not all science fictions are destined to become scientific realities.

# 15. LONGEVITY NOW

**Long Life to You**

AT THE ONSET OF THIS INVESTIGATION into the mysteries of long life, I suggested the Methuselah factors might be all around us in plain sight if we would only seek them without preconceptions. That has proven to be the case. There are more longevous people in populous areas than in remote isolated regions. They do not consume exotic substances and elixirs, but ordinary familiar food. They are rarely involved in complex regimens or obscure cults. Instead they are mostly found walking vigorously in conventional society. Far from being reclusive or psychologically odd, they are usually highly respected members of their communities. Better educated people have a significant longevity advantage over the lesser educated, the affluent over the poor. Proximity to modern medicine is a plus, not an iatrogenic minus.

The pragmatic challenge presented by the longevity agenda is that although its components are relatively easy to describe, they are hard to live by. Anyone considering them will be beset by a flurry of reasonable doubts. He or she will wonder: How can I possibly remember the various prolongevous pluses and anti-longevous minuses? I'm too old for this. I'm too young. Anyway, isn't it probable that after trying it for a while, I'll just revert to my former habits? Despite what Georgakas says, I think this is really about deprivation. My life is hard enough as it is. I'm not interested in mortgaging present time for some hypothetical future. Maybe prolongevity isn't so practical after all, at least not for me.

Having heard such concerns many times, I think it might be helpful if I ended my explication of the longevity agenda by discussing some of the ways in which I've tried to implement it in my own life. I don't offer my personal solutions, most certainly not my compromises, as models. They are not. But they do illustrate the adjustments everyone must make as our real worlds collide with our best intentions. As for the age issue, that's easy to deal with. The younger one is when one begins a longevity program, the sooner premature aging is halted. Caloric restriction, in particular, has always had its most dramatic effects the earlier it was initiated. On the other hand, when people over 75 have been put on longevity agendas, they have shown immediate significant health gains.[1] A statistical irony to bear in mind is that as you age chronologically, the older you are at any given moment the greater the probability that you will exceed the average life span by an increasingly longer period of time.

My biggest personal challenge has always been exercise. I never cared much for athletics as a child, and I managed to hit 190 pounds, much of it fat, while still in my 20s. Consequently I've frequented health clubs throughout my adult life. The first one was in the 1950s when I was still a college student in my native Detroit. The gym I went to was operated by a former Mr. Michigan. In retrospect I see that his workouts were geared to power lifting and were not at all useful for longevity. Since then I've participated in many health club classes and observed even more of them. I've seen a high incidence of injuries resulting from these classes. Very often this was partly the fault of instructors who had become bored with repeating basic routines all day long five and six days a week. They had a marked tendency to put in workout movements more suitable for professional dancers than the average person and they set a pace that put unnecessary stress on the joints and other vulnerable parts of the body.

I've also been involved in formal swimming and jogging programs, but they never ceased to be something of a chore. I always found that I seemed to spend as much or more time getting to an exercise site, suiting up, warming up, and showering as I spent actually exercising. Over the years this has led me to put more emphasis on informal walking. My major problem has been sheer laziness. I have ample time to walk an hour each day, and I enjoy walking, but I am so interested in my work that I often put off walking until later in the day and then end up doing it much too briefly or not doing it at all.

I am more successful when I can walk with a purpose. I've developed various sequences in which I leave my house to do my daily post office stop and other errands in circuits of approximately a mile and a half. During my frequent business trips into Manhattan, I avoid the subway whenever feasible and walk between various destinations. New York happens to be highly suitable for this kind of walking; I've clocked many Manhattan miles without ever feeling bored. For vacations I usually opt for a place with hiking trails or a long shore line. I also like to visit cities that I can canvass on foot. I do more walking in the summer than in the winter, and I augment my walking with home exercises, repeatedly lifting three to 15 pound weights for upper body strength.

Meeting dietary goals has been far easier for me. I was raised on Mediterranean cooking, which is now recognized as one of the healthiest ethnic cuisines. So it's been relatively easy for me to adopt a predominantly vegetarian diet, which is the kind of food I genuinely prefer. At present I eat lamb or fish once or twice a week at most. In the summer many of my vegetables come from a small organic garden. I fertilize it with animal manure and compost from a plastic bin which I fill with non-meat and non-dairy leftovers and trimmings. These low-cost bins are easy to find in garden supply stores. I control pests by using predatory insects that are harmless to humans and obtainable through mail order. I've also been fortunate to find Michael Sobsey, a greengrocer in nearby Hoboken who specializes in high quality organic and lightly sprayed produce. He is extremely conscientious about valid labeling.

The weakest area of my diet involves sweets and caffeine. At one time I was drinking more than a pot of coffee every day and eating sweets at nearly every meal. I've worked myself down to one or two cups of coffee a day and one sweet. Lowering coffee intake has been made easier by the general improvement in my diet. The more prolongevous my diet became, the more frequent my adverse reactions to too much coffee.

I have now largely restricted my coffee intake to a formal afternoon break from work which takes me out of the house or office. The coffee is usually accompanied by a blueberry muffin or toasted bagel with jelly. I never put myself under time pressure during these breaks. I either arrange to meet with someone I want to talk with about non-business matters or I take along something to read. In short, the coffee break is genuine downtime. I know that coffee consumption is antilongevous, but I don't think my minimal present intake is going to rob me of even a year of life. The stress reduction from my coffee break may even make up for the damage. I also take vitamin B to counterattack the vitamin B depletion caused by coffee consumption.

I've never done a strict caloric accounting of my total diet, but my weight has remained at about 170 for nearly 20 years. Moreover, even though it's normal for people to lose bone and muscle and gain in fat as they grow older, I've been able to achieve the opposite through diet and exercise. One of my goals in the next decade is to bring my weight down to the fleeting 158 it hit one hot summer afternoon in the early 1970s when I'd just finished an hour of swimming laps and relaxing in a sauna. I hope to accomplish this by taking off a pound or two each year, primarily through increased exercise. Part of my informal weight management involves increasing exercise the day after I know I've overeaten and limiting that day's fuel to fruits and salads.

Although I think my diet is quite wholesome, I use supplements. I believe this is essential because of the toxic nature of our society, particularly since I live in an industrial area. I take two capsules of Added Protection, a multi-vitamin/mineral supplement with a nutritional wallop much heftier than the usual drugstore brands. This supplementation was prescribed for me by my physician who believes two a day are useful for a healthy person and up to six a day for a person who is ill. In addition to the multi, I take 400 milligrams of E, a gram of calcium-magnesium, and various doses of evening primrose and fish oils. The oils are taken mostly to moisten my unusually dry skin. I also take at least one gram of vitamin C a day (my multi gives another half gram). This is far in excess of the RDA, but I have found C gives me a boost when I feel run down and definitely helps stave off colds. If that is due to the placebo effect, so be it. I rarely take medication of any kind, not even aspirin or ibuprofen.

My experience has been that when beginning some new aspect of the longevity agenda or refining one in progress, an all-or-nothing, now-or-never attitude is counterproductive. Time is always required for physical and psychological alternatives to real change. False starts and restarts are to be expected. Habits that have been acquired over a lifetime cannot be breezily expunged in an instant makeover. Trial and error are an inevitable and essential part of the process. The direction and permanency of change is far more critical than its pace or degree at any given time. I've also discovered that incremental gains are highly interactive. Better fuels facilitate better exercise habits and those habits make it easier to eliminate additional bad fuels. The surge of well-being that follows the elimination of negative factors or the addition of positive ones provides considerable psychological support for the next round of change.

If I didn't have a prolongevous mindset, I would never have undertaken a work like *The Methuselah Factors*. Because of unfortunate events in my life, I have had an unusually early and intense concern with health. Both my father and my mother died from heart disease in their early 50s. My father was a chain smoker and my mother was considerably overweight. In contrast, my grandfather, who acted as a father to me, lived to his early 80s. He spent the last 20 years of his life gardening and he exercised daily with a variety of devices. I've also had very close friends who died of alcoholism and workplace poisoning.

As a result of these and other experiences with premature dying, it should not be surprising that I've never smoked and that I have a relatively low tolerance for anyone not willing to confront the life-threatening dangers posed by our toxic society. I don't allow people to smoke when they are with me. Nor do I tolerate other antilongevous behavior. Whenever possible, I avoid social situations where I know there will be noise, smoke, and other toxic conditions. I haven't paid much of a social price for this, as I have gathered a social circle of friends who either share my views or willingly accommodate them.

I also make it a point to support the environmental cause in any way I can and to actively oppose any politician who waffles on environmental protection and regulation of industry, whatever the rationale. I use as many recyclable products as possible in my home and office, even though they are often more expensive in terms of immediate dollars and cents. I wear clothes made of natural materials. I don't own an electric car, but I will do so as soon as they are economically feasible. I don't have any illusions that my modest efforts have a significant impact on the environment, but I have the moral satisfaction of not being an accomplice to terracide.

I've gone to considerable effort to find a physician committed to holistic medicine. I see him once a year for blood tests that chart my body chemistry. On the rare occasions when additional tests are needed, we always choose those which are the least invasive. This usually means avoiding tests and instruments commonly used in ways I consider reckless. Through my physician's nutritional emphasis, I learned about the cancer-fighting properties of cruciferous vegetables (broccoli, kale, brussels sprouts, asparagus, cauliflower, and other members of the cabbage family) years before they were formally recommended by the American Cancer Society.

Despite my enthusiasm for alternative medicine, I have found that there are times when conventional, even high-tech medicine, offers the best treatment. In the mid-1980s, I began to get leg pains in the morning. Ultimately I learned that osteoarthritis had developed in a leg slightly misshapen from birth. I undertook a series of treatments including supplements, chiropractic manipulation, acupuncture, water aerobics, electrical pulses, and stationary cycling. I was able to slow, but could not stop, the advance of the disease. A slight limp eventually worsened until my entire body was becoming twisted. Even with a cane, I could not walk more than a few blocks. The best solution at that point was hip replacement. I did my usual research and put myself in the care of one of the world's leading surgeons in that specialty. The operation was a success. I was walking normally within a matter of weeks.

This experience also illustrates the advantages of living at this time in this particular society. If I had been afflicted two decades earlier or if I had been living in a country with underdeveloped medical technology, my walking days would have been over and premature aging virtually guaranteed. Instead I am walking as much and as fast as ever. My longevity prospects may even have been increased by a rededication to regular exercise. Experiences similar to mine are found in many accounts of the long living who too frequently are mistakenly considered to be a biological elite immune to the usual maladies. Many people who have had serious bouts with disease have gone on to become centenarians.[2]

Keeping up with emerging health research is also relatively easy in our society. I subscribe to two useful, inexpensive newsletters: the *University of California at Berkeley Wellness Letter* published by the School of Public Health and the *Harvard Medical School Health Letter*.[3] Both of these newsletters give conservative advice. Thus, if both endorse some supplement or activity, I feel quite comfortable about adopting it. The reverse does not hold true. If either newsletter expresses caution or uncertainty about some new finding I am interested in, I look up the original study. The *Nutrition Action Newsletter*[4] put out by the Center for Science in the Public Interest is much lighter reading but does an excellent job of nutritionally evaluating brand name products. In 1994 it made nutritional headlines by exposing the high fat content of popcorn sold in movie theaters and of many typical Chinese restaurant dishes.

The best sources for information about cutting-edge alternative medical practices relevant to longevity are found in the books and nationally syndicated radio programs of health crusader Gary Null.[5] I consider him the most reasonable and most altruistic commentator of his kind. He reports on all issues in depth and provides exhaustive documentation. His reporting on non-surgical and non-toxic cancer treatments is outstanding. I am also impressed by his courageous exposures of corporate and government disinformation. Mass media is usually totally unreliable as a source of health information. Considerable confusion and much harmful advice often results from the attempts of commentators to be shocking, amusing, or ironic. A noteworthy exception to this generalization is the work of the *New York Times* health writers. Like the writers for the institutionally-backed newsletters, they tend to be cautious in their reporting, but they handle breaking stories conscientiously and always identify their sources, many of which are obscure academic journals which even a prolongevous enthusiast like myself might not read regularly.

Jane E. Brody, the leading health writer for the *Times*, has been particularly sensitive to women's health issues and to the shifting recommendations of professional and governmental health agencies. A good example of this concern was a full-page story of Feb. 8, 1995 in which Brody highlighted a 14-year study of 121,170 female nurses conducted by the Harvard School of Public Health and the Harvard Medical School. A basic finding was that the greater the amount of added body weight as one grew older the greater the risk of heart disease and death, with observable risk beginning with a gain of even ten pounds. This conclusion was a major repudiation of the 1990 guidelines of the U.S. Department of Agriculture and the Health and Human Services Administration, which had stated that mid-life weight gain was not harmful.

Brody also quoted Dr William Castelli, the director of the Framingham Study, as stating that people who met the ideal weights in the 1959 Met Life Tables had the best chance of avoiding heart disease and early death. Castelli also noted that not one of the 10,000 persons studied since 1948 who maintained a cholesterol count of under 150 had had a heart attack. A similar observation was made by Dr Walter Willet, the director of the nurses study, who affirmed that when thin smokers and others who had lost weight from diseases such as cancer and AIDS are removed from longevity charts based on weight, leaner people have a decided advantage in life expectancy. Castelli and Willet both expressed the belief that the federal government had erred in its 1990 upward revision of ideal body weights; they were confident the guidelines would be changed given the new data.

In a Personal Health column adjacent to her analysis of the nurses study, Brody reported on a 20-member panel of exercise specialists convened by the American College of Sports Medicine and the Federal Centers for Disease Control and Prevention. The panelists announced that, "physical activity itself, not necessarily optimal fitness, is the main protector in lowering the risk of developing a host of chronic health problems, including coronary heart disease, hypertension, diabetes, osteoporosis, colon cancer, anxiety, and depression." In other words the panel had discovered that the benefits that had previously been thought to accrue only if one got the heartbeat up to 60 to 90% of its capacity for twenty minutes at least three times a week were available to those who simply did continuous physical activity of any kind for a minimum of 30 minutes a day.

These observations confirm what has been evident time and again in the longevity research I've been citing in these pages. The nurses study is especially valuable because it is the largest study dealing exclusively with women. Feminist critics have rightly pointed out that although women make up more than 50 percent of the general population, they remain underrepresented in most health studies, particularly those dealing with heart disease. In terms of longevity studies, although women handily outlive men in every culture and climate, there has been no systematic investigation to determine the genetic or social basis of this phenomenon.

In like manner, there has been little work done on the relationship of longevity and race. This is largely due to the problematic definition of what constitutes a racial category. Whatever the starting definition, any research will soon encounter numerous individuals of mixed racial heritage whose racial classification must be considered arbitrary. What can be stated is that examples of centenarians are available for all races as conventionally defined. In the United States there are also pertinent life-span statistics. In 1900 there was a 15-year life-span advantage for Americans defined as "white" compared to those defined as "non-white". That gap has steadily closed over the course of the century and as of 1995, the longevity differences between racial categories is not statistically significant. Moreover, women defined as "non-white" had longer life spans than males defined as "white". These data strongly suggest that any longevity differences between racial categories are due to social factors and that the longevity advantage of being female is not affected by racial classification.

Highly encouraging for all health-conscious Americans is that the life expectancy for Americans in 1995 has increased to a little over 75 years. It would be reasonable to assume that any American following even a modest prolongevity agenda should be living much longer than this statistical average. This hypothesis is supported by data involving the life expectancy of groups pre-selected for their good health habits. As early as 1960, Seventh Day Adventist males had already achieved a life expectancy of 80.5. Twenty years later when the American life expectancy for the general population was 71.8 for males and 78.6 for females, Mormons of both sexes in various locations and categories had life expectancies ranging from 86.5 to 92.4. And in Dallas, Texas, a population chosen for its physical fitness had a male life expectancy of 88.4 and a female life expectancy of 98.1![6]

The weight of all the data I've offered throughout this book indicates that choice rather than chance is now the dominant factor in how long any American is likely to live. The longevity letter lying on the communal desk has been opened and its contents analyzed. Valid longevity habits have been divorced from the mumbo-jumbo of folklore and fraud. Just when and how one chooses to access this longevity pathway is also no mystery. The time to begin is when you are psychologically ready. The place to begin is where the most harm is now being done. May you live to be as old as Moses!

# GLOSSARY

ACTUARY  An individual who computes insurance premiums on the basis of risk probabilities determined from statistical records.

AEROBIC  Utilizing oxygen.

ANOREXIA NERVOSA  An eating disorder, chiefly in young women, characterized by an aversion to food and obsession with weight loss, and manifested in self-induced starvation and excessive exercise.

ANTIOXIDANT  A substance which inhibits the conversion of an element into its oxide.

ARRESTATE  The body's sense of appetite, a sense which can be highly influenced by psychological and cultural factors and which can be psychologically readjusted.

ARTERIOSCLEROSIS  A condition in which the walls of the arteries harden, thicken, and lose elasticity owing to mineral and fatty deposits.

ATHEROSCLEROSIS  The most common form of arteriosclerosis. A condition in which plaques containing cholesterol and fatty material build up on the inner lining of the arteries and obstruct or block the flow of blood.

BASAL METABOLISM  The total of all chemical reactions within the body when it is resting in a fasting state.

BHA (butylated hydroxyanisole)  An antioxidant found in many processed foods or their packaging. It is considered safer than BHT but needs additional testing.

BHT (butylated hydroxytoluene)  An antioxidant used in many processed foods or their packaging. It may cause cancer and allergic reactions.

BIOLOGICAL AGING  The age of an organism indicated by its systemic fitness.

CARBOHYDRATES   A class of organic compounds required by the body for heat and energy which may also contain essential nutrients, such as vitamins and minerals.

CELLS   The structural units of all living things.

CENTENARIAN   Anyone at least 100 years of age.

CHOLESTEROL   An organic alcohol that is a universal tissue constituent. Found deposited in the vessel walls in atherosclerosis.

CHRONOLOGICAL AGE   The age of an organism indicated by the number of solar years it has existed.

DEVELOPED WORLD   Used in this book to indicate the United States, Canada, Europe, and Japan.

DIURETICS   Substances which stimulate an increase in the output of urine and thus temporarily cause loss of water in the body.

DNA (deoxyribonucleic acid)   A long string of atoms found in the nucleus of each cell. It controls all the characteristics of living things and transmits heredity.

ENZYMES   Proteins found in the cell which control most metabolic chemical reactions.

FATS   Foods composed of carbon, hydrogen, and oxygen which have more energy-producing power weight for weight than either carbohydrates or proteins.

FREE RADICALS   Unstable molecular fragments which last only a few thousandths of a second.

GENE   The unit of heredity transmitted in the chromosome.

GERIATRICS   A branch of medical science concerned with treating the diseases most prevalent among older people.

GERONTOLOGY   A branch of learning concerned with the study of aging in all its facets.

HORMONES   Chemical substances released into the bloodstream by the endocrine glands to stimulate body growth, resistance to stress, sexual functions, and other important bodily reactions.

IMMUNOLOGICAL SYSTEM   All those parts of the body which act to protect it from foreign substances.

LACTOVEGETARIAN  A vegetarian whose diet includes some dairy products.

LATE MATURITY  Used in this book to indicate persons who are at least 70 but have not reached 80 years of age.

LONGEVITY  Generally indicates great duration of life and in this book indicates a minimum age of 90 years.

MINERALS  Inorganic substances found in nature that are neither animal nor plant.

MINIMUM DAILY REQUIREMENT (MDR)  A standard developed by the Food and Drug Administration to indicate the daily amount of each identified essential nutrient which prevents symptoms of an actual deficiency disease in most persons.

NONAGENARIAN  Any person over the age of 90 but not yet 100 years of age.

OLD  In this book indicates a person more than 80 but not yet 90 years of age.

PHAGOCYTE  A blood cell that destroys foreign particles, bacteria and cells.

PITUITARY  A small endocrine gland located at the base of the skull.

PLACEBO  A pill, injection, or other treatment containing no active medication.

PLACEBO EFFECT  A physical reaction resulting from a placebo.

PROLONGEVOUS  Used as an adjective to indicate something which favors longevity and used as a noun to indicate persons who consciously plan for long life.

PROTEINS  Nitrogenous organic compounds essential to bodily growth and maintenance.

RECOMMENDED DAILY ALLOWANCE (RDA)  A standard established by the National Academy of Sciences to indicate the amount of a known nutrient needed by a healthy person.  This standard is used to help determine the United States Recommended Daily Allowances (USRDA), a value used for nutritional labeling by the Food and Drug Administration. The USRDA uses higher estimates of nutritional needs than the RDA because it is to be used as a guideline by the general population.

RNA (ribonucleic acid) A long chain of atoms produced by the DNA to direct the formation of proteins.

SENILITY A vague term with no precise scientific measure which generally refers to decaying mental ability.

SOMATYPE Bodily shape.

SUPERCENTENTARIAN Used in this book to indicate anyone over 115 years of age.

SUPERLONGEVOUS Used in this book to indicate anyone over the age of 110 but less than 115 years of age.

SYNDROME A group of symptoms that characterizes a particular condition.

TRACE ELEMENT A mineral required by the body in minute quantities.

TRIGLYCERIDE A major storage form of fatty acids, and the major constituent of fatty tissue.

VEGAN A "pure" vegetarian whose diet excludes all animal products (milk, cheese, eggs, and so on) with the exception of human milk for infants.

VITAMINS Organic compounds needed for growth and life maintenance.

# $\mathcal{N}$OTES AND FURTHER READING

Due to the diverse nature of individual chapters, other materials consulted (but not cited) have been added to the notes for some chapters under the heading "Additional Sources". Books and articles on the general subject of longevity are listed with the references for "Rethinking the First Ninety-Nine," Chapter 8.

## Chapter 1: *Longevity Lore*

1. A good treatment of immortality episodes in the Gilgamesh myth and commentary can be found in Theodor H. Gaster, *The Oldest Stories in the World* (Boston: Beacon Press, 1952), pp 21-51.

2. Gerald J. Gruman, *A History of Ideas About the Prolongation of Life* (Philadelphia: The American Philosophical Society, 1966). Similar material is available in Alex Comfort, *The Process of Aging* (Lond: Weidenfeld and Nicolson, 1965).

3. An analysis of the changing causes of death in the US along with appropriate charts may be found in Alexander Leaf, *Youth in Old Age* (NY: McGraw-Hill, 1975), pp xiii-xviii.

4. Speculations on the subject were summarized by Jane E. Brody in "Genetic Explanation Offered for Women's Health Superiority," *NYT*, Jan 29, 1980, p C1.

5. Herbert A. de Vries, *Report on Jogging and Exercise for Older Adults* (DC: HEW, 1968); _____, "Physiological Effects of an Exercise Training Regimen Upon Men Aged 52-88," *Journal of Gerontology*, 25 (1970), pp 325-36; and for exercise guidelines for those over 60, _____, *Vigor Regained* (Englewood Cliffs, NJ: Prentice-Hall, 1974).

## Chapter 2: *Oldest of the Old*

1. Information about Grandma Filkins has been provided by A. Ross Eckler, who has interviewed some of her descendants. Her obituary in the *Herkimer Evening Telegram*, is dated Dec 4, 1928, but appeared about a week later. A modest obit, *NYT*, Dec 5, 1928, identified her as the oldest woman in New York State.

2. William J. Thoms, *The Longevity of Man* (Lond: Frederic Norgate, 1879). The 1873 edition was also consulted.

3. The entire autopsy report can be found as an appendix in Thoms.

4. Leslie Stephen and Sidney Lee, *The Dictionary of National Biography* (Lond: Oxford University Press, 1950), X, p 737.

5. T. E. Young, *On Centenarians* (Lond: Charles and Edwin Layton, 1899). The 1905 edition was also consulted.

6. *Ibid,* pp 38-42.

7. Maurice Ernest, *The Longer Life* (Lond: Adam, 1938). The author Anglicized his name during World War I, and some of his work may be found under "Ernst."

8. *Ibid,* p 39.

9. *Ibid,* p 33.

10. Obit, Li Chung Yun, *NYT*, May 6, 1933, p 13.

11. Renewed popular interest in ginseng in the 1970s led to more laboratory analysis of the plant in the US and the Soviet Union. No conclusive results have been forthcoming. However, prolonged use of ginseng has been linked to insomnia, nervousness, diarrhoea, and skin eruptions: Ronald K. Siegel, "Ginseng Abuse Syndrome," *Journal of the American Medical Association*, 241 (1979), pp 1614-15. Ironically, Asian food faddists of the late 18th and 19th centuries considered American-grown ginseng to be superior in medicinal powers to other ginseng. This led to a brisk international trade in American ginseng: Leonard Slazinski, Letter and Citation in *Journal of the American Medical Association*, 242 (1979), p 616.

12. At my request the call was placed by Robert Trumbull of the *NYT* Tokyo Bureau . He also wrote about Izumi in "Japan Hails Elders Amid New Concern for Them", *NYT*, Sept 16, 1979, p 19. Norman McWhirter, editor of the *Guinness Book of World Records*, provided material independently confirming this data.

13. Rouch did not know that Dollo might be the oldest person in the world until he was told that by the author during a 1977 interview on Rouch's films. The information on Dollo that follows is based on material provided by Rouch at that time and later in a follow-up interview by Barbara Margolis.

14. "The Man Who Spoke with Lincoln," unsigned article in *Ebony*, Feb, 1963, pp 79-84.

15. Mark Thrash obit, *NYT*, Dec 17, 1943, and Martha Graham obit, *NYT*, June 25, 1959. Additional information from A. Ross Eckler.

16. Ernest, p 37.

17. Zhores Medvedev's major challenge to Soviet data can be found in

"Caucasus and Altay Longevity: A Biological or Social Problem?" *The Gerontologist,* Vol 14, No 5 (Oct 1974), pp 381-87, and in "Aging and Longevity," *The Gerontologist,* Vol 15, No 3 (June 1975), pp 196-201. A general assessment of Soviet methodology can be found in his *Soviet Science* (NY: Norton, 1978). Medvedev has furnished additional data to the author through a long interview and correspondence.

## Chapter 3: *The Long-Living People of Abkhasia*

1. The following seven persons were interviewed by American researchers between 1966 and 1976. Holding the birth year constant, the age claims given at different times varied by 7 to 30 years with the highest ages given in 1975/1976. Ages claimed for Solomon Arshab were 127 and 140; for Alexa Tsvijba, 95 and 125; for Tandal Dzoupha, 97, 102, 104, and 114; for Makhtil Targil, 94, 104, 109, and 118; and for Sheilach Butba, 111, 120, and 128. Kamachich Kvichenyva, who claimed to be 127, was certain she was only two years older than Sheilach Butba, whose highest claim would make her 130 and whose lowest claim would make her 113. This escalating aging and inconsistent claim pattern is typical for nearly all age claims in the region checked against more than one source. There is no reason to accept the lowest claimed age as any more valid than the highest as the underlying pattern is age escalation.

2. Leaf, p 8.

3. Sula Benet, *How to Live to Be 100* (NY: Dial Press, 1975), pp 1-6.

4. Sula Benet, *Abkhasians* (NY: Holt, Rinehart, 1974), pp 16-17, 29.

5. Peter Young, "161 Years Old and Going Strong," *Life,* Vol 61, No 12 (Sept 16, 1966), pp 121-29.

6. Henry Gris and Milton Merlin, *May You Live to Be 200!* (So. Brunswick and NY: A. S. Barnes, 1978), pp 167-84. Gris did all the traveling and research and Merlin did much of the actual writing.

7. *Ibid,* p 172.

8. *Ibid,* p 183.

9. I had two formal interviews with Dr Gogoghian in October of 1978, and I was able to visit the institute on a number of occasions. Unless otherwise noted, all interviews on Abkhasians took place in the first two weeks of Oct, 1978.

10. G. N. Schinava, N. N. Sachuk, and Sh. D. Gogohiya, "On the Physical Condition of the Aged People of the Abkhasian ASSR," *Soviet Medicine,* 5 (1964), is cited and partly reproduced in Benet, *Abkhasians, p 14.*

11. Before the age of egg implants and other hi-tech reproductive medicine, the oldest recorded age at which a woman became a mother was a

little over 57 years. The oldest recorded age at which a man became a father was in the early 90s.

12. Oddly enough the museum was not on the official tour of Intourist, the state agency which dealt with all tourist matters at that time.

13. John Abercrombey, *A Trip Through the Eastern Caucasus* (Lond: Edw. Stanford, 1889), p 23.

14. Essad Bey, *Twelve Secrets of the Caucasus* (NY: Viking, 1931), p 271.

15. Contemporary Abkhasian writers published include Fazil Eskander, *The Beginning: Short Stories* (Sukhumi: Alashara, 1978).

16. Benet, *How*, p 42.

17. *Ibid*, p 43.

18. Elie Metchnikoff, *The Prolongation of Life* (Lond: Heinemann, 1910), p 175.

19. Benet, *How*, p 48.

20. *Ibid*, p 42.

21. Benet, *Abkhasians*, p 15.

22. When I contacted the Graham organization, I was informed it did not handle individual appeals because that would be construed by the then-Soviet Union as political interference. After the fall of the Soviet Union, John and some of his family and friends emigrated to the US and the UK.

ADDITIONAL SOURCES

Alexander A. Bogomoletz, *The Prolongation of Life* (NY: Duell, Sloan & Pearce, 1946).

Samuel Rosen, Nicolai Prebrajensky, Simeon Khechinashvili, *et al*, "Epidemiologic Hearing Studies in the USSR," *Archives of Otolaryngology*, Vol 91, No 5 (1970), pp 424-28.

Chapter 4: *Soviet Centenarians*

1. Gris and Merlin, *op cit*, p 143.

2. Benet, *How*, p 59. Also, even the oldest claimed supercentenarians had only great-grandchildren (four generation families) in N. Varina (translator), "Secrets of the Centenarians", excerpt from *Literaturnaya Gazeta*, publication of the Soviet Writers' Union in *Atlas World Press Review*, Vol 25, No 1 (Jan 1978), p 46.

3. Bogomoletz, *op cit*, is generally uncritical of age claims. A similar problem plagues Nodar N. Kipshidze, *et al*, "The Longevous People of Soviet

Georgia," in *Realistic Expectations for Long Life,* ed. Gari Lesnoff-Caravaglia (NY: Human Science Press, 1987) and Argir Kirkov Hadjihristev, *Life-Styles for Long Life: Longevity in Bulgaria* (Springfield, Ill: Charles C. Thomas, 1988).

4.  Dimitry F. Chebotaryov (*sic*) and Nina N. Sachuk, "Sociomedical Examination of Longevous People in the USSR," *Journal of Gerontology*, Vol 19, No 4 (Oct 1964), pp 435-40; and N. Sachuk, "The Geography of Longevity in the USSR," *Geriatrics*, Vol 20, No 7 ( July, 1965), pp 605-6.

5.  Gris and Merlin, pp 278-99, contains a transcript of a taped interview with Chebotarev which brings together in one place ideas and observations that can also be found in numerous writings and other interviews.

6.  Chebotaryov, "Sociomedical," pp 435-40; Sula Benet, *How*, p 52.

7.  After an examination of life tables from a variety of statistical statements, L. I. Dublin, A. J. Lotka, and M. Spiegelman, *Length of Life* (NY: Ronald Press, 1949) conclude on p 117, "These studies indicate that the difference in expectation of life at about age 25 between persons with a better record of parental longevity and those with a poor record may be anywhere between two to four years."

8.  Dorothy Gallagher, *Hannah's Daughters* (NY: Crowell, 1976), genealogy on p 280, photos on pp 332 and 333, and Hannah's life story on pp 13-102.

9.  Alexander Graham Bell, "Who Shall Inherit Long Life?" *National Geographic*, XXXV, No 6, (June, 1919), pp 504-14.

10.  Sula Benet, *Abkhasians.* Pitskelauri is quoted as saying that 90% of Georgian women marry and bear children before age 25, in Patrick M. McGrady, Jr, *The Youth Doctors* (NY: Coward McCann, 1968), p 295.

11.  Benet, *How*, pp 145-146.

12.  *Ibid*, p 59.

13.  *Ibid*, pp 55-56.

14.  Reported by L. F. Kovalenko of the Institute of Gerontology in Benet, *How*, p 58.

15.  Christopher Wren, "Soviet Centenarians," *NYT*, Sept 9, 1977.

16.  Gris and Merlin, p 145.

17.  Benet, *How*, p 43. For purposes of comparison, it is important to note that the correction found most plausible for raw US census data on centenarians is 95%.

18.  Gris and Merlin, pp 278-302, 323-26. Also Dan Fisher, "Soviets Aiming for Lifespans of 400 Years," *LA Times*, Aug 13, 1977, p 1.

19.  Gris and Merlin, pp 321-323.

20.  Zhores Medvedev, *Soviet Science* (NY: Norton, 1978), p 65.

21.  Extensive advertising campaign of 1979 in New York City area.

ADDITIONAL SOURCES

Dorothy A. Halpern, "Profile: Alexander A. Bogomoletz," in *American Review of Soviet Medicine*, Vol 1, No 2 (Dec, 1943), pp 173-75.

W. C. McKain, "Observations on Old Age in the Soviet Union," in *Gerontologist*, Vol 7 (1967), No 1.

Edward Podolsky, *Red Miracle: The Story of Soviet Medicine* (NY: Beechhurst Press, 1947).

Chapter 5: *Longevity in the Mountains*

1. Michael James, *NYT*, Sept 28, 1956.
2. David Davies, *The Centenarians of the Andes* (NY: Doubleday, 1975) pp 99-109.
3. *Ibid*, p 105.
4. *Ibid*, p 107.
5. *Ibid*, p 87.
6. *Ibid*, p 113-24.
7. Grace Halsell, *Los Viejos* (Emmaus, Pa: Rodale, 1976), p 16.
8. *Ibid*, p 87.
9. *Ibid*, p 157.
10. An outstanding film that deals with old people in the Andes is *The Spirit Possession of Alejandro Mamani*, a documentary made by anthropologists in the Bolivian highlands. It deals with an 81-year-old Aymara Indian living under conditions similar to those in Vilcabamba. Although physically strong, Mamani is obsessed by the fear of evil spirits, illness, and abandonment. His paranoia eventually extends to distrusting his own relatives and friends, with financial concerns playing a role in his alienation. A grim epilogue to the film informs the viewer that after the anthropologists left the area, Alejandro Mamani committed suicide by leaping from a high cliff.
11. Alexander Leaf, *Youth*, and "Every Day Is a Gift When You Are Over 100," *National Geographic*, Vol 143, No 1 (Jan, 1973), pp 92-119.
12. Leaf, *Youth*, p 49.
13. Walter Sullivan, "Scientists Seek Key to Longevity," *NYT*, Feb 11, 1973, p 1.
14. Richard B. Mazess and Sylvia H. Forman, "Longevity and Age Exaggeration in Vilcabamba, Ecuador", in *Journal of Gerontology*, Vol 34, No 1 (Jan, 1979) pp 94-98.
15. *Ibid*, p 97.
16. Walter Sullivan, "Very Old People in the Andes Are Found to Be

Merely Old," *NYT*, March 17, 1878, p 18.

17. International report summarized in Richard B. Mazess, "Health and Longevity in Vilcabamba, Ecuador," *Journal of the American Medical Association*, Vol 240, No 16 (Oct 13, 1978), p 1781. Also see Mazess, "Bone Mineral in Vilcabamba, Ecuador," *American Journal of Roentgenology*, 130 (April, 1978), pp 671-74.

18. Wendell C. Bennett and Robert M. Zingg, *The Tarahumara* (Chgo: Univ of Chgo Press, 1935), pp 349-50.

19. James Norman, "The Tarahumaras," *National Geographic*, Vol 149, No 5 (May 1976), p 717.

20. Gris and Merlin, p 144.

21. Alexandru Ciuca, "Longevity and Environmental Factors," *Gerontologist*, Vol 7, No 4 (1967), pp 252-56.

22. Suha Beller and Erdman Palmore, "Longevity in Turkey," *Gerontologist*, Vol 14, No 5 (Oct, 1974), pp 373-76.

23. J. N. Morris, J. A. Heady, *et al*, "Coronary Heart Disease and Physical Activity of Work," *Lancet*, 2 (1953), pp 1053-57, 1111-20.

24. M. J. Karvonen *et al*, "Longevity of Endurance Skiers," *Medicine and Science in Sports*, 6 (1974), pp 49-56.

25. John Langone, *Long Life* (Boston: Little, Brown, 1978), p 217.

26. Ralph S. Paffenbarger, Alvin L. Wing, and Robert T. Hyde, "Physical Activity as an Index of Heart Attack Risk in College Alumni," *American Journal of Epidemiology*, Vol 108, No 3 (Sept 1978), pp 161-75.

27. R. S. Paffenbarger, Jr, and W. E. Hales, "Work Activity and Coronary Heart Mortality," *New England Journal of Medicine*, 292 (1975), p 545. See also Ralph S. Paffenbarger *et al*, "Work Activity of Longshoremen as Related to Death from Coronary Heart Diseases and Stroke," *New England Journal of Medicine*, Vol 282, No 20 (May 14, 1970), pp 1109-14.

28. J. N. Morris and M. D. Crawford, "Coronary Heart Disease and Physical Activity of Work. Evidence of a National Necropsy Survey," *British Medical Journal*, 2 (1958), pp 1485-96, and J. N. Morris, C. Adam, S. Chave, *et al*, "Vigorous Exercise in Leisure Time and the Incidence of Coronary Heart Disease," *Lancet*, 1 (1973), pp 333-39.

ADDITIONAL SOURCES

Samuel M. Fox and John P. Naughton, "Physical Activity and the Prevention of Coronary Heart Disease," *Preventive Medicine*, 1 (1972), pp 92-120.

Harold A. Kahn, "The Relationship of Reported Coronary Heart Disease Mortality to Physical Activity of Work," *American Journal of Public*

*Health*, 52 (1963), pp 1058-67.

Philip Sturgeon, Suha Beller, and Eleanor Bates, "Study of Blood Type Group Factors in Longevity," *Journal of Gerontology*, Vol 24, No 1 (1963), pp 90-94.

Henry Longstreet Taylor, Ernest Kleptear, Ancel Keys, *et al*, "Death Rates Among Physically Active and Sedentary Employees of the Railroad Industry," *American Journal of Public Health*, 52 (1962), pp 1697-1707.

Chapter 6: *The Hunzakuts*

1. John Keay, *The Gilgit Game* (Hamden, Ct: Archon, 1979) provides good background to the British exploration and seizure of Hunza.

2. Robert McCarrison, *Studies in Deficiency Diseases* (Lond: Henry Frowde and Hodder & Stoughton, 1921).

3. G. T. Wrench, *The Wheel of Health* (London: C. W. Daniel, 1938).

4. James Hilton, *Lost Horizon* (NY: Morrow, 1933) p 69.

5. J. I. Rodale, *The Healthy Hunzas* (Emmaus, Pa: Rodale, 1949).

6. Jay Milton Hoffman, *Hunza* (Valley Center, Cal: Professional Press Publishing, 1968), p 1.

7. Albert Abarbanel, "The Healthiest People in the World," in *American Mercury*, Sept, 1954, pp 43-44.

8. Allen Banik and Renee Taylor, *Hunza Land* (Long Beach, Cal: Whitehorn Publishing, 1960).

9. E. O. Lorimer, *Language Hunting in the Karakoram* (Lond: Allen & Unwin, 1939).

10. Wilfred Skrede, *Across the Roof of the World* (NY: Norton, 1954).

11. John Clark, *Hunza: Lost Kingdom of the Himalayas* (Lond: Hutchinson, 1957).

12. Jean Bowie Shor, *After You, Marco Polo* (NY: McGraw-Hill, 1955) and Jean and Frank Shor, "At World's End in Hunza," in *National Geographic*, CIV, No 4 (Oct, 1953), pp 485-518.

13. Leaf, *Youth*, pp 27-42.

14. Robert McCarrison, "Faulty Food in Relation to Gastro-Intestinal Disorder," Sixth Mellon Lecture delivered before the Society for Biological Research, Univ of Pittsburgh School of Medicine, Nov 18, 1921, 27 pages.

15. Firsthand accounts of the war appear in Col. Algernon Durand, *The Making of a Frontier* (Lond: Thomas Nelson, 1908) and in E. F. Knight, *Where Three Empires Meet* (Lond: Longman Green, 1893). Dr. John Clark has written me that Mir Nazim Khan claimed in his autobiography that he had withdrawn from a very strong position in order to ensure a British victory. As a reward for

his treachery he was given the place of his deposed brother. This is at odds with the British accounts, which credit the Pathan troops for scaling a wall the defenders had thought unassailable.

16. McCarrison, "Faulty," p 10.

17. McCarrison, *Studies*, p 9.

18. Robert McCarrison, "The Relationship of Diet to the Physical Efficiency of Indian Races," in *The Practitioner* (Lond), Jan, 1925, pp 90-100.

19. G. W. Leitner, *Results of a Tour in Dardistan, Kashmir, Little Tibet, Ladak, Zanskar, Etc in 1866* (Lond: Trubner, 1868-73), 4 Vols.

20. Major J. Biddulph, *Tribes of the Hindoo Koosh* (Calcutta: Office of the Superintendent of Government Printing, 1880).

21. John Clark, "Hunza in the Himalayas," in *Natural History*, LXXII, No 6 (Oct, 1963), pp 38-46. I have corresponded with and phone-interviewed Dr Clark to obtain additional data. Among other comments, Dr Clark said that goiter and cretinism were still rare in Hunza when he was there. He thought that goiter was just becoming common as the last residual iodine was being washed from the soil. He notes that appendicitis is generally not found in most parts of Asia except among people who have lived in the West.

22. Wrench, p 101.

23. Barbara Mons, *High Road to Hunza*, (Lond: Faber & Faber, 1958), p 104.

24. Leaf, *Youth*, p 37.

25. Wrench, p 27.

26. Sir Francis Younghusband, *Dawn in Asia* (Lond: John Murray, 1930), p 34.

27. Lorimer, p 184.

28. Telephone interview, 1979.

29. Mons, p 106.

30. Walter R. Lawrence, *The Valley of Kashmir* (Lond: Henry Frowde, 1895), p 227.

31. Rodale, p 200.

32. John Keay, *The Gilgit Game* contains numerous accounts. See also his excellent bibliography of 19th-century exploration of the area.

33. R. C. F. Schomberg, *Between the Oxus and the Indus* (Lond: Martin Hopkinson, 1935), p 137. Similar incident reported by McCarrison.

34. M. Auriel Stein, *Sand-Buried Ruins of Kohtan* (Lond: T. Fisher Unwin, 1903), p 51. Similar incident reported by the Shors.

35. Younghusband, p 192.

36. Stein, p 174.

37. Leaf, *Youth*, p 34.

38. Brian Jeffries, "Civilization Closing In on Shangri-La," in *LA Times*,

June 9, 1974, Section 8, p 9, and "No More Shangri-La," *Washington Post*, Sept 26, 1974, p A10.

39. Audry Topping, "Opening a New Road to China: The Karakoram Highway," in *NYT Magazine*, Dec 2, 1979, p 136.

ADDITIONAL SOURCES

William Martin Conway, *Climbing and Exploration in Karakoram-Himalayas* (Lond: T. Fisher Unwin, 1894), 4 Vols.

George Curzon, *The Pamirs* (Lond: Royal Geographical Soc, 1896).

Frederick Drew, *The Northern Barrier of India* (Lond: Edw. Stanford, 1877).

P. T. Etherton, *Across the Roof of the World* (Lond: Constable, 1911).

_____, five articles on the health of the Hunzakuts, pp 133-75, in *The Pakistan Journal of Medical Research*, April 1966.

George Scott Robertson, *The Kafirs of the Hindu-Kush* (Lond: Lawrence & Bullen, 1896).

R. C. F. Schomberg, *Unknown Karakoram* (Lond: Martin Hopkinson, 1936).

Eric Shipton, *Mountains of Tartary* (Lond: Hodder & Stoughton, 1951).

H. M. Sinclair, *The Work of Robert McCarrison* (Lond: Faber & Faber, 1952). A collection of McCarrison's essays.

Renee Taylor as told to by His Highness Mir Mohd Jamal Khan, *Come Along to Hunza (The History of Shangri-La)* (Minneapolis: T. S. Denison, 1974).

_____ and Milford J. Nobbs, *Hunza: The Himalayan Shangri-La* (El Monte, Cal: Whiteman, 1962).

_____, *Hunza Health Secrets for Long Life and Happiness* (Englewood Cliffs, NJ: Prentice-Hall, 1964).

Lowell Thomas, *Book of the High Mountains* (NY: Julian Messner, 1964).

Jenny Visser-Hooft with contributions by P. C. Visser, *Among the Kara-Korum Glaciers in 1925* (Lond: Edw. Arnold, 1926).

Chapter 7: *Serendipitous Sheringham and Cambridgeshire*

1. "English Village Soil Linked To Longevity," in *NYT*, Oct 6, 1977, p 72, is typical.

2. 1971 Census of England and Wales, Norfolk Part I, H. M. Stationery Office, 1973, pp 18-27.

3. This and other interview material in the present chapter were obtained in Sept, 1978. The ages of all the centenarians discussed in the chapter were confirmed by a telegram from the Queen. This verification occurs when the claim of someone approaching 100 is brought to the attention of Buckingham

Palace. The claim is then checked through official governmental records. If the age is valid, a telegram is sent on the appropriate birthday. The system, which involves the prestige of the Monarch, has established a record of reliability. Since none of the centenarians discussed in this chapter claimed an extreme age, I did not think it necessary to verify their ages independently.

4. 1971 Census, 1, pp 18-27.

5. In addition to interview material, background on Mr Cornelius is available in the files of the *Eastern Daily Press* and *North Norfolk News*. These were written from 1974 to 1979 at the time of his birthday.

6. A. Campbell Erroll, *A History of the Parishes of Sheringham and Beeston Regis* (Norwich, England: Rigby Printing, 1970), his major work. Also: "Life and Death in Norfolk Villages," Part I, Sheringham typescript, Norwich Public Libraries, Local Collection, Norwich, and typescripts and other materials given to me by Mr Erroll.

7. "Life and Death in Norfolk Villages, Part III—A Village Community in 1791."

8. I tabulated all deaths recorded in the church from 1800 to 1978.

9. Author's investigation.

ADDITIONAL SOURCES

R. W. Apple, Jr, "Britain's Notable Nonagenarians," in *NYT Magazine*, Nov 11, 1979, pp 50-72.

*All Saints Upper Sheringham*, a pamphlet printed by Ashlock Magazine Center (Home Words), Lond, 1960.

Chapter 8: *Rethinking the First Ninety-Nine*

1. Osborn Segerberg, Jr, *Living to Be 100* (NY: Scribner, 1982).

2. Belle Boone Beard, *Centenarians: The New Generation* (NY: Greenwood Press, 1991).

3. Jim Heynen, *One Hundred Over 100* (Saskatoon, Saskatchewan: Western Producer Prairie Books, 1990). Photographs by Paul Boyer of each centenarian interviewed.

4. Harvey Lehman, *Age and Achievement* (Princeton, NJ: Princeton Univ Press, 1930) and Ruth A. Hubbell, "Men and Women Who Have Performed Distinctive Service After the Age of 74," *Wilson Bulletin for Librarians*, 9 (Feb, 1935), pp 297-305.

5. Sharon Johnson, "Welthy Fisher: Woman with a Mission," *NYT*, April 2, 1978, p 54, and "Spreading the Word," *NYT*, September 18, 1979. Her

autobiography is titled *To Light a Candle* (NY: McGraw-Hill 1962).

6. Harold M. Schmeck Jr, "Research Attempts to Fight Senility," *NYT*, July 31, 1979, and "Memory Loss Curbed by Chemical in Foods," *NYT*, Jan 9, 1979, p C1.

7. Belle Boone Beard, "Some Characteristics of Recent Memory in Centenarians," *Journal of Gerontology*, Vol 23, No 1 (Jan 1968), pp 23-31. More general: Dr Arthur S. Freese, *The End of Senility*, (NY: Arbor House, 1978) and Belle Boone Beard, *Social Competence of Centenarians* (Athens, Ga: Social Science Research Inst, Univ of Georgia, 1967).

8. Stephen Jewett, "Longevity and the Longevity Syndrome," *The Gerontologist*, Vol 12, No 1 (Spring, 1973), pp 91-99.

9. John Court, "Want to Live to Be 120?" *Atlas*, Vol 16, No 4 (Oct, 1968), pp 54-55.

10. Herbert A. de Vries and Gene M. Adams, "Comparison of Exercise Responses in Old and Young Men," *Journal of Gerontology*, Vol 27, No 3 (1972), and de Vries, "Prescription of Exercise for Older Men from Telemetered Exercise Heart Rate Data," *Geriatrics*, April, 1971.

11. Lewis (*sic*) Cornaro, *The Immortal Mentor* (Trenton, NJ: Daniel Fenton, 1810).

12. Luigi Cornaro, *How to Live for a Hundred Years and Avoid Disease* (Oxford: Alden Press, 1935). Includes "Letter from a Nun of Padua" and Joseph Addison, *Spectator #105*.

13. Clive M. McCay, L. A. Maynard, *et al*, "Retarded Growth, Life Span, Ultimate Body Size and Age Changes in the Albino Rat After Feeding Diets Restricted in Calories," *Journal of Nutrition*, Vol 18, No 1 (1939).

14. See discussion and citations in Nathaniel Altman, *Eating for Life* (Wheaton, Ill: Theosophical Publishing, 1977), pp 21-23, 37.

15. One of the studies correlating wine consumption with heart disease is A. A. St Leger, A. L. Cochrane, and F. Moore, "Factors Associated with Cardiac Mortality in Developed Countries with Particular Reference to the Consumption of Wine," *Lancet*, May 12, 1979, pp 107-20.

16. James Crichton-Browne, *The Doctor Remembers* (Lond: Duckworth, 1938); A. Gueniot, *How to Live to Be a Hundred* (Valletta, Malta, 1933); and Hermann Weber, *On Longevity and the Means for the Prolongation of Life* (Lond: Macmillan, 1939). Also useful: James Crichton-Browne, *The Prevention of Senility and a Sanitary Outlook* (Lond: Macmillan, 1905) and *Delusions in Diet* (NY: Funk & Wagnalls, 1910).

17. A film has been made of the Nearings at their farm in Maine in which they discuss their way of life and the ideals that have molded it. It offers lively interviews full of good humor and views of their newly completed stone

house. At the time of the film Scott was 93 and Helen was 73. *Living the Good Life*, produced by Bullfrog Films; 30 mins. The film has won a number of awards.

18. The film, titled *Happy Birthday, Mrs Craig*, has been shown on television. The centenarian speaks vigorously throughout the film, recalling the early days of black pioneers in the West. Equally notable are her continued advocacy of change and her relationship to her family, which numbers five generations. Produced by Richard Kaplan Productions, Inc; 1 hr.

ADDITIONAL SOURCES

William G. Bailey, *Human Longevity from Antiquity to the Modern Lab: A Selected, Annotated Bibliography* (NY: Greenwood Press, 1987).

Sir Richard Bulstrode, *Miscellaneous Essays* (Lond: John Browne, 1715) and *Letters* (Lond: R. Sare, 1712).

Alex Comfort, *A Good Age* (NY: Crown, 1976).

E. V. Cowdrey, *Aging Better* (Springfield, Ill: Charles C. Thomas, 1972).

Robert S. De Ropp, *Man Against Dying* (NY: St Martins, 1966).

Irene Gore, *Add Years to Your Life and Life to Your Years* (NY: Stein & Day, 1973).

Joan Gomez, *How Not to Die Young* (NY: Stein & Day, 1972).

W. Forbes Gray, *Five Score: A Group of Famous Centenarians* (Lond: John Murray, 1931).

Joel Kurtaman and Philip Gordon, *No More Dying* (LA: J. P. Tarcher, 1976).

Helen Nearing, *Loving and Leaving the Good Life* (Post Mills, Vt: Chelsea Green, 1992).

Helen and Scott Nearing, *Living the Good Life* (NY: Shocken, 1970) and *Continuing the Good Life* (NY: Shocken, 1979).

Adrian M. Ostfeld and Don C. Gibson, eds, *Epidemiology of Aging*, DC: Dept of Health, Education and Welfare Pub No (NIH) 75-711, 1972.

Charles Reinhardt, *120 Years of Life* (Lond: London Publicity, 1910).

George Soule, *Longer Life* (NY: Viking, 1958).

Eric Weiser, *The Years in Hand* (NY: Abelard-Schuman, 1967).

Ruth Winter, *Ageless Aging* (NY: Crown, 1973).

Chapter 9: *The Longevous Personality*

1. M. Friedman and R. H. Rosenman, *Type A Behavior and Your Heart* (NY: Knopf, 1974).

2. Hans Selye, *The Stress of Life* (NY: McGraw-Hill, 1976), revised

edition.

3. See discussion in Alex Comfort, *The Process of Aging* (Lond: Weidenfeld & Nicolson, 1965), p 69.

4. *Ibid*, p 67.

5. E. Pfeiffer, A. Verwoerdt, and H. S. Wang, "Sexual Behavior in Aged Men and Women," in E. Palmore, ed, *Normal Aging* (Durham, NC: Duke Univ Press, 1970). See also Gustave Newman and Claude R. Nichols, "Sexual Activities and Attitudes in Older Persons," *Journal of the American Medical Association*, 173 (1960), pp 33-35, and Jane E. Brody, "Survey of Aged Reveals Liberal Views on Sex," *NYT*, April 22, 1980, p C1.

6. Diana S. Woodruff, *Can You Live to Be 100?* (NY: Chatham Square, 1977), pp 155-65.

7. Jules V. Quint and Bianca R. Cody, "Pre-eminence and Mortality: Longevity of Prominent Men," *The American Journal of Public Health*, Vol 60, No 6 (June, 1970), pp 1118-24.

8. Metropolitan Life Insurance Company, "Longevity of Corporate Executives," *Statistical Bulletin* 55 (1974), pp 2-4.

9. G. Gallup and E. Hill, *The Secrets of Long Life* (NY: Bernard Geis, 1960).

10. O. Carl Simonton, Stephanie Matthews-Simonton, and James Creighton, *Getting Well Again* (LA: J. P. Tarcher, 1978). A wider, equally informed view can be found in Kenneth R. Pelletier, *Mind as Healer, Mind as Slayer* (NY: Delacorte, 1977).

11. Norman Cousins, "What I Learned From 3,000 Doctors," reprinted from *The Saturday Review* in *Prevention*, Vol 30, No 6 (June, 1978), p 109.

12. *Ibid*, p 109.

ADDITIONAL SOURCES

David Hendin, *Death as a Fact of Life* (NY: Norton, 1973).
Brian Inglis, *The Case for Unorthodox Medicine* (NY: Putnam, 1965).
Gay Luce and Julius Segal, *Sleep* (NY: Coward McCann, 1966).
Nathaniel Weyl, "Survival Past the Century Mark," in *Mankind Quarterly*, 17 (1977), pp 163-65.

Chapter 10: *Dr. Two Legs*

1. John T. Davis, *Walking* (NY: Bantam, 1979), pp 85-87. A good introduction to the psychological and physiological benefits of walking.

2. *Journal of the American Medical Association*, Dec 1994.

3. T. R. Dawber, *The Framingham Study: The Epidemiology of Atherosclerotic Disease* (Cambridge, MA: Harvard Univ Press, 1980).

4. Alfred Rosenfeld, *Prolongevity II* (NY: Knopf, 1985), p 80. Updates *Prolongevity* published in 1976. Author originated or at least popularized the term *prolongevity.*

5. *Desirable Weight Tables for Men and Women*, Metropolitan Life Insurance Company, 1959. These are produced at intervals of approximately 20 years. As published, the weights include indoor clothing and shoes. Following the system used by Kenneth Keyes in *How to Live Longer-Stronger-Slimmer* (NY: Frederick Fell, 1966), the charts have been adapted to the nude body by subtracting 5 pounds of clothing for women (Metropolitan Life allows 2-4 pounds) and 8 pounds for men (Metropolitan Life allows 5-7 pounds). Heights are given for bare feet instead of one-inch heels for men and two-inch heels for women.

6. Clarence M. Agress, *Energetics* (NY: Grosset & Dunlap, 1978).

7. *Royal Canadian Air Force Exercise Plans for Physical Fitness* (NY: Bantam, 1972).

8. Kenneth H. Cooper, *Aerobics* (NY: Bantam, 1968).

9. John N. Leonard, J. L. Hofer, and N. Pritikin, *Live Longer Now* (NY: Grosset & Dunlap, 1974). Nathan Pritikin with Patrick M. McGrady, Jr, *The Pritikin Plan for Diet and Exercise* (NY: Grosset & Dunlap, 1979).

10. Truman Clark, "Master's Movement," *Runner's World*, Vol 14, No 7 (July, 1979), pp 80-95, has a number of charts showing running records for those from 40 to 100. Additional information on Iordanidis provided by Yannis Iordanidis from news clippings. Walking feats can be found in Davis, *Walking* and various other feats by old people in the *Guinness Book of World Records.*

11. See Pritikin with McGrady, pp 89-90 and Carol Lawson, "Behind the Best Sellers," *NYT*, July 1, 1979.

ADDITIONAL SOURCES

Grant Swinup, *Energetics* (LA: Sherbourne Press, 1970).

Sir Percival Horton-Smith Hartley, "The Longevity of Oarsmen," *British Medical Journal*, 1 (April, 1939), p 657.

C. Harley Hartung, John F. Foreyt, Robert E. Mitchell, *et al*,"Relation of Diet to High-Density-Lipoprotein Cholesterol in Middle-Aged Marathon Runners, Joggers, and Inactive Men," *New England Journal of Medicine*, Vol 302, No 7 (Feb 14, 1980), pp 357-61.

Anthony P. Polednak, *The Longevity of Athletes* (Springfield, Ill: Charles C. Thomas, 1979).

Yehuda Shoenfeld, Gad Keren, Tavia Shimoni, *et al,* "Walking—a Method for Rapid Improvement of Physical Fitness," *Journal of the American Medical Association,* 243 (1980), pp 2062-63.

## Chapter 11: *Food As Fuel*

1. Nathaniel Altman, *op cit,* summarizes major vegetarian concepts.
2. Dean Ornish, *Program for Reversing Heart Disease* (NY: Ballantine, 1991) and *Stress, Diet, & Your Heart* (NY: Signet, 1984) are aimed at the general reader with comprehensive bibliographies.
3. Roy Walford, *Maximum Life Span* (NY: Avon, 1984) and *The 120 Year Diet: How to Double Your Vital Years* (NY: Pocket Books, 1988) are aimed at the general reader with comprehensive bibliographies.
4. Some studies indicate that a B-12 deficiency can develop in vegetarians who eat no meat or dairy products. Vegans dispute this. See Altman, *Eating*, p 150.
5. Letitia Brewster and Michael F. Jacobson, *The Changing American Diet* (DC: Center for Science in the Public Interest, 1978).
6. Altman, pp 33-38, has extensive discussion and bibliography.
7. Joseph H. Highland, Marcia E. Fine, *et al, Malignant Neglect* (NY: Knopf, 1979), pp 150-51, and Richard D. Lyons, "Chemical Tied to Cancer Is Banned as Cattle Feed," *NYT,* June 30, 1979, p 6.
8. Highland, pp 55-81.
9. Easy-to-read summary in Jane E. Brody, "Personal Health: Alcohol Offers Some Benefits to Health as Well as Drawbacks," *NYT,* Oct 3, 1979. See also St Leger, *op cit,* and Jane E. Brody, "Women and Alcohol," *NYT,* Sept 15, 1993, p C13.

ADDITIONAL SOURCES

Charles H. Hennekins, B. Rosner, and D. S. Cole, "Daily Alcoholic Consumption and Fatal Coronary Heart Disease," *American Journal of Epidemiology,* 107 (1978), pp 1906-200.
Charles H. Hennekins, Walter Willet, Bernard Rosner, *et al,*"Effects of Beer, Wine, and Liquor in Coronary Death," in *Journal of the American Medical Association,* 242 (1979) pp 1973-74. Contains a good section on additional sources. See also editorial in same issue.
William McQuage and Ann Aikman, *The Longevity Factor* (NY: Simon & Schuster, 1979).
Nevin S. Scrimsaw, "Protein Requirements—Strengths and Weaknesses of the

Committee Approach," *New England Journal of Medicine*, Vol 29, No 3 (Jan 15, 1976), pp 134-42, and No 4 (January 22, 1976), pp 198-203 contain dissenting views on some aspects of the World Health organization's recommendations, particularly in relation to young adults.

Univ of Cal, Berkeley, *Wellness Letter* editors, *Wellness Encyclopedia* (Boston: Houghton Mifflin, 1991).

### Chapter 12: *Biochemical Individuality*

1. Roger J. Williams, "Nutritional Individuality," *Human Nature*, Vol 1, No 6 (June, 1978), pp 46-53.

2. Linus Pauling, *Vitamin C and the Common Cold* (San Francisco: W. H. Freeman, 1970).

3. H. L. Newbold, *Vitamin C Against Cancer* (NY: Stein & Day, 1979) is very enthusiastic about the use of C in fighting diseases, particularly cancer. The book is most valuable in its transcripts of interviews with prominent physicians and researchers.

4. Newbold includes a section on negative effects of megadoses of C in some patients and how to avoid those effects, as well as different forms of C and their effects. Included in an appendix is the important study by Ewan Cameron and Linus Pauling, "Supplemental Ascorbate in the Supportive Treatment of Cancer: Prolongation of Survival Times in Terminal Human Cancer," originally published in *Proceedings* of the National Academy of Science, USA, Vol 73 (Oct, 1976), pp 3685-89, Medical Science.

5. Individuals using C as medicine generally add one gram every other day. They cease adding with the first signs of mild diarrhoea. They further report that after a time diarrhoea ensues with the previously-tolerated dose, and they begin to lower by a gram every other day until the reaction ceases.

6. Priscilla W. Laws, *Medical and Dental X-Rays; A Consumer's Guide to Avoiding Unnecessary Radiation Exposure* ( DC: Public Citizen, Health Research Group, 1974).

7. "Excess X-Ray Radiation Found," *NYT*, Dec 5, 1979, p A12.

8. Harold Elrick, James Crakes, and Sam Clarke, *Living Longer and Better* (Mountain View, Cal: World Publications, 1978), p 153, and Hans J. Kugler, *Dr Kugler's Seven Days to a Longer Life* (NY: Stein & Day, 1978).

### ADDITIONAL SOURCES

Ivan Illich, *Medical Nemesis* (Lond: Calder & Boyars, 1975).

Edward C. Lambert, *Modern Medical Mistakes* (Bloomington, Ind: Indiana

Univ Press, 1978).

Robert Mendelsohn, *Confessions of a Medical Heretic* (Chgo: Contemporary, 1979).

*Recommended Dietary Allowances*, 8th Ed Rev (DC: Nat'l Academy of Sciences, 1974).

Nathan W. Shock, ed, *Aging: Some Social & Biological Aspects* (Freeport, NY: Books for Libraries, 1960).

Leonard Tushnet, *The Medicine Men* (NY: St Martin's 1971).

## Chapter 13: *The Toxic Society*

1. Bayard Webster, "Acid Rain: An Increasing Threat," *NYT*, Nov 6, 1979, p C1, is a good summary article. Webster describes the composition of the rain: "Sulfur dioxide, which comprises about 60% of the acid components of the rains, is created almost entirely by the combustion of coal and oil in power plants, smelters, steel mills, factories, and space heaters. Nitrogen oxide, which makes up 35% of the acid in the rains, originates in the exhausts of internal combustion engines, mostly in automobiles, and in the emissions from high-temperature fossil fuel combustion." See also Alan J. Otten, "Industrial Countries Will Meet Next Week in Attempt to Curb Destructive Acid Rains," *Wall St Journal*, Nov 9, 1979.

2. Two excellent references to the many problems involved are Samuel S. Epstein, *The Politics of Cancer* (San Francisco: Sierra Club, 1978) and Highland and Fine, *op cit.*

3. David Burnham, "Utility in Michigan Faces $450,000 Fine," *NYT*, Nov 10, 1979, p 9.

4. Elizabeth Whelan, *Preventing Cancer* (NY: Norton, 1978), pp 52-76. See also David L. Levin, Susan S. Devesa, *et al*, *Cancer Rates and Risks* (DC: Dep't of Health, Education and Welfare Publication No NIH 75-691).

5. Whelan, p 213.

6. *Cancer Facts and Figures*, The American Cancer Society, 1977.

7. Harold Elrick, *et al*, p 182.

8. How this works in discouraging regulation of toxins and radiation can be seen in Harry Schwartz, "A Look at the Cancer Figures," *Wall Street Journal*, Nov 15, 1979, p 26.

9. Quoted in *Energy Matters*, Vol 1, No 2 (June 1979), p 1.

10. Jay M. Gould and Benjamin A. Goldman, *Deadly Deceit* (NY: Four Walls Eight Windows, 1994), pp 13-28.

11. M. C. Hatch, *et al*, "Cancer Near the Three Mile Nuclear Plant: Radiation Emissions," *American Journal of Epidemiology* 132 (September

1990), pp 397-412.

12. Molly Ivins, "Denver Uncertain over Old Uranium Site," *NYT*, Feb 20, 1979, p A13.

13. Howell Raines, "An Unwelcome Alabama Guest: Radioactive Gas in Many Homes," *NYT*, March 16, 1979, p A13.

14. "Ex-Heads of Atomic Plant Admit Deliberate Release of Gases in '59," *NYT*, Nov 11, 1979, p 63.

15. Molly Ivins, "Utah Uneasy over Leukemia-Atomic Tests Study," *NYT*, Feb 23, 1979. See also Joseph L. Lyon *et al*, "Childhood Leukemia and Nuclear Fallout," in *New England Journal of Medicine*, 300 (1979), pp 402-7. Editorial on the study in same issue.

16. Useful consumer guides for those concerned about possible water pollution are "Manual for Evaluating Public Drinking Water Supplies," available free from the Water Supply Division of the Environmental Protection Agency, Washington, DC 20460, and "Safe Drinking Water for All: What You Can Do," from the League of Women Voters Education Fund.

ADDITIONAL SOURCES

Robert Alex Baron, *The Tyranny of Noise* (NY: St Martin's, 1970).

Flaminio Cattebeni, Aldo Cavallaro, and Giovanni Galli, eds, *Dioxin, Toxicological and Chemical Aspects* (NY: Spectrum Publications, 1978).

Edwin Chen, *PBB: An American Tragedy* (Englewood Cliffs, NJ: Prentice-Hall, 1979).

Laurie Garrett, *The Coming Plague* (NY: Farrar, Straus, and Giroux, 1994).

Ron M. Linton, *Terracide* (Boston: Little, Brown, 1970).

William H. McNeill, *Plagues and Peoples* (NY: Doubleday, 1977).

William Irwin Thompson, ed, *Gaia: A Way of Knowing* (San Francisco: Lindisfarne, 1981).

Chapter 14: *Redefining the Biological Limits*

1. The best-known work of the group that calls itself the Immortalists is Alan Harrington, *The Immortalist* (Millbrae, Cal: Celestial Arts, 1969).

2. Leonard Hayflick, *How and Why We Age* (NY: Ballantine, 1994).

3. Rosenfield, *Prolongevity II*.

4. Robert Prehoda, *Extended Youth* (NY: Putnam, 1968).

5. "Study Links Heavy Use of a Pain Reliever to Kidney Failure," *NYT*, Dec 22, 1994, B12. Summarizes *New England Journal of Medicine* article of the same week.

6. Patrick M. McGrady, Jr, *The Youth Doctors* (NY: Coward McCann, 1968), pp 53-58. An excellent survey of 20th-century rejuvenation schemes.

7. Michel Gauguelin, *How Atmospheric Conditions Affect Your Health* (NY: Stein & Day, 1971).

ADDITIONAL SOURCES

Ernest Becker, *The Denial of Death* (NY: Free Press, 1973).

Victor Bogomoletz, *The Secret of Keeping Young* (Lond: Arco, 1954).

Michael W. Fox, *Superpigs and Wondercorn* (NY: Lyons & Burford, 1992).

Daniel Hershey, *Lifespan* (Springfield, Ill: Charles Thomas, 1964).

Saul Kent, *The Life-Extension Revolution* (NY: Morrow, 1980).

Albert Krueger and David S. Sobel, "Air Ions & Health," in David S. Sobel, ed, *Ways of Health* (NY: Harcourt Brace Jovanovich, 1979).

P. B. and J. S. Medawar, *The Life Science* (NY: Harper & Row, 1977).

Osborn Segerberg, Jr, *The Immortality Factor* (NY: Dutton, 1974).

Nathan W. Shock, ed, *Perspectives in Experimental Gerontology* (Springfield, Ill: Charles C. Thomas, 1966).

Nathan W. Shock, *Trends in Gerontology* (Stanford, Cal: Stanford Univ Press, 1951).

Lee Weston, *Body Rhythm* (NY: Harcourt Brace Jovanovich, 1979).

## Chapter 15: *Longevity Now*

1. New support for this finding occurs constantly. A scientific assessment is found in *New England Journal of Medicine* 330 (1994), pp 1769 & 1819. Popular treatment in Jane E. Brody, Personal Health columns, *NYT*, July 14, 1993, p C12 and Aug 10, 1994, p C8.

2. Jim Heynen, *One Hundred Over 100*, is very revealing in this respect.

3. *University of California Wellness Letter*, Box 420148, Palm Coast, FL 32142; *Harvard Health Letter*, Box 420300, Palm Coast, FL 32142.

4. *Nutrition Action Newsletter*, CSPI, Suite 300, 1875 Connecticut Ave, NW, DC 20009.

5. Gary Null, *Natural Living Journal*, PO Box 495, Huntington, NY 11743-0495.

6. See tables in Hayflick, p 323.

ADDITIONAL SOURCES

Herman Brotman, "Comparison of Life Expectancy, 1900 and 1974," *Gerontologist*, Feb 1977, pp 208-9.

Erdman Palmore and Frances C. Jeffers, *Prediction of Life Span* (Lexington, Mass: Heath Lexington Books, 1971).

Anthony Pearl and Ruth Dewitt Pearl, *The Ancestry of the Long-Lived* (Baltimore: Johns Hopkins Univ Press, 1934).

# BIBLIOGRAPHY

## BOOKS

Abercrombey, John. *A Trip Through the Eastern Caucasus.* Lond: Edw. Stanford.

Agress, Clarence M. *Energetics.* NY: Grosset & Dunlap, 1978.

Altman, Nathaniel. *Eating for Life.* Wheaton, Ill: Theosophical Publishing, 1977.

Beard, Belle Boone. *Centenarians: The New Generation.* NY: Greenwood Press, 1991.

_____ . *Social Competence of Centenarians.* Athens, Ga: Social Science Research Inst, Univ of Ga, 1967.

Bailey, Wm. G. *Human Longevity from Antiquity to the Modern Lab: A Selected, Annotated Bibliography.* NY: Greenwood Press, 1987.

Bacon, Robert Alex. *The Tyranny of Noise.* NY: St Martins,1970.

Becker, Ernest. *The Denial of Death.* NY: Free Press, 1973.

Benet, Sula. *Abkhasians.* NY: Holt, Rinehart, 1974.

_____ . *How to Live to Be 100.* NY: Dial Press, 1975.

Banik, Allen & Renee Taylor. *Hunza Land.* Long Beach, Cal: Whitehorn Publishing, 1960.

Bennett, Wendell C. and Rbt. M. Zingg. *The Tarahumara.* Chgo: Univ of Chgo Press, 1935.

Bey, Essad. *Twelve Secrets of the Caucasus.* NY: Viking, 1931.

Bogomoletz, Alexander A. *The Prolongation of Life.* NY: Duell, Sloan & Pearce, 1946.

Bogomoletz, Victor. *The Secret of Keeping Young.* Lond: Arco, 1954.

Brewster, Letitia and Michael F. Jacobson. *The Changing American Diet.* Washington, DC: Ctr for Science in the Public Interest, 1978.

Bulstrode, Sir Richard. *Miscellaneous Essays.* Lond: John Browne, 1715.

_____ . *Letters.* Lond: R. Sare, 1712.

Cattebeni, Flaminio, Aldo Cavallaro and Giovanni Galli, eds. *Dioxin, Toxicological and Chemical Aspects.* NY: Spectrum Publications, 1978.

Chen, Edwin. *PBB: An American Tragedy.* Englewood Cliffs, NJ: Prentice

Hall, 1976.

Clark, John. *Hunza: Lost Kingdom of the Himalayas.* Lond: Hutchinson, 1957.

Comfort, Alex. *The Process of Aging.* Lond: Widenfeld & Nicholson, 1965.

_____. *A Good Age.* NY: Crown, 1976.

Conway, Wm. Martin. *Climbing and Exploration in Karakoram-Himalayas.* Lond: T. Fisher Unwin, 1894. 4 vols.

Cooper, Kenneth H. *Aerobics.* NY: Bantam, 1968.

Cornaro, Lewis (*sic*) *The Immortal Mentor.* Trenton, NJ: Daniel Fenton, 1810.

_____, Luigi. *How to Live for a Hundred Years and Avoid Disease.* Oxford: Alden Press, 1935.

Cowdrey, E.V. *Aging Better.* Springfield, Ill: Charles C. Thomas, 1972.

Crichton-Browne, James. *The Doctor Remembers.* Lond: Duckworth, 1938.

_____. *The Prevention of Senility and a Sanitary Outlook.* Lond: Macmillan, 1905.

_____. *Delusions in Diet.* NY: Funk & Wagnalls, 1910.

Curzon, George. *The Pamirs.* Lond: Royal Geographical Soc, 1896.

Davies, David. *The Centenarians of the Andes.* NY: Doubleday, 1975.

Davis, John T. *Walking.* NY: Bantam, 1979.

Dawber, T. R. *The Framingham Study: the Epidemiology of Atherosclerotic Disease.* Cambridge, Mass: Harvard Univ Press, 1980.

De Ropp, Robert S. *Man Against Dying.* NY: St Martins, 1966.

De Vries, Herbert A. *Report on Jogging and Exercise for Older Adults.* Washington, DC: US Admin on Aging, HEW, 1968.

Dublin, L. I., A. J. Lotka and M. Spiegelman. *Length of Life.* NY: Ronald Press, 1949.

Durand, Algernon. *The Making of a Frontier.* Lond: Thos. Nelson, 1908.

Drew, Frederick. *The Northern Barrier of India.* Lond: Edw. Stanford, 1877.

Elrick, Harold, James Crakes and Sam Clarke. *Living Longer and Better.* Mt View, Cal, World Publications, 1978.

Epstein, S. *The Politics of Cancer.* San Francisco: Sierra Club, 1978.

Ernest, Maurice. *The Longer Life.* Lond: Adam, 1938.

Erroll, A. Campbell. *A History of the Parishes of Sheringham and Beeston Regis.* Norwich, England: Rigby Printing, 1970.

Etherton, P. T. *Across the Roof of the World.* Lond: Constable, 1911.

Eskander, Fazil. *The Beginning: Short Stories.* Sukhumi, Abkhaz Republic: Alashara, 1978.

Fisher, Welthy. *To Light a Candle.* NY: McGraw-Hill, 1962.

Fox, Michael W. *Superpigs and Wondercorn.* NY: Lyons & Burford, 1992.

Friedman, M. and R. H. Rosenman. *Type A Behavior and Your Heart.* NY: Knopf, 1974.

Freese, Dr Arthur A. *The End of Senility.* NY: Arbor House, 1978.

Gallagher, Dorothy. *Hannah's Daughters.* NY: Crowell, 1976.

Gallup, G. and E. Hill. *The Secrets of Long Life.* NY: Bernard Geis, 1960.

Garrett, Laurie. *The Coming Plague.* NY: Farrar Straus & Giroux, 1994.

Gaster, Theodor H. *The Oldest Stories in the World.* Boston: Beacon Press, 1952.

Gauguelin, Michael. *How Atmospheric Conditions Affect Your Health.* NY: Stein & Day, 1971.

Gomez, Joan. *How Not to Die Young.* NY: Stein & Day, 1972.

Gore, Irene. *Add Years to Your Life and Life to Your Years.* NY: Stein & Day, 1973.

Gould, Jay M. and Benjamin A. Goldman. *Deadly Deceit.* NY: Four Walls Eight Windows, 1994.

Gray, W. Forbes. *Five Score: A Group of Famous Centenarians.* Lond: John Murray, 1931.

Gris, Henry and Milton Merlin. *May You Live to Be 200!* So Brunswick & NY: A. S. Barnes, 1978.

Gruman, Gerald J. *A History of Ideas about the Prolongation of Life.* Phil: Amer Philos Soc, 1966.

Gueniot, A. *How to Live to Be a Hundred.* Valletta, Malta, 1933.

Hadjihristev, Argir Kirkov. *Life-Styles for Long Life: Longevity in Bulgaria.* Springfield, Ill: Charles C. Thomas, 1988.

Halsell, Grace. *Los Viejos.* Emmaus, Pa: Rodale, 1976.

Harrington, Alan. *The Immortalist.* Millibrae, Cal: Celestial Arts, 1969.

Hayflick, Leon. *How and Why We Age.* NY: Ballantine, 1994.

Hershey, Daniel. *Lifespan.* Springfield, Ill: Charles Thomas, 1964.

Heynen, Jim. *One Hundred over 100.* Saskatoon, Saskatchewan: Western Producer Prairie Bks, 1900.

Hendin, David. *Death as a Fact of Life.* NY: Norton, 1973.

Highland, Jos. H., Marcia E. Fine *et al. Malignant Neglect.* NY: Knopf, 1979.

Hilton, James. *Lost Horizon*. NY: Morrow, 1933.

Hoffman, Jay Milton. *Hunza*. Valley Ctr, Cal: Professional Press Publishing, 1968.

Illich, Ivan. *Medical Nemesis*. Lond: Calder & Boyars, 1975.

Inglis, Brian. *The Case for Unorthodox Medicine*. NY: Putnam, 1965.

Keay, John. *The Gilgit Game*. Hamden, Ct: Archon, 1979.

Kent, Saul. *The Life-Extension Revolution*. NY: Morrow, 1980.

Kipshidze, Nodar, *et al*, "The Longevous People of Soviet Georgia" in *Realistic Expectations for Long Life*, ed. Gari Lesnoff-Caravaglia. NY: Human Science Press, 1987.

Knight, E. F. *Where Three Empires Meet*. Lond: Longman, Green, 1893.

Krueger, Albert and David S. Sobel. "Air Ions & Health" in David S. Sobel, ed., *Ways of Health*. NY: Harcourt Brace Jovanovich, 1979.

Kugler, Hans J. *Dr Kugler's Seven Days to a Longer Life*. NY: Stein & Day, 1978.

Kurtaman, Joel and Philip Gordon. *No More Dying*. LA: J. P. Tarcher, 1976.

Lambert, Edw. C. *Modern Medical Mistakes*. Bloomington, Ind: Indiana Univ Press, 1978.

Langone, John. *Long Life*. Boston: Little, Brown, 1978.

Lawrence, Walter R. *Valley of Kashmir*. Lond: Henry Frowde, 1895.

Laws, Priscilla W. *Medical and Dental X-Rays; a Consumer's Guide to Avoiding Unnecessary Radiation Exposure*. Washington, DC: Public Citizen, Health Research Group, 1974.

Leaf, Alexander. *Youth in Old Age*. NY: McGraw-Hill, 1975.

Lehman, Harvey. *Age and Achievement*. Princeton, NJ: Princeton Univ Press, 1930.

Leitner, G. W. *Results of a Tour in Dardistan, Kashmir, Little Tibet, Ladok, Zanskar, Etc in 1866*. Lond: Trubner, 1868-73. 4 vols.

Leonard, John N., J. L. Hofer and N. Pritikin. *Live Longer Now*. NY: Grosset & Dunlap, 1974.

Linton, Ron M. *Terracide*. Boston: Little, Brown, 1970.

Luce, Gay and Julius Segal. *Sleep*. NY: Coward McCann, 1966.

Lorimer, E. O. *Language Hunting in the Karakoram*. Lond: Allen & Unwin, 1939.

McCarrison, Rbt. *Studies in Deficiency Diseases*. Lond: Henry Frowde & Hodder & Stoughton, 1921.

McGrady, Patrick M., Jr. *The Youth Doctors.* NY: Coward McCann, 1968.

McNeill, Wm. H. *Plagues and Peoples.* NY: Doubleday, 1977.

McQuage, Wm. and Ann Aikman. *The Longevity Factor.* NY: Simon & Schuster, 1979.

Medawar, P. B. and J. S. *The Life Science.* NY: Harper & Row, 1977.

Medvedev, Zhores. *Soviet Science.* NY: Norton, 1978.

Mendelsohn, Rbt. *Confessions of a Medical Heretic.* Chgo: Contemporary, 1979.

Metchnikoff, Elie. *The Prolongation of Life.* Lond: Heinemann, 1910.

Mons, Barbara. *High Road to Hunza.* Lond: Faber & Faber, 1958.

Nearing, Helen. *Loving and Leaving the Good Life.* Post Mills, VT: Chelsea Green, 1992.

_____ and Scott Nearing. *Living the Good Life.* NY: Shocken, 1970.

_____. *Continuing the Good Life.* NY: Shocken, 1979.

Newbold, H. L. *Vitamin C Against Cancer.* NY: Stein & Day, 1979.

Ornish, Dean. *Program for Reversing Heart Disease.* NY: Ballantine, 1991.

_____. *Stress, Diet & Your Heart.* NY: Signet, 1984.

Palmore, Erdman and Frances C. Jeffers. *Prediction of Life Span.* Lexington, Mass: Heath Lexington Bks, 1971.

Pauling, Linus. *Vitamin C and the Common Cold.* San Francisco: W. H. Freeman, 1970.

Pearl, Anthony and Ruth Dewitt Pearl. *The Ancestry of the Long-Lived.* Baltimore: Johns Hopkins Univ Press, 1934.

Podolsky, Edward. *Red Miracle: The Story of Soviet Medicine.* NY: Beechhurst Press, 1947.

Pelletier, Kenneth R. *Mind as Healer, Mind as Slayer.* NY: Delacorte, 1977.

Polednak, Anthony P. *The Longevity of Athletes.* Springfield, Ill: Charles C. Thomas, 1979.

Prehoda, Rbt. *Extended Youth.* NY: Putnam, 1960.

Pritikin, Nathan, with Patrick M. McGrady, Jr. *The Pritikin Plan for Diet and Exercise.* NY: Grosset & Dunlap, 1979.

*Recommended Dietary Allowance.* 8th Ed Rev. Washington, DC: Nat'l Academy of Sciences, 1974.

Reinhardt, Charles. *120 Years of Life.* Lond: London Publicity, 1910.

Robertson, George Scott. *The Kafirs of the Hindu-Kush.* Lond: Lawrence & Bullen, 1896.

Rodale, J. I. *The Healthy Hunzas.* Emmaus, Pa: Rodale, 1949.

Rosenfeld, Alfred. *Prolongevity II.* NY: Knopf, 1985.

*Royal Canadian Air Force Exercise Plans for Physical Fitness.* NY: Bantam, 1972.

Schomberg, R. C. F. *Between the Oxus and the Indus.* Lond: Martin Hopkinson, 1935.

Segerberg, Osborn Jr. *Living to Be 100.* NY: Scribner, 1982.

_____. *The Immortality Factor.* NY: Dutton, 1974.

Selye, Hans. *The Stress of Life.* NY: McGraw-Hill, 1976.

Shipton, Eric. *Mountains of Tartary.* Lond: Hodder & Stoughton, 1951.

Shock, Nathan W., ed. *Aging: Some Social & Biological Aspects.* Freeport, NY: Bks for Libraries, 1960.

_____, ed. *Perspectives in Experimental Gerontology.* Springfield, Ill: Charles C. Thomas, 1966.

_____. *Trends in Gerontology.* Stanford, Cal: Stanford Univ Press, 1951.

Simonton, O. Carl, Stephanie Matthews-Simonton and James Creighton, *Getting Well Again.* LA: J. P. Tarcher, 1978.

Sinclair, H. M. *The Work of Robert McCarrison.* Lond: Faber & Faber, 1952.

Skrede, Wilfred. *Across the Roof of the World.* NY: Norton, 1954.

Soule, George. *Longer Life.* NY: Viking, 1958.

Stein, M. Auriel. *Sand-Buried Ruins of Kohtan.* Lond: T. Fisher Unwin, 1903.

Stephen Leslie and Sidney Lee. *Dict Nat'l Biog.* Lond: OUP, 1950. Vol X.

Swinup, Grant. *Energetics.* LA: Sherbourne Press, 1970.

Taylor, Renee, as told to by Mir Mohd Jamal Khan. *Come Along to Hunza (The History of Shangri-La).* Minneapolis: T. S. Denison, 1974.

_____ and Milford J. Kobbs. *Hunza: The Himalayan Shangri-La.* El Monte, Cal: Whiteman, 1962.

_____. *Hunza Health Secrets for Long Life and Happiness.* Englewood Cliffs, NJ: Prentice-Hall, 1964.

Thomas, Lowell. *Book of the High Mountains.* NY: Julian Messner, 1964.

Thompson, Wm. Irwin, ed. *Gaia: A Way of Knowing.* San Francisco: Lindisfarne, 1981.

Thoms, Wm. J. *The Longevity of Man.* Lond: Frederic Norgate, 1873 & 1879.

Tushnet, Leonard. *The Medicine Man.* NY: St Martins, 1971.

Walford, Roy. *Maximum Life Span.* NY: Avon, 1984.

_____ . *The 120 Year Diet: How to Double Your Vital Years.* NY: Pocket Books, 1988.

Weber, Hermann. *On Longevity and the Means for the Prolongation of Life.* Lond: Macmillan, 1939.

Weiser, Eric. *The Years in Hand.* NY: Abelard Schuman, 1967.

Weston, Lee. *Body Rhythm.* NY: Harcourt Brace Jovanovich, 1979.

Winter, Ruth. *Ageless Aging.* NY: Crown, 1973.

U of Cal Berkeley. *Wellness Encyclopedia.* Boston: Houghton Mifflin, 1991.

Whelan, Elizabeth. *Preventing Cancer.* NY: Norton, 1978.

Woodruff, Diana S. *Can You Live to Be 100?* NY: Chatham Square, 1977.

Wrench, G. T. *The Wheel of Health.* Lond: C. W. Daniel, 1938.

Young, T. E. *On Centenarians.* Lond: Charles & Edwin Layton, 1899 & 1905.

Younghusband, Sir Frances. *Dawn in Asia.* Lond: John Murray, 1930.


PERIODICALS

Abarbanel, Albert. "The Healthiest People in the World." *American Mercury,* Sept, 1954.

Apple, R. W., Jr. "Britain's Notable Nonagenarians." *NYT Magazine,* Nov 11, 1979.

Beard, Belle Boone. "Some Characteristics of Recent Memory in Centenarians." *Journal of Gerontology,* Vol 23, No 1 (Jan, 1968).

Bell, Alexander Graham. "Who Shall Inherit Long Life?" *Nat'l Geographic,* XXXV, No 6 (June, 1919).

Beller, Suha and Erdman Palmore. "Longevity in Turkey." *Gerontologist,* Vol 14, No 5 (Oct, 1974).

Brody, Jane E. "Genetic Explanation Offered for Women's Health Superiority." *NYT,* Jan 20, 1980, p C1.

_____ . "Survey of Aged Reveals Liberal Views on Sex." *NYT,* April 22, 1980, p C1.

_____ . "Personal Health: Alcohol Offers Some Benefits to Health as Well as Drawbacks." *NYT,* Oct 3, 1979.

_____. "Women and Alcohol." *NYT*, Sept 15, 1993, p C13.

_____. Personal Health Columns, *NYT*, July 14, 1993, p C12; Aug 10, 1994, p C8.

Brotman, Herman. "Comparison of Life Expectancy, 1900 and 1974." *Gerontologist*, Feb, 1977.

Burnham, David. "Utility in Michigan Faces $450,000 Fine." *NYT*, Nov 10, 1979, p 9.

Cameron, Ewan and Linus Pauling. "Supplemental Ascorbate in the Supportive Treatment of Cancer: Prolongation of Survival Times in Terminal Human Cancer." *Proceedings* of the Nat'l Academy of Science, 73 (Oct, 1976).

Chebotaryov, Dimitry (*sic*) and Nina N. Sachuk. "Sociomedical Examination of Longevous People in the USSR." *Journal of Gerontology*, Vol 19, No 4 (Oct, 1964).

Ciuca, Alexandru. "Longevity and Environmental Factors." *Gerontologist*, Vol 7, No 4.

Clark, John. "Hunza in the Himalayas." *Natural History*, LXXII, No 6 (Oct, 1963).

Clark, Truman. "Master's Movement." *Runner's World*, Vol 14, No 7 (July, 1979).

Court, John. "Want to Live to be 120?" *Atlas*, Vol 16, No 4 (Oct, 1968).

Cousins, Norman. "What I Learned from 3,000 Doctors." *Prevention*, Vol 30, No 6 (June, 1978).

De Vries, Herbert A. "Physiological Effects of an Exercise Training Regimen Upon Men Aged 52-88." *Journal of Gerontology*, 25 (1970).

_____ and Gene M. Adams. "Comparison of Exercise Responses in Old and Young Men." *Journal of Gerontology*, Vol 27, No 3 (1972).

_____. "Prescription of Exercise for Older Men from Telemetered Exercise Heart Rate Data." *Geriatrics*, April, 1971.

"English Soil Linked to Longevity." *NYT*, Oct 6, 1977, p 72.

"Excess X-Ray Radiation Found." *NYT*, Dec 5, 1979, p A12.

Fox, Samuel M. and John P. Naughton, "Physical Activity and the Prevention of Coronary Heart Disease." *Preventive Medicine*, 1 (1972).

Halpern, Dorothy. "Profile: Alexander A. Bogomoletz." *American Review of Soviet Medicine*, Vol 1, No 2 (Dec, 1943).

Hartung, C. Harley, *et al.* "Relation of Diet to High-Density-Lipoprotein

Cholesterol in Middle-Aged Marathon Runners, Joggers, and Inactive Men." *New England Journal of Medicine*, Vol 302, No 7 (Feb 14, 1980).

Hatch, M. C. *et al.* "Cancer Near the Three Mile Nuclear Plant: Radiation Emission." *American Journal of Epidemiology*, Vol 132 (Sept, 1990).

Hennekins, Chas. H., Walter Willet, Bernard Rosner, *et al.* "Effects of Beer, Wine and Liquor in Coronary Death." *Journal of the American Medical Ass'n*, 242 (1979).

_____, B. Rosner and D. S. Cole. "Daily Alcoholic Consumption and Fatal Coronary Heart Disease." *American Journal of Epidemiology*, 107 (1978).

Horton-Smith, Sir Percival Hartley. "The Longevity of Oarsmen." *British Medical Journal*, 1 (April, 1939).

Hubbell, Ruth A. "Men and Women Who Have Performed Distinctive Service After the Age of 74." *Wilson Bulletin for Librarians*, 9 (1935).

Ivins, Molly. "Denver Uncertain over Old Uranium Site." *NYT*, Feb 20, 1979, p A13.

_____. "Utah Uneasy over Leukemia–Atomic Tests Study." *NYT*, Feb 23, 1979.

Jeffries, Brian. "Civilization Closing In on Shangri-La." *LA Times*, June 9, 1974, Sec 8, p 9.

_____. "No More Shangri-La," *Washington Post*, Sept 26, 1974, p A10.

Jewett, Stephen. "Longevity and the Longevity Syndrome." *Gerontologist*, Vol 12, No 1 (Spring, 1973).

Johnson, Sharon. "Welthy Fisher: Woman with a Mission." *NYT*, April 2, 1978, p 54.

_____. "Spreading the Word." *NYT*, Sept 18, 1979.

Karvonen, M. J., *et al.* "Longevity of Endurance Skiers." *Medicine and Science in Sports*, 6 (1974).

Kahn, Harold A. "The Relationship of Reported Coronary Heart Disease Mortality to Physical Activity of Work." *American Journal of Public Health*, 52 (1963).

Lawson, Carol. "Behind the Best Sellers." *NYT*, July 1, 1979.

Leaf, Alexander. "Every Day is a Gift When You are Over 100." *Nat'l Geographic*, Vol 143, No 1 (Jan 1973).

Lyon, Joseph L., Melville R. Klauber, *et al.* "Childhood Leukemia and

Nuclear Fallout." *New England Journal of Medicine*, 300 (1979).

Lyons, Richard D. "Chemical Tied to Cancer is Banned as Cattle Feed." *NYT*, June 30, 1979, p 6.

McCay, Clive M., L. A. Maynard, *et al.* "Retarded Growth, Life Span, Ultimate Body Size, and Age Changes in the Albino Rat After Feeding Diets Restricted in Calories." *Journal of Nutrition*, Vol 18, No 1 (1939).

McCarrison, Rbt. "Faulty Food in Relation to Gastro-Intestinal Disorders." 6th Mellon Lecture, Univ of Pittsburgh School of Medicine, Nov 18, 1921.

_____. "The Relationship of Diet to the Physical Efficiency of Indian Races." *The Practitioner* (Lond), Jan, 1925.

McKain, W. C. "Observations on Old Age in the Soviet Union." *Gerontologist*, Vol 7, No 1 (1967).

"The Man Who Spoke with Lincoln." *Ebony*, Feb 1963.

Mark Thrash Obituary, *NYT*, Dec 17, 1943.

Martha Graham Obituary, *NYT*, June 25, 1959.

Mazess, Richard B. "Health and Longevity in Vilcabamba, Ecuador." *Journal of the American Medical Ass'n*, Vol 240, No 16 (Oct 13, 1978).

_____. "Bone Mineral in Vilcabamba, Ecuador." *American Journal of Roentgenology*, 130 (April, 1978).

Medvedev, Zhores. "Caucasus and Altay Longevity: A Biological or Social Problem?" *The Gerontologist*, Vol 14, No 5 (Oct, 1974).

_____. "Aging and Longevity." *The Gerontologist*, Vol 15, No 3 (June, 1975).

Metropolitan Life Insurance Co. "Longevity of Corporate Executives." *Statistical Bulletin*, 55 (1974).

Morris, J. N., J. A. Heady, *et al.* "Coronary Heart Disease and Physical Activity of Work." *Lancet*, 2 (1953).

_____ and M. D. Crawford, "Coronary Heart Disease and Physical Activity of Work. Evidence of a National Necropsy Survey." *British Medical Journal*, 2 (1958).

_____ *et al.* "Vigorous Exercise in Leisure Time and the Incidence of Coronary Heart Disease." *Lancet*, 1 (1973).

*New England Journal of Medicine*, 330 (1994).

Newman, Gustave and Claude R. Nichols. "Sexual Activities and Attitudes in Older Persons." *Journal of the American Medical Ass'n*, 173 (1960).

Norman, James. "The Tarahumaras". *Nat'l Geographic*, Vol 149, No 5 (May 1976).

Otten, Alan J. "Industrial Countries Will Meet Next Week in Attempt to Curb Destructive Acid Rains." *Wall St Journal*, Nov 9, 1979.

Paffenbarger, Ralph S., Alvin L. Wing and Rbt T. Hyde. "Physical Activity as an Index of Heart Attack Risk in College Alumni." *American Journal of Epidemiology*, Vol 108, No 3 (Sept, 1978).

_____ and W. E. Hales. "Work Activity and Coronary Heart Mortality." *New England Journal of Medicine*, 1975.

_____ *et al*. "Work Activity of Longshoremen as Related to Death from Coronary Heart Diseases and Stroke." *New England Journal of Medicine*, Vol 282, No 20 (May 14, 1970).

*Pakistan Journal of Medical Research*. Five articles on Hunzakut health. April, 1966.

Quint, Jules V. and Bianca R. Cody. "Pre-eminence and Mortality: Longevity of Prominent Men." *American Journal of Public Health*, Vol 60, No 6 (June 1970).

Raines, Howell. "An Unwelcome Alabama Guest: Radioactive Gas in Many Homes." *NYT*, Mar 16, 1979, p A13.

Rosen, Samuel, Nicolai Prebrajensky, Simeon Khechinashvili *et al*. "Epidemiologic Hearing Studies in the USSR." *Archives of Otolaryngology*, Vol 91, No 5 (1970).

Sachuk, N. "The Geography of Longevity in the USSR." *Geriatrics*, Vol 20, No 7 (July, 1965).

St Leger, A. A., A. L. Cochrane, and F. Moore. "Factors Associated with Cardiac Mortality in Developed Countries with Particular Reference to the Consumption of Wine." *Lancet*, May 12, 1979.

Schinava, N., N. Sachuk, and Sh. D. Gogohiya. "On the Physical Condition of the Aged People of the Abkhasian ASSR." *Soviet Medicine*, 5 (1964).

Schmeck, Harold M., Jr. "Research Attempts to Fight Senility." *NYT*, July 31, 1979.

_____. "Memory Loss Curbed by Chemical in Foods." *NYT*, Jan 9, 1979, p C1.

Schwartz, Harry. "A Look at the Cancer Figures." *Wall St Journal*, Nov 15, 1979.

Scrimsaw, Nevin S. "Protein Requirements—Strengths and Weaknesses of the Committee Approach." *New England Journal of Medicine*, Vol 29, No 3 (Jan 15, 1976) and No 4 (Jan 22, 1976).

Shoenfeld, Yehuda *et al.* "Walking—A Method for Rapid Improvement of Physical Fitness." *Journal of the American Medical Ass'n*, 243 (1980).

Shor, Jean and Frank. "At World's End in Hunza." *Nat'l Geographic*, CIV, No 4 (Oct, 1953).

Siegel, Ronald K. "Ginseng Abuse Syndrome." *Journal of the American Medical Ass'n*, 241 (1979).

Slazinski, Leonard. Letter on ginseng & Citation, *Journal of the American Medical Ass'n*, 242 (1979).

"Study Links Heavy Use of a Pain Reliever to Kidney Failure," *NYT*, Dec 22, 1994, p B12.

Sturgeon, Philip, Suha Beller and E. Bates, "Study of Blood Type Group Factors in Longevity." *Journal of Gerontology*, Vol 24, No 1 (Jan, 1969).

Sullivan, Walter. "Scientists Seek Key to Longevity." *NYT*, Feb 11, 1973, p 1.

_____. "Very Old People in the Andes are Found to Be Merely Old." *NYT*, Mar 17, 1978, p 18.

Taylor, Henry Longstreet, Ernest Kleptear, Ancel Keys, *et al.* "Death Rates Among Physically Active and Sedentary Employees of the Railroad Industry." *American Journal of Public Health*, 52 (1962).

Topping, Audry. "Opening a New Road to China: the Karakoram Highway." *NYT Magazine*, Dec 2, 1979.

Trumbull, Rbt. "Japan Hails Elders Amid New Concern for Them." *NYT*, Sept 16, 1979, p 19.

Varina, N., trans. "Secrets of the Centenarians." *Atlas World Press Review*, Vol 25, No 1 (Jan, 1978).

Webster, Bayard. "Acid Rain: An Increasing Threat." *NYT*, Nov 6, 1879, p C1.

Weyl, Nathaniel. "Survival Past the Century Mark." *Mankind Quarterly*, 17 (1977).

Williams, Roger J. "Nutritional Individuality." *Human Nature*, I, No 6 (June, 1978).

Wren, Christopher. "Soviet Centenarians." *NYT*, Sept 9, 1977.

Young, Peter. "161 Years Old and Going Strong." *Life*, Vol 61, No 12 ( Sept 16, 1966).

# INDEX

## A

Abalava, Thense, 58
Abbott, George 151
Abkhasia, 32, 34, 35, 37-66, 159, 161, 197; alcohol, 63; body type, 52; climate, 53, 70; diet, 51-52; genetics, 52-53; history, 38, 49; language, 58-59; life span, 49; life style, 48, 51; literacy, 56-57, 76; longevity data, 47-48; physical activity, 51, 52, 159; State Museum, 54-55; respect for elders, 50-51; Soviet of Elders, 50; sport, 52.
Academy of Medical Science, USSR, 69
Acetaminophen, 264
Acupuncture, 230
Additives, 203-206, 210
Adenosine triphosphate (ATP), 78-79
Afghanistan, 116
African-Americans, 25-27, 135, 150
Aga Khan, 115
Agha, Zaro, 21
Aging causes, 256-259
Ahmed, Sahoor, 107, 108
Air ions, 266
Air pollution, 236-237, 241

Alcohol, 22, 63, 93, 145, 158, 208-209, 215
Alexander, Judge Albert R., 139
Alexander the Great, 37, 99, 101
American Cancer Society, 239
*American Mercury* magazine, 99
Angiosarcoma, 235
Anorexia nervosa, 144
Antacids, 228
Anthony, Charles, 17
Antibiotics, 228
Antireticular cytotoxic serum, 79
Archer, Elizabeth, 129
Aristotle, 187
Armenia, 31, 67, 73
Arundel, Thos Howard, 14th Earl, 15
Asbestos, 235, 238, 243
Ascorbic acid, see Vitamin C
Aslan, Ana, 79-80
Aspirin, 222
Atkins diet, 197
Atomics International, 246
Atomic testing, see Radiation
Austro-Hungarian Empire, 27
Auto-immunity, 257-258
Ayvazov, Makhum, 74
Azerbaijan, 11, 32, 35, 67, 72-74

## B

Babylon, 1

Bacon, Roger, 8
Bada, Jeffrey, 33-34, 45
Ballet, 176
Baltimore Longitudinal Study of
    Aging, xii, 133
Banik, George, 98-99
Barbiturates, 228
Barbusse, Henri, 55
Bavaria, 27
Beard, Belle Boone, 133, 135
Beer, 209
Bell, Alexander Graham, 71-72
Beller, Suha, 91
Benet, Sula, 29, 42, 43, 57-60, 62,
    65, 72-77, 15;*The Abkhasians*,
    59; *How to Live*, 58
Bennett, Wendell, 89-90
Beria, Lavrenti, 49
Bidulph, Major, 104
Biofeedback, 263
Bis-chlormethyl ether, 235
Black lung, 235
Blindness, 140
Blumenbach, Johann, 37
Body weight, 179-183, chart, 181;
    reduction, 182-183
Bogomoletz, Alexander A., 79
Boyle, Robert H., 233
Brahmins, 109
Brezhnev, Leonid, 49, 55
British Museum, 96
Brown lung, 235
Bulgaria, 29
Bull, Horace,128-129
Butba, Sheilach, 59
Butkov, O. G., 58

C
Caffeine, 209-211
Calcium, 223-224

Caloric intake, prolongevous,
    196, 214-215,
*Cambridge Evening News*, 128
Cambridgeshire, 125-130
Canada, centenarians, 14; pollution,
    233
Canadian Air Force exercises, 187
Cancer, and additives, 203-206;
    aging, 242; artificial sweeten-
    ers, 207-208; beef, 195;
    bladder, 239, 251; breast, 195,
    201, 242; colonic, 195, 242;
    digestive tract, 251; dyes, 205,
    235; environmental
    pollutants, 233-254; esopha-
    geal, 210, 239; fats, 242; high-
    protein diet, 200-201; kidney,
    251; larynx, 239; lung, 239,
    242; meat adulterants, 201;
    mouth, 239; pancreas, 239;
    radiation, 226-227, 246-248;
    remissions, 169, 170-71;
    selenium, 218-219; skin, 185,
    244; smoking, see tobacco
    smoke; stress, 169; tea, 210;
    urinary tract, 251; vaginal, 201;
    vitamin C, 221
*Candid Camera*, 170
carbohydrates, 192, 215
Carnegie Collection of High
    Altitude Butterflies, 105
Carpathian Mts, 90-91
Carpio, Miguel, 82, 85-86
Carroll, Lewis, 243
Casals, Pablo, 140
Cataracts, 140
Cato, 138
Caucasians, 37
Caucasus, 6, 93, 265; longevity
    claims and studies, 28-35, 37-

66; *passim*, 67-77
Cell transplants, 259, 265
Cereals, whole-grain, 197, 206
Cervantes, Miguel de, 135; *Don Quixote*, 135, 145
Chagall, Marc, 140
Chapman, James, 129
Charles I, 15
Chastney, Ivy and Reggie, 123
Chebotarev, Dimitri, 69-70, 78, 80
Chemical dumps, 252
Chernobyl, 245
Chicago Museum of Natural History, 105
Chick, Dame Harriet, 128
China, 230; physician-patient relationship, 224
*China Syndrome, The*, 245
Chital, 112
Cholesterol, 51, 69, 85, 198
Churchill, Winston, 124
Clark, John, 100, 105, 106, 107, 108, 110, 111, 114, 115
Climatics and longevity, 53, 70
Cloning, 262-263
Cocoa, 210
Coffee, 209, 210, 211-212, 272
Cola, 210
Comfort, Alex, 261-262
Committee of One Hundred, 136
Consumers Power Co., 236
Cooking processes, 198, 202, 216
Cooper, Kenneth, 187
Cornaro, Luigi, 142-146, 150
Cornelius, Frederick, 118-120
Cosmetics, 248
Cousins, Norman, 169-171; *Anatomy of an Illness*, 170; *The Healing Heart*, 170
Craig, Lula Sadler, 150

Craske, Stanley, 122-123
Creighton, James, 169
Crichton-Browne, Sir James, 142, 146, 147
Crustaceans, 202-203
Cryonics, 260-261
Cubitt, Mrs. M.E., 124
Cuyahoga River, pollution of, 254
Cyclamates, 207

**D**

Dairy products, 193, 198-99, 206
Dales, The, 118-124
Dannon Yogurt Co., 29
Davies, David, 82-83, 84, 117
DDT, 206
Degenerative diseases, in athletes, 173; role of sugar, 207; role of water pollution, 251
Delaney Sisters, Bessie and Sarah, 135, *Having Our Say*, 135; *Delaney Sisters' Book of Wisdom*, 135
Denis, "Chick," 118
Derbent, 58
Descartes, René, 8, 15
Desmond, Countess of, 13, 15
Devenny, Rbt, 124, 125
Diascuria, 38
Dickens, Charles, 243
Diets, 19, 51-52, 69, 192; diet guidelines, 214-215
Diethylstilbestrol (DES), 201
Digitalis, 228
Dioxin, 249-250
Diuretics, 228
DNA, 257, 267-268
Dogon people, 23-24
Dogras, 109
Dollo, Anai, 23-25, 34

Drakenberg the Dane, 19-20, 58
Duke University, Chapel Hill Study
of Aging, 133

E

Eating habits, 211-213
*Ebony* magazine, 25
Eckler, A. Ross, 12-13
Ecuador, 6, 29, 81-94
Elizabeth II,119
Empelton, Alice, 125-127, 128, 129
Emphysema, 239
Environment, 233-254
Environmental Protection Agency,
251
Ernest, Maurice, 19-21
Erroll, A. Campbell, 120-122
Eskimo, 140
Essed Bey, 56
Estonia, 31
Evacuation, 212
Evans, Flo, 125
Exercise, 92, 93, 173-190, 270-271;
advocates of, 146-148; aerobics,
183; agenda for longevity, 173-
193; benefits to skeletal
system, 174-175; bowling, 176;
gardening, 187; golfing, 176;
hiking, 185; horseback riding,
185; ice skating, 185; jogging,
177; recommended program,
187-88; roller skating, 185;
running, 177; skiing, 185-186;
skiing cross country, 185;
skipping rope, 198; sledding,
186; swimming, 177-178, 184-
185; tennis, 177; walking, 174,
183-184, 186-187, 188; weight-
lifting, 177-178

F

Fanon, Frantz, 84
Fasting, 196, 200, 231-232
Fats, 192-193, 196, 214-215
Filkins, Delina, 6, 11-13, 14, 26,
74, 199
Finland, 93, 185
Fish, 202-203
Fisher, Welthy Honsinger, 136, 137
Flagg, Ernest, 148
Fluorocarbons, 244
Folk remedies, 230-231
Fonda, Jane, 183
Food, 191-216; food devitalization,
197; food dyes, 205; food
pyramid, 193
Food and Drug Administration,
199, 201, 204-205
Forman, Sylvia H. 85-87
*Fortune* magazine, 165
Framingham Longitudinal Study,
133
Frank, Dr. Jerome D., 171
Franklin, Benjamin, 8
Friedman, Dr. M., 156

G

Gagarin, Yuri, 55
Gallagher, Dorothy, 71; *Hannah's
Daughters,* 71
Gallup, George, 166
Gandhi, Mahatma, 98, 137
Gardening, 187, 272
Genetic engineering, 261-263
Genetic influence on longevity, 5-6,
50, 52-53, 70-72, 87
Genghis Khan, 37
George V, 124
Georgia, 29, 31, 32, 67, 68, 73, 77,

160-161; average life spans, 49; centenarian statistics, 74

*Gerontologist, The* 30

Gerovital, 79-80

Germany, 233

Ghazanfar, Ali, Mir of Hunza, 115-116

Ghazan Khan, Mir of Hunza, 103

Gilgamesh, 1

Gilgit, 95, 96, 107, 108, 109, 110

Goethe, J. W. von, 135; *Faust*, 135

Gogoghian, Shoto, 39-40, 41, 45-54, 60, 62, 66

Goldman, Benjamin, 245-246

Goiter, 229

Gori, 58-59

Gould, Jay and Benjamin Goldman, 245-246; *Deadly Deceit*, 245

Graham, Billy, 61

Graham, Henry and Martha, 26

Grains, 197-206

Gray Panthers, 162

Great Britain, 6, 13, 117-130

Greece, 3, 61, 187, 200

Gregory, Mrs. J.B., 71

Grice, John Henry, 123

Gris, Henry, 43-44, 65

Grombtchevski, Capt, 103

Gruman, Gerald, 1-2, *History of Ideas about the Prolongation of Life*, 1

Gueniot, Alexandre, 142, 146, 147

*Guiness Book of World Records*, 11, 12, 26

**H**

Hair dyes, see Cosmetics

Halsell, Grace, 83-85, 98; *Los Viejos*, 84

Hardy, Thomas, 137-138

*Harvard Medical School Health Letter*, 275

Hayflick, Leonard, 258; *How and Why We Age*, 259

Health Education & Welfare, Dept of, 226-227

Health Research Group, 226

Health literature, 229-230

Hearing difficulties, 139-140; and noise, 253-254

Heart attacks, 156, 169-170; bypass surgery, 196; disease, 51, 104, 156, 167-170; cholesterol, 51, 69, 85; noise, 252-253; pollutants, 254; high protein, 201; walking, 189

Hearth, Amy Hill, 135

Hebrew legends, 3, 8

Heredity, see Genetic influence

*Herkimer Evening Telegraph*, 12

Heynen, Jim, 133, 135

High blood pressure, see Hypertension

Hilton, James, 98, *Lost Horizon*, 98

Ho Chi Minh, 55

Hoffman, Jay, 98-99

Hoffman-La Roche, 250

Holistic medicine, 169, 170, 171

Holmes, Oliver Wendell, 139

Hubbell, Ruth, 136

Hudson, Henry, 25

Hudson River, pollution of, 251

Humphry, G.M., 19

Hunter College-CUNY, 29

Hunza, 6, 7; customs, 101-102; diseases, 104-110; exercise, 95-116; treatment of aged, 102

Hypertension, 175; sodium, 208, 228

**I**

Iatrogenic disease, 227
Ibsen, Henrik, 138
Immune system, 257-258
India, 137; legends, 2
Industrial toxicity, 234-237, 244,
  248, 250-254
Institute for the Study of Man, 29
Institute of Actuaries, 18
Institute of General Genetics,
  (USSR), 79
Iodine deficiency, 229
Iordanidis, Demetrios, 189
Ireland, 93
Iron, 222-223
Izumi, Shigechiyo, 22-23, 209

**J**

Jackson, Andrew, 42
Jamal Khan, Mir of Hunza, 103
Janda, Judy, 44, 60, 62
Japan, cancer, 242; Family Registra-
  tion Act, 22; longest-lived man,
  22-23, longevity myths, 3
Jats, 109
Jeaps, Florence, 127, 128
Jenkins, Henry, 13
Jewett, Stephen, 141-142
Jogging, see Exercise
Jones, Mother, 136
Joubert, Pierre, 14, 19, 20, 64, 74


**K**

Kaslantzia, Mikhail, 64-66
Katchelavo, Riso, 39-41, 66
Keay, John, 95
Kiev, 68-69, 73, 80;
  Gerontological Institute, 68
Kipling, Rudyard, 95, 109-110;

*Kim*, 110; *Man Who Would be
King*, 110
Kobachia, Yelif, 54
Komarov, L.V., 78-79, 80
Kuhn, Maggie, 162
Kvichenya, Kamachich, 59, 76-77

**L**

Lactovegetarians, 91, 147, 148, 198
Lauchuck, May, 192
Laws, Priscilla, 226
Lazuria, Khfaf, 34, 41-45, 59, 64, 74,
  76, 102
Leaf, Alexander, 29; on Caucasus
  research, 42, 43, 65, 100, 107,
  111; Hunza research, 100;
  Vilcabamba research, 85
Lehman, Harvey, 135
Leitner, G.W., 104
Lermontov, Mikhail, 37
Li Chung Yun, 21-22
*Life* magazine, 43
Life spans, average, 132-133;
  Abkhasian, 49; American
  athletes, 173; American clergy,
  162-163; black Americans, 25;
  capitalist bloc nations, 32-33;
  Rumania, 90-91; Scandinavia,
  185; USSR, 29-32, 49
Lincoln, Abraham, 25
Liquids, 208
Literacy House, Lucknow, 137
Lithuania, 73
London transport workers, 92-93
Lorimer, David, 99, 100, 108, 110,
  115
Love Canal, 252
Lymphocytosis, 266
Lynchberg College, 133

**M**

Mahmood, Safdar, 106-107
Makhadzir Raids, 43
Mali, 23-24
Marriage and longevity, 69,
162-164
Marx Brothers, 170
Matthews-Simonton, Stephanie, 169
Maugham, Somerset, 138, 265
Mazess, Richard, 86-87
McCarrison, Rbt, 95, 96-97, 100,
103-104, 107, 108, 109, 110,
111, 128; *Studies in Deficiency
Disease*, 97
McCay, Clive, 144
McMurray, Lavinia, 71
Meat, 194-195; adulteration, 202;
balanced diet, 215; cancer, 193;
genetic alteration, 201
Medlen, Mrs. Karl, 72
Medvedev, Roy, 29
Medvedev, Zhores A., 29-34, 74,
79-80
Meiji, Emperor, 22
Memory, 138-139
Mental abilities, 135-138
Mesothelemia, 235
Metchnikoff, Eli, 27, 58; *Prolonga-
tion of Life*, 58
Methuselah, 3
Metropolitan Life Insurance
Co. Weight Chart, 181
Mexico, 6, 88-89
Michelangelo, 141
Microwave ovens, 248
Migraines, 157
Minerals, 104, 199, 222-224, 228-
229, 264
Mislimov, Shirali, 11, 33, 34,

72, 74
Mississippi River, pollution, 251
Mohammed Nazim Khan, Mir of
Hunza, 103
Mohammed Safdar Ali Khan,
Mir of Hunza, 100
Monet, Claude, 138
Monkey glands, 264-265
Mons, Barbara, 100, 106-107, 110,
115
Monsanto Chemical Co., 203
Morgan, Sarah Ellen, 129
Moses, Anna Mary "Grandma",
138
Mountain people studies, 91-94
Moyers, Bill, 171, *Healing and the
Mind*, 171
Musgrove, Mrs., 119
Muscle building, 178, 200

**N**

Nagirs, 112-114
Napoleon Bonaparte, 21
Nat'l Academy of Sciences, 199
Nat'l Committee for the Artificial
Prolongation of Human Life
(USSR), 78
Nat'l Committee on Radiation
Protection and Measurement,
226
*Nat'l Enquirer*, 44
*Nat'l Geographic* Magazine, 90, 94
Nat'l Geographic Society, 29
Nat'l Institute of Mental Health
Longitudinal Study, 133
Nat'l Radium Institute, 246
Native Americans, 2
Navajo, 244
Nearing, Helen and Scott, 142, 147-

150; *Living the Good Life*, 147;
*Continuing the Good Life*, 147-
148
Neve, Margaret Ann, 20
*New England Journal of Medicine,
The*, 170
New Jersey "cancer alley", 237
New Orleans, 251
*New York Times, The*, 21, 85, 149,
277-278
Niehans, Paul, 265
Noise, 253-254
Norman, James, 90
Norway, 233
Novosti News Agency, 54
Nuclear radiation, 235-248
Nuclear Regulatory Commission,
236
Null, Gary, 276-277
*Nutrition Action Newsletter*, 276

O
Obesity, see Body Weight
O'Keeffe, Georgia, 140
Orchard House, Sawston, 125-127
Organic foods, 205
*Organic Gardening* magazine, 84
Ornish, Dean, 133, 195-196
Osteoporosis, xi
Overstrand retirement home, 124
Overweight, see Body Weight

P
Pakistan, 95, 107, 115
Palmore, Erdman, 91
Pannell, Dr. Walter, 150
Parr, Thomas, 13, 15-16, 33, 58, 60,
68
Pathans, 109, 112
Pauling, Linus, 220-221, 222

*People Are Funny*, 98
Pereira, Javier, 81-82
Pesticides, 206-207, 249-250
Peter the Great, 58
Physical fitness programs, 187-188
Picasso, Pablo, 140
Pichi, Paolini, 192
Pius XII, 265
Placebos, 168-169
Plunkett, Katherine, 20
Poe, Edgar Allen, xi
Pollution, 233-254
Polo, Marco, 100
Polychlorinated biphenyls (PCBs),
203
Polynesian legends, 3
Pouder, Ann, 20
Poultry, 202, 215
Prehoda, Rbt, 264
*Prevention* magazine, 84
Pritikin, Nathan, 133, 189, 195-196
Pritikin Plan, 187, 197
Processed foods, 205-206
Project 2000, 78
Protein, 199-201, 262
Psychosomatic diseases, 168-169
Punjab, 107, Punjabis, 109
Pushkin, Alexander, 37

R
Rabelais, 145
Radiation, 226-228
Radiation Protection and Measure-
ment, Nat'l Committee on, 226
Rajputs, 109
Rennie, Rachel, 126-127, 128
Respect for elders, 50, 55, 59-60, 66
Respiratory diseases, 237-242
Retirement, 160-162; communities,
163

RNA, 257
Robinson Brick & Tile Co., 246
Rodale, J.A., 98, 105, 110; Rodale
    Press, 84
Roman Empire, xiv
Roman legends, 3
Rondanini *Pieta*, 141
Rosenfeld, Albert, 261;
    *Prolongevity II*, 261
Rosenman, Dr R.H., 156
Rouch, Jean, 23-24
Rousseau, Jean Jacques, 17
Rubinstein, Arthur, 140
Rumania, 80, 90-91
Runcieman, Rosie, 123
Russell, Bertrand, 136
Russian Revolution, 49, 64-65

S

Saccharin, 207-208
Salt, see Sodium
Satis, Cardinal de, 146
*Saturday Review, The*, 170
Saunders, "Colonel" George B., 162
Scarsdale diet, 197
Scotland, 18; centenarian claims, 20
Sea Marge, Overstrand, 124-125
Segerberg, Osborn, 133, 135
Selenium, 83, 117, 119
Sellers, James, 128-129
Selye, Hans, 157-158, 167
Senility, 134, 221
7th-Day Adventists, 195
Seveso, Italy, 250
Sexual activity, 163-164; sexual
    rejuvenation, 265
Shakespeare, Wm., 144
Shannocks, 122
Shaw, George Bernard, 124
Sheringham, Cambridgeshire,

117-124, 129-130
Sherpas, 112
Shor, Jean and Frank, 100, 110-111,
    115
Siberia, 32
Sierra Madre Range, 6, 93
Sikhs, 109
Simonton, O. Carl, 169-170
Skin cancer, 185, 244
Sleep patterns, 155-156
Smith, Charlie, 25-26, 27
Smoke detectors, 248
Smoking, see Tobacco smoke
Sobsey, Michael, 272
Sodium, 208, 228
Sodium nitrate, 201
Sophocles, 135
Soviet Union, 6, 20, 31, 32, 33-34,
    48, 49; longevity programs, 78-
    80; longevity studies and
    claims, 28, 35, 37-66, 67-81;
    marriage and longevity, 68, 72
Sports, 176, 185-86; vegetarian
    athletes, 200
Spurling, Arthur "Chammy," 150
Ssu-ma, Ch' ien, 2
State Mutual Assurance Co., 238
Steloff, Francis, 150-151
Stilwell, Joseph, 100
Stokowski, Leopold, 140
Stone, I.F., 162
Strauss, Richard, 140
Stress, 156-161
Strokes, 157
Sugar,206- 207, 213
Sukhumi Institute of Gerontology,
    62
Sun Yat-sen, Mme, 137
Supercentenarian , xii
Superlongevous, xii

Sweden, 233
Synthetic foods, 264

**T**
Tache, Joseph, 14
T'ai chi chuan, 186
Tamerlane, 37
Tanguay, Cyprien, 15
Taoists, 4
Tarahumara Indians, 6, 88-90, 94
Targil, Makhtil, 76
Tarrant, Brenda and Norman, 127
Taylor, Renée, 99
Tea, 210
Temur, Vanacha, 62-64
Tennessee Valley Authority, 246
Terrazas, Aurelio, 89
Terry, Walter, 129
Teutonic legends, 3
Thomas, Lowell, 98
Thoms, Wm. J., 13-18, 19, 20, 57,
    122-123, 131
Thrash, Mark, 26
Three Mile Island, 245-246
*Tiflissky Listok*, 58
Titian, 140
Tobacco smoke, 43, 83, 93, 142,
    238-242, 274; and alcohol, 208-
    209; cancer, 239-242; coronary
    disease and emphysema, 239;
    stress, 158
Toledo, José David, 85
Torres, José, 90
Toxins, see Pollution
Toxic Substance Control Act, 203
Trace elements, 2, 83
Truman, President Harry S., 188
Turkestan, 100
Turkey, 6; centenarian claims, 21,
    91-92; Turks, 42, 43
Tylenol, 264

**U**
Ukraine, 70
Ulcers, 157
United Nations Food and
    Agricultural Organizations,
    199
United States, 164-165;
    centenarian claims, 25-27;
    centenarian statistics, 279;
    degenerative diseases in, 5, 173
    diet in, 192-193, 199-200, 204-
    208; longevity studies, 70-71,
    93, 131-134, 141-146, 195,
    279; marriage and longevity,
    163-164; meat additives,
    201-202; weight, 179-182;
    retirees, 161-162
University College, London
    gerontological unit, 82
*University of California at Berkeley
    Wellness Newsletter*, 276
Upper Sheringham Village, 6, 117-
    124
Uranium, 234
USSR, see Soviet Union

**V**
Vegetarian animals, 200
Vegetarian diets, 195-197, 199-201,
    232; athletes, 200; average life
    span, 195; fat, 193; fiber, 212;
    fresh food, 197; natural food,
    199, 205-206
Verdi, Giuseppe, 140, *Otello*, 140
Vietnam, 249
Vilcabamba Valley, Ecuador, 6,
    81-94
Vinyl chloride, 234
Vitamin A, 106, 229
Vitamin B, 209, 228, 272; complex,
    106

Vitamin C (ascorbic acid), 170-171,
220-222, 229, 273
Vitamin D, 223, 229; deficiency,
106
Vitamin E, 209, 219-220, 221, 222,
229, 259, 273
Vitamins and memory, 138
Vouba, Biga, 47

W
Wagner, Richard, 140
Wald, George, 244
Walford, Roy, 196-197; *Maximum
Life Span*, 197
Walking, see Exercise
Warren, Dolly, 150
Washington, George, 143
Water pollution, 250-252
Weaver, Eula, 189
Weber, Hermann, 142, 146
Weight reduction, see Body Weight
*Wellness Encyclopedia, The*, 214
West family, 123
Whelan, Elizabeth, 241-242
*Who's Who in America*, 165
Williams, Horace, 128
Wilson, Polly, 127, 128
Wine, 143, 209
Wingo, Plennie, 189
Wolfe, Sidney M., 226
Women, Abkhasia, 41, 44, 47, 48,
136; lung cancer, 239; iron,
223; Hunza, 101-102;
longevity superiority, 30, 46-
47, 49, 74, 279; pregnancy, 250
Wrench, G.T., 98, 100, 105, 106;
*The Wheel of Health*, 97

X
X-rays, 226-227

Y
Yasin, 112
Yemenis, 244
Yoga, 9, 263
Yogurt, 27, 29
Young, T.E., 18-19, 20, 57
Younghusband, Francis Edward,
112-114

Z
Zingg, Robert, 89-90
Zukor, Adolph, 139

NATIONAL UNIVERSITY
LIBRARY      SAN DIEGO

Vitamin C (ascorbic acid), 170-171,
220-221, 226, 227
Vitamin D, 223, 226, deficiency,
106
Vitamin K, 200, 219, 220, 221, 226,
296, 270, 273
Vitamins and minerals, 136
Vodka, diet, 47, 228

W
Wagner, Richard, 140
Wald, George, 214
Walford, Roy, 196-197, Maximum
Life-span, 197
Walking, see Exercise
Warren, Dolly, 156
Washington, George, 147
Water pollution, 255, 252
Weaver, Eula, 189
Weber, Herman, 147, 140
Weight reduction, see Body Weight
Wellness Encyclopedia, The, 218
West family, 123
Whelan, Elizabeth, 241-242
Who's Who in Nutrition, 165
Williams, Homer, 128
Wilson, Polly, 127, 128
Wine, 143, 209
Winpo, Blondie, 189
Wolfe, Sidney M., 226
Women: Athletics, 41, 44, 45, 48,
130; lung cancer, 239; iron,
223; menace, 101-102;
longevity superiority, 30, 46,
47, 49, 74, 275; Pregnancy, 250
Wrench, G. T., 98, 100, 105, 106,
The Wheel of Health, 97

X

Y
Yeast, 312
Yemenis, 241
Yoga, 9, 265
Yogurt, 27, 29
Young, T. K., 18-19, 20, 37
Younghusband, Francis, Ed., and,
112-114

Z
Zingg, Robert, 89-90
Zukot, Arol b, 139

NATIONAL UNIVERSITY
LIBRARY    SAN DIEGO